MARYLAND
Real Estate
PRACTICE & LAW

Donald A. White

TWELFTH EDITION

Dearborn™
Real Estate Education

This publication is designed to provide accurate and authoritative information in regard to the subject matter covered. It is sold with the understanding that the publisher is not engaged in rendering legal, accounting, or other professional service. If legal advice or other expert assistance is required, the services of a competent professional should be sought.

President: Mehul Patel
Executive Director of Product Development: Kate DeVivo
Managing Editor: Anne Huston
Managing Editor: Tony Peregrin
Development Editor: Leah Strauss
Director of Production: Daniel Frey
Production Editor: Caitlin Ostrow
Senior Production Artist: Virginia Byrne
Creative Director: Lucy Jenkins
Director of Product Management: Melissa Kleeman

Published by Dearborn™ Real Estate Education
30 South Wacker Drive
Chicago, Illinois 60606-7481
(312) 836-4400
www.dearbornRE.com

Printed in the United States of America

08 09 10   10 9 8 7 6 5 4 3 2 1

ISBN-13: 978-1-4277-7922-9
ISBN-10:   1-4277-7922-8

Contents

CHAPTER 5
Interests in Real Estate   84

CHAPTER 6
How Ownership Is Held   87

CHAPTER 7
Legal Descriptions   97

CHAPTER 8
Real Estate Taxes and Other Liens   101

CHAPTER 9
Real Estate Contracts   109

CHAPTER 10
Transfer of Title   132

Preface

As a student entering a real estate course, you face exciting challenges. You must learn a large body of theory and then apply it to practice. You will want to know legal principles and real estate theory so well that when you get your license, you will be able to do the right thing almost automatically.

If you fail to understand and appreciate law and theory, you can suffer devastating financial and legal consequences. On the other hand, if you build your educational foundation in real estate well, you should be able to make the money you want and not lose the money you make through costly mistakes.

The purpose of this volume is to present clearly many of the laws and operating requirements for real estate brokerage in the State of Maryland. It builds on basic information presented in Dearborn™ Real Estate Education's real estate principles texts. The author has made a serious effort to avoid duplicating information presented in the principles texts. Therefore, you should study each subject area in *both* the basic text and in this book (see Table P.1 under "How to Use This Book"). Online information can be accessed using the Web addresses available throughout the text and in Appendix D in the back of the book.

As you finish each chapter and before you go on to the next, be certain that you are able to answer *and* understand each question presented. An answer key for all of the tests is included at the end of the book.

You will want to make frequent use of Appendix D, Maryland Real Estate–Related Web Sites. It contains several carefully chosen "hub" sites that give you access to multiple official sources for real estate law and regulation at various levels of government.

While the author has exercised care in providing information pertaining to the laws governing the practice of real estate in Maryland, the reader is urged to consult with legal counsel regarding any statutory enactment and should not rely solely on this publication as legal authority for compliance with any statute.

Throughout your real estate course, you'll be studying and taking tests in preparation for the Maryland Real Estate Licensing Examination. That examination is prepared and administered for the State Real Estate Commission by an independent testing service, PSI Examination Services Inc., Las Vegas, Nevada. *Maryland Real Estate Practice & Law* is designed to familiarize you with the subject matter you will find on that examination. The questions at the end of each chapter are prepared in a multiple-choice format similar to the one used in the licensing examination.

About the Author

Maryland Real Estate Practice & Law (12th edition) is written by Donald A. White, DREI, of Silver Spring, Maryland. Mr. White has been a Maryland real estate licensee since 1967 and has held an associate broker license since 1972. He holds degrees in music (BS MusEd), in religious education (MRE), and in business (MA). He is professor emeritus in the Department of Business at Prince George's Community College, where he has taught real estate licensing courses continuously since 1972. He served several terms as chair of the Education Committee of the Prince George's Association of REALTORS®. A past president of the Maryland Real Estate Educators Association, he is presently a member of the Educational Advisory Committee to the Education Committee of the Maryland Real Estate Commission.

The author holds the Distinguished Real Estate Instructor (DREI) designation from the Real Estate Educators Association, of which he is a charter member. He has taught frequently in REALTOR® continuing education seminars. He also was the principal author of *Questions and Answers on Maryland Real Estate* and coauthor, with Maurice Boren, of the *Study Guide to Maryland Real Estate License Examinations*.

How to Use This Book

The conversion table below provides a quick and easy reference for using *Maryland Real Estate Practice & Law* in conjunction with various principles books. For instance, *Maryland Real Estate Practice & Law's* Chapter 16, "Closing the Real Estate Transaction," may be read in conjunction with Chapter 22 in *Modern Real Estate Practice*, Chapter 17 in *Real Estate Fundamentals*, and Chapter 12 in *Mastering Real Estate Principles*.

TABLE P.1

Chapter Conversion Table

Maryland Real Estate Practice & Law (12th edition)		Modern Real Estate Practice (book and software)	Real Estate Fundamentals	Mastering Real Estate Principles
1.	Maryland Real Estate License Law and Regulations	—	—	16
2.	Real Estate Agency	4	7	13
3.	Real Estate Brokerage	5	7	13
4.	Listing and Buyer Representation Agreements	6	7, 8	15
5.	Interests in Real Estate	7	3	7
6.	How Ownership Is Held	8	5	9
7.	Legal Descriptions	9	2	6
8.	Real Estate Taxes and Other Liens	10	3, 10	5, 25
9.	Real Estate Contracts	11	8	14
10.	Transfer of Title	12	4	10
11.	Title Records	13	6	11
12.	Real Estate Financing	14, 15	12, 13	Unit VII
13.	Leases	16	9	8
14.	Environmental Issues and the Real Estate Transaction	21	16	3
15.	Fair Housing	20	15	17
16.	Closing the Real Estate Transaction	22	17	12

Acknowledgments

The author appreciates constructive suggestions on the updating and revision of this text provided by the following reviewers: Sharyn J. Kotrosa, instructor, Long and Foster Real Estate Inc.; Pam Nunzio, professional development trainer and senior instructor, Weichert Institute of Real Estate; and Linda L. Wise, Coldwell Banker Residential Brokerage/Southern Maryland Association of REALTORS®.

He also extends thanks to Elizabeth Gill White for her sharp eye and encouragement.

CHAPTER

1

very Important chapter

Maryland Real Estate License Law and Related Regulations

■ KEY TERMS

administrative law

affiliates

associate brokers

clock hours

Code of Maryland
    Regulations (COMAR)

common law

irrevocable consent

jointly and severally liable

judicial activism

latent defects

natural persons

nonresidential property

precedent

real estate

real estate broker

real estate brokerage
    services

red flags

salespersons

statutes

strict construction

■ OVERVIEW

In this chapter, you will learn some of the history of brokerage regulation in Maryland; learn which Maryland statutes and regulations govern the industry today; come to understand the structure, duties, and powers of the Maryland Real Estate Commission; and begin to appreciate the mechanics of obtaining, maintaining, and upgrading a brokerage license. You will also delve into various requirements and prohibitions that guide the everyday life of a real estate licensee.

■ HISTORY AND SOURCES OF MARYLAND LICENSE LAW

The *Maryland Real Estate Brokers Act*, a law designed to protect the public interest, became effective June 1, 1939. Since then, there have been frequent revisions.

1

All the work of real estate licensees is affected by this important statute. It is therefore the basis of much of this chapter.

The Maryland Real Estate Brokers Act appears as Title (Chapter) 17 in the *Business Occupations and Professions* Article of the Annotated Code of Maryland. In this book, this statute is referred to as the "Brokers Act" and as "Title 17."

Real estate brokerage is governed both by statutory law, such as the Brokers Act mentioned above, and by administrative law, found in the **Code of Maryland Regulations (COMAR).** Regulations governing the practice of real estate brokerage are passed and enforced by the Maryland Real Estate Commission—a body within the executive branch of government. The Maryland Real Estate Brokers Act was enacted by the legislative branch of Maryland government: the General Assembly. Therefore, it is an example of legislative (statutory) law.

In addition to statutes and regulations, some aspects of **common law** apply to real estate brokerage in Maryland. Common law is called *the unwritten law* because it is not written by a legislative body; rather, it is found in numerous volumes of decisions from courts of appeal. Such decisions are needed when no relevant statute exists or when an existing statute is challenged as unconstitutional. They also arise in cases of ambiguity where uncertainty of language or intent makes a statute difficult to apply.

On occasion, older laws no longer seem to make sense to the courts called on to give their opinions. Judges who then "modernize" the law are practicing **judicial activism**. This is in contrast to **strict construction**, which takes statutes at their face value and supports the original intention of their writers. For example, in 1965, the U.S. Supreme Court held that the Civil Rights Act of 1866 still applied literally—word for word—and was still the law of the land almost a century after it was written. Their decision is an example of strict construction.

Statutes are *voted into law* by legislative bodies, but common law is *handed down* by judges. Decisions made by courts of appeal become binding on lower courts within their judicial area. The higher the court of appeal making a decision, the more numerous the courts in which that decision becomes the standard—the **precedent**—for decisions made later in those lower courts.

The Maryland Real Estate Commission, one of the largest licensing boards within the Department of Labor, Licensing, and Regulation, adopts and enforces regulations to implement the Brokers Act. These regulations are **administrative law.** Regulations apply statutes to particular situations. The Code of Maryland Regulations (COMAR) contains regulations adopted by all 18 of Maryland's licensing boards.

The Brokers Act and regulations from COMAR relating to real estate can be found in many college and public libraries in bound volumes in the legal reference section. They are also available to the public at the Web site of the Real Estate Commission: *www.dllr.state.md.us/license/occprof/recomm.html*.

The statutes and regulations discussed in this book are those enacted at the time of its publication, including changes taking effect on or before October 1, 2008.

■ DEFINITIONS OF TERMS [§17-101]

As used in Title 17, certain terms have specific definitions that apply to either a section of the law or the entire statute. For example, a **real estate broker** is defined as an individual who provides **real estate brokerage services.** Those services are then defined as any of the following:

- For consideration, and for another person: selling, buying, exchanging, or leasing any real estate or collecting rent its use
- For consideration, assisting another person to locate or obtain for purchase or lease any residential real estate
- Engaging regularly in a business of dealing in real estate or leases or options on real estate
- Engaging in a business the primary purpose of which is promoting the sale of real estate through a listing in a publication issued primarily for promotion of real estate sales
- Engaging in the business of subdividing land located in any state and selling the subdivided lots
- For consideration, serving as a consultant for any of the activities in this list

Although Maryland law generally defines *persons* as "individuals, receivers, trustees, guardians, personal representatives, fiduciaries, or representatives of any kind and any partnership, firm, association, or other entity," only **natural persons** (individuals) may hold real estate licenses granted by the State. However, a broker's license, rather than showing the broker's actual name, may show the name under which the broker is operating—typically a company name. This is called the broker's *designated name*.

In the statute and in this book, *Commission* refers to the State Real Estate Commission. When the term *licensed* is used, it refers to the status of an individual licensed by that Commission.

■ LICENSES AND CERTIFICATES ISSUED BY THE COMMISSION (TITLE 17, SUBTITLE III)

The Commission issues three levels of license for those delivering real estate brokerage services: broker, associate broker, and salesperson. It also issues branch office certificates. Currently, there are almost 56,000 active licenses, including all three levels (see Table 1.1). This does not include inactive and expired licenses. Licenses may be kept on inactive status no longer than four years, after which they expire. Expired licenses are then held four years from the date of their expiration, during which time they may be reinstated as discussed later in this chapter. Persons named on inactive or expired licenses may not perform acts of real estate brokerage.

In addition to the three basic levels of license, each level has subtypes. Broker licenses may be resident, nonresident, reciprocal, or temporary/for commercial only. Associate broker and salesperson licenses include resident, nonresident, and reciprocal (Maryland has reciprocal licensing agreements with Pennsylvania and

TABLE   1.1

Overview of Active and Inactive Licenses and Certificates Granted by the Commission by January 1, 2008

LICENSE LEVEL	SUBTYPE	NUMBER
Broker	Resident	4,960
	Nonresident	
	Reciprocal	31
	Temporary (Commercial)	0
Associate Broker	Resident	3,261
	Nonresident	
	Reciprocal	8
Salesperson	Resident	46,900
	Nonresident	
	Reciprocal	103
	Special exception to be branch office manager without 3 years' experience	0
	Total	55,996
Inactive	All levels	4,384
Branch Offices	n/a	773
TOTAL	Total	60,380

(From published minutes of Commission meeting, January 20, 2008)

Oklahoma). In addition to these three subtypes, associate brokers and salespersons may also be registered to manage branch offices.

To have an active license, every salesperson and associate broker must be affiliated with and under the authority of a licensed broker. When individuals affiliate with brokers, they enter into either an employee or nonemployee relationship with them. Almost all licensees affiliated with brokers today are in a nonemployee relationship with their brokers. Even though many **affiliates** meet the IRS requirements for "qualified real estate agent"—also called "statutory nonemployees"—and are self-employed from the point of view of income taxation, they are all still subject to supervision and control by their broker.

Throughout this book, *affiliate* (the noun) refers either to a licensed associate broker or a licensed salesperson. **Associate brokers** are individuals who have met the educational, experience, and testing requirements for becoming real estate brokers but who request licenses that authorize them to provide real estate brokerage services only *under a broker* with whom they affiliate as associate brokers. Despite their education and experience, their duties and authority are no greater than those of salespersons. **Salespersons** are individuals who aid brokers with whom they are affiliated in providing real estate brokerage services. Salespersons are general agents of their broker.

Affiliates meet the Internal Revenue Service requirements for staututory nonemployee (self-employed) status when their broker does not withhold federal or state income taxes, Social Security, or Medicare assessments. Also, the broker does not make any contribution to affiliates' Social Security accounts. Affiliates' paychecks are "net" to them; they are responsible for all their own taxes. Section 3508 of the IRS Code specifies that such "Qualified Real Estate Agents" may report their income as self-employed persons using Schedule 1040C. To be recognized as a qualified real estate agent, affiliates must

- be licensed real estate agents (hold an active real estate license);
- receive "substantially all"—meaning no less than 90 percent—of their brokerage remuneration based on production rather than upon hours worked; and
- act pursuant to written contracts with their brokerage firms stating that they will not be treated as employees for federal tax purposes.

Real estate, as used in the Brokers Act, is defined as any interest in real property anywhere. Such interests include, but are not limited to, interests in condominiums, time-share estates, and time-share licenses, as those terms are defined in the *Real Property* Article, as well as fee and life estates.

In the Brokers Act, the term *state* refers to any state in the United States, its territories, possessions, or the District of Columbia. In this book, when *State* is capitalized, it refers to the State of Maryland. In the statute, *Department* refers to the Department of Labor, Licensing, and Regulation under whose authority the Commission operates. *Secretary* refers to the chief executive of that department.

Persons Not Subject to the Brokers Act When Performing Acts of Real Estate Brokerage [§17-102]

Certain persons who perform real estate activities are required neither to hold brokerage licenses nor to be governed by the provisions of the Brokers Act. However, like all persons in the State, they are governed in their real estate dealings by other laws, such as those in the *Real Property* Article. Examples are

- persons acting under a judgment or order of a court;
- public officers performing the duties of their office;
- landlords or owners of any real estate, unless their primary business is providing real estate brokerage services;
- persons engaging in a single transaction selling or leasing real estate, if they are acting under a power of attorney executed by the owner of that real estate;
- auctioneers who are licensed by various jurisdictions within Maryland when selling any real estate at public auction; and
- persons acting as receivers, trustees, personal representatives, or guardians.

Persons Who Must Conform to the Act When Performing Acts of Real Estate Brokerage but Are Not Required to Hold Brokerage Licenses [§17-301(b)]

In contrast, other persons, when performing acts of real estate brokerage, are governed by and must conform to the relevant requirements of the Brokers Act, although they need not hold real estate licenses. They are

- financial institutions in the leasing or selling of property they have acquired through foreclosure or by receiving a deed or an assignment in lieu of foreclosure;
- lawyers who are not regularly engaged in the business of providing real estate services and who do not advertise that they conduct such business;
- homebuilders in the rental or initial sale of homes they have constructed (although homebuilders and their salespersons must be registered with the Home Builder and Home Builder Sales Representative Registration Unit of the Consumer Affairs Division in the Office of the Attorney General);

- agents of a licensed real estate broker or of an owner of real estate, while managing or leasing that real estate for that broker or for the property's owner;
- persons who negotiate the sale, lease, or transfer of businesses when the sale does not include any interest in real property other than the lease for the property where the business operates; and
- owners who subdivide and sell not more than six lots of unimproved property they own in any one calendar year (although if they or their family has owned the property for ten years or more, there is no limit on the number of lots they may sell).

■ THE MARYLAND REAL ESTATE COMMISSION [§17-201–§17-214]

The Maryland Real Estate Commission is one of several commissions within the Department of Labor, Licensing, and Regulation. It consists of nine members; five are licensee members chosen, one each, from the Eastern Shore, Baltimore Metropolitan Area, Baltimore City, Southern Maryland, and Western Maryland. They must have held Maryland real estate licenses for at least ten years and have resided in the areas from which they are appointed for at least five years, both immediately prior to their appointment. The other four members are consumer members who shall not have had an ownership interest in or received compensation from an entity regulated by the Commission in the year just before their appointment.

Members are appointed by the Governor with the advice of the Secretary and the advice and consent of the Senate. Membership terms, which are staggered to ensure regulatory continuity, begin on June 1 and end four years later, either with reappointment or on the appointment of a qualified replacement. Members may be removed before the end of their terms by the Governor in cases of incompetence or misconduct.

Each year, members of the Commission elect from among themselves a chairperson to preside at their meetings. This officer is covered by a surety bond. The Commission meets each month with a majority of the members then under appointment constituting a quorum. These meetings are open to the public.

The Commission has adopted bylaws for the conduct of its meetings and regulations for the conduct of hearings and for issuance of licensing applications. With ten days' advance written notice, a member of the public may speak before the Commission.

The Commission's Executive Director, who is appointed by and serves at the pleasure of the Secretary, is not a member of the Commission. Neither is the Executive Director the chairperson of the Commission. The Executive Director, a State employee who is also covered by a surety bond, attends and participates in the monthly meetings, directs the day-to-day operations of the Commission, and supervises its office staff and field inspectors between monthly meetings.

Duties and Powers [§17-209, §17-212]

The Commission's primary duties are administration and enforcement of the Brokers Act through the licensing process. To carry out this duty, the Commission is empowered to

- investigate complaints of unlicensed brokerage activity,
- investigate complaints about licensee behavior,
- conduct hearings and administer oaths,
- issue subpoenas for attendance of witnesses or production of evidence,
- take depositions, and
- seek injunctions (in certain circumstances).

The Commission acts as Police

The Commission adopts, maintains, and enforces General Regulations and a Code of Ethics that set forth standards of conduct for all individuals who are under the authority of the Brokers Act. The Code of Ethics and the General Regulations are part of COMAR—the Code of Maryland Regulations. The Code of Ethics addresses licensees' relations with the client, the public, and with other licensees. It is quite different from the Code of Ethics of the National Association of REALTORS®. However, the two codes are complementary in that neither contradicts the other.

The Commission must investigate any written, sworn complaint alleging that an unauthorized person has provided real estate brokerage services. The Commission has statutory authority to hold hearings on such a complaint and to impose a financial penalty not to exceed $5,000 for the first proven violation, $15,000 for the second, and $25,000 for a third or subsequent violation. (An "unauthorized person" is one who neither holds a required license nor is exempt from the requirement to have one.)

Authority over Nonlicensees [§17-613 (c)]

The Commission is empowered to hold hearings and assess fines not only on licensees but also on certain nonlicensees who violate any part of the Brokers Act. See §17-301(b) discussed above.

Other Powers and Duties [§17-208–§17-214]

2 or 3 ?'s

The Commission has many other powers and duties. In the course of its operation, it routinely

- issues, renews, suspends, or revokes licenses;
- orders investigations and holds hearings as needed;
- after hearings, reprimands and/or fines licensees who have violated law or regulation;
- collects and retains license fees;
- collects fines and pays them into the General Fund of the State;
- submits an annual report of its activities to the Secretary;
- certifies, on request of any person and payment of the required fee, the licensing status and qualifications of any person who is the subject of the request;
- approves the content of educational courses for licensing and for continuing education;
- adopts regulations and a code of ethics to implement Title 17;
- convenes hearing boards (panels) of three members, at least one of whom must be a consumer member and one a professional member (licensee) from among the commissioners; and
- maintains and administers a Guaranty Fund to reimburse members of the public as much as $25,000 for actual losses caused by licensees and their employees. *Actual Losses*

■ REQUIREMENTS FOR LICENSURE

Before providing real estate brokerage services in the State, individuals generally must be licensed by the Commission either as real estate brokers or as associate brokers or salespersons affiliated with and working under the authority of licensed brokers. Licenses are granted for a two-year term beginning on their date of issuance.

Brokers [§17-305]

To qualify for the real estate broker license, applicants must

- be of good character and reputation and at least 18 years of age;
- have completed a 135-hour course in real estate—including 3 clock hours of real estate ethics—approved by the Commission;
- have been licensed as real estate salespersons actively and lawfully for at least three years; and
- have passed the broker prelicensing examination.

For applicants who are qualified to practice law in this state, the Commission waives the education and experience requirements but not the examination requirement. Broker education requirements for all others are in addition to the salesperson (60-hour) requirements they may have previously met. However, an individual who has been engaged in real estate practice as a licensed real estate broker in another state for at least three of the five years immediately preceding submission of application is considered to have satisfied the broker educational requirements.

Associate Brokers [§17-304]

To qualify for the associate real estate broker license, an applicant must meet the education and experience requirements for a broker license. The applicant must also obtain written commitment from a licensed real estate broker to accept the applicant as an associate broker of the firm when all other associate broker requirements have been satisfied.

Salespersons [§17-305]

To qualify for issuance of the salesperson license, an applicant must

- be of good character and reputation;
- be at least 18 years of age;
- successfully complete a basic (60-hour) course in real estate—including 3 clock hours of real estate ethics—approved by the Commission;
- pass the required examination; and
- obtain written commitment from a licensed real estate broker to accept the applicant as a salesperson of the firm when all other salesperson licensing requirements have been satisfied.

General Rules [§17-307]

Applicants must successfully complete prelicensing education requirements before taking salesperson or broker examinations. General Regulation .26 states that after passing both parts (General and State) of the exam, application for licensure must be made within one year or re-examination will be required. The Commission's application forms must be used. The required fees are shown in Table 1.2.

Requirements for Nonresidents [§17-514]

Salesperson, associate broker, and broker applicants who are not residents of the State must submit to the Commission their **irrevocable consent.** This consent allows a licensee to be served with official documents without the server's having

TABLE 1.2

Usual License Fees

	Original License Fee	Guaranty Fund Assessment*	Total Original Fees	Renewal or Exchange of License Fee
Broker	$95	$20	$115	$95
Associate Broker	$65	$20	$85	$65
Salesperson	$45	$20	$65	$45

raise

The proper fees must accompany every application. These fees, originally established by statute, are now subject to annual change by the Commission. Applicants are also required to pay the testing service a $65 examination fee to register, take, or retake all or part of either real estate examination. Standard examination registration fees, which are neither refundable nor transferable, may be paid by check, money order, company check, or cashier's check. Cash is not accepted.

Fees for other services:

Not Correct

Certificate of License History	$10	Reinstatement of License/Late Fee	$100
Broker Business Address Change	5	Transfer to Another Broker	10
Broker Business Name Change	5	Time-share Registration	100
Branch Office License	5	Duplicate License or Pocket Card	5
Personal Name Change	5	Dishonored Check	25
Reactivate Inactive License	10		

* The Guaranty Fund initial assessment, paid on issuance of the first license to an applicant, is not paid on renewals unless needed to replenish the Guaranty Fund. This has happened only once in the past 30 years.

to travel to a foreign (out-of-state) jurisdiction to present them. Applicants are required to submit any additional documentation that the Commission requires to determine their professional competence, good character, and reputation. Broker applicants must also submit or pay for a credit report.

Licenses for Nonresidents to Perform Commercial Brokerage [§17-536–§17-540]

In the above sections, a "nonresident real estate broker" is a person licensed by a jurisdiction other than Maryland to provide real estate brokerage services there. That broker may be either an individual, a partnership, joint venture, limited liability company, limited liability partnership, or corporation, depending on the jurisdiction. "Nonresident real estate salespersons" (and associate brokers) are individuals who are licensed, not by the Commission but by another state, to provide real estate brokerage services under a nonresident real estate broker—in this context, a broker who has complied with detailed requirements for a temporary license to perform acts of brokerage involving Maryland commercial property. Nonresident brokers may qualify for such a license only if their own state grants similar privileges to Maryland licensees. The nonresident broker may deal with commercial property only through and under a licensed Maryland real estate broker with whom the nonresident has a written agreement detailing their entire relationship for specific proposed transactions.

The onerous requirements for a temporary license imposed by these sections may be one reason that not one temporary commercial broker or salesperson license was issued between October 1, 2003, and December 31, 2007. In addition, interstate cobrokering on Maryland real property of all kinds is much simpler when the broker from the other state procures a standard nonresident license described in §17-514 above.

Waiver of Requirements for Licensure [§17-308]

The Commission may waive any requirement for individual licenses for applicants who hold comparable or equivalent licenses granted by another state if those applicants pay the required application fees, meet the relevant requirements, and submit certification of license history from the other state. If applicants are seeking broker licenses based on their comparable licenses in another state, they must provide adequate evidence of actively maintaining brokerage offices there.

Reciprocity [§17-3A-01–§17-3A-10]

To facilitate transactions involving parties from other states seeking to buy, rent, or sell property in Maryland and Maryland residents seeking to buy, rent, or sell in other states, the 2006 legislative session made provisions for reciprocal real estate brokerage licensing. Under the terms of any reciprocal licensing agreement, the Brokers Act requires the following:

- That each state recognize the previous education, experience, and examination of applicants for any of the licensure classes authorized in the applicants' home state as satisfying the requirements for licensure in the reciprocal state
- That applicants submit consent to service of process, in a form required by the Commission (similar to the irrevocable consent required of traditional nonresident applicants by §17-514)
- That applicants verify that they have read and agree to comply with all laws of the state for which they are seeking reciprocal licensure
- That applicants, other than brokers, provide certification from their broker that the broker is currently licensed and will actively and personally supervise the applicants performing real estate brokerage services in the state where they would be receiving the reciprocal licensure
- That neither state requires additional continuing education to renew reciprocal licenses
- That applicants furnish to Maryland Certificates of Licensure or Records of Good Standing from the state from which the applicants are applying. Such statements must contain the applicants' names, addresses, licensure classifications, and history of past or present disciplinary proceedings. Applicants themselves must give written statements as to whether they are subjects of any disciplinary proceedings or criminal investigations anywhere and whether they have been convicted in the United States of any felony or certain misdemeanors or of any crimes that violate the Maryland Brokers Act.
- Each state requires that brokers holding reciprocal licenses, who later open principal places of business in the state that granted them reciprocal licenses, promptly notify that state and obtain a standard nonresident license within 90 days after establishing those principal places of business. Applicants for standard nonresident licenses may be required to pass the state portion of a licensure examination required by the state granting the reciprocal licenses.
- States have the right, for cause, to deny applications for reciprocal licensure.

Maryland has signed reciprocity agreements with Pennsylvania and Oklahoma, and is negotiating with other states. Many states have multiple reciprocity agreements, often found on each state's Web site. In each situation, the details of the "reciprocity" may be very different from those of the Maryland program. The

Maryland Real Estate Commission appears to be proceeding with great care to establish the reciprocity authorized by the 2006 legislation. Barriers to agreement between states sometimes include unwillingness to renew without the reciprocal license holder's completing the host state's continuing education requirements, passing a host state's law exam, or taking the same number of prelicensure hours as required by the host state. Maryland law seeks mutual concession in all these areas. As noted in Table 1.1, 142 reciprocal licenses of various levels had been issued by the end of 2007.

Pocket Cards and License Certificates [§17-309]

License certificates and pocket cards issued by the Commission show

- the name of the licensee,
- the designated name of the licensed real estate broker with whom a salesperson or associate broker is affiliated,
- the date the license will expire, and
- the licensing registration number of the licensee.

Certificates and pocket cards issued for affiliates are sent to their brokers. Pocket cards are detached and given to affiliates when they sign their own license certificates. The signed license certificates are retained and displayed in the office out of which each licensee operates. Although no such requirement is explicitly stated anywhere in the Brokers Act or in any regulation, the Commission has informed the author that licensees are expected to carry their pocket cards whenever they engage in real estate brokerage activity.

Real estate broker licenses authorize their holders to provide real estate brokerage services to the public. Persons who hold associate broker and salesperson licenses may never provide real estate brokerage services in their own name or in the name of any broker with whom they are not affiliated. They may only provide brokerage services in the name of the broker under whom they are licensed. Individuals on inactive status have no broker. Their licenses and pocket cards have been returned to the Commission. While inactive, their performing acts of real estate brokerage is a violation of law—a misdemeanor punishable by fine and/or imprisonment.

Exchange of Licenses and Additional Licenses and Affiliations [§17-311–§17-313]

A licensed real estate broker may also hold licenses as a real estate salesperson or associate broker, affiliated under another licensed real estate broker. This requires submission of additional proper applications to the Commission and payment of additional license fees. A broker in one company who works at the same time for the broker of another company as an affiliate must obtain a commitment for such affiliation from that other broker and must inform that broker of the other license. A broker may operate more than one real estate company, but for each additional real estate brokerage company, the broker must obtain a separate real estate broker's license. Therefore, it is legally possible for an individual to hold two or more broker licenses simultaneously.

Licensees who hold salesperson, associate broker, or broker licenses may exchange those licenses for other levels of license by complying with procedures established by the Commission and paying the required additional fees. Affiliates may obtain additional licenses and become affiliated with additional Maryland brokers by obtaining a commitment from each additional broker, paying the required additional licensing fees, and giving notice of such multiple relationships to all their brokers.

Reinstatement after Nonrenewal [§17-314]

Reinstatement of an expired license is possible within the four years following the date of its expiration. It presently requires that applicants show proof of meeting all applicable continuing education requirements for the period since expiration and pay past-due renewal fees as well as $100 reinstatement fees. They must also meet the requirement of good character and reputation. Neither timely nor late renewal of a license affects the power of the Commission to bring charges for prior acts or conduct.

4 year inactive

Transfer of Affiliation [§17-311]

Affiliates may apply to the Commission to transfer their affiliation from one broker to another after obtaining from the new broker a commitment stating that, on termination of the current affiliation and issuance of new license certificates and pocket cards, they will become affiliated with the new broker. They shall also submit to the Commission, either from their former brokers or from themselves, a statement confirming termination of their prior relationship with their transfer applications. It is advisable in every case, although not clearly required by law or regulation, that the former broker be informed of the details of the transfer.

Dishonored Checks [§17-521]

In the event of a dishonored check, licensees are not considered to have properly renewed their licenses until they pay both the original amount of the renewal fees and a collection fee of $25 for each dishonored check.

If bounce

■ LICENSE TERM, TRANSFER, AND RENEWAL [§17-314]

A broker and the broker's affiliates' license renewal notices and application forms are mailed to the broker's main office not later than one month before licenses expire. The notices state

- the dates on which the current licenses expire;
- the dates by which the Commission must receive the renewal applications, if licensees use hard-copy (paper) applications for renewal; and
- the amount of the renewal fees (see Table 1.2).

Although the preferred mode of application for renewal is online—a method that enables instantaneous and less expensive processing—the Commission continues to accept and process hard-copy renewal and upgrade applications.

Continuing Education Requirements [§17-315]

Continuing education for license renewal is measured in **clock hours,** with credit allowed only for approved, individual courses of not less than 1.5 and not more than 6 hours in length. A *clock hour* is defined in the Business Occupations and Professions Article as 50 minutes of actual class time for each 60-minute hour [§1-101].

Completion of the required number of continuing education hours in specific subjects is required for renewal of any level of license. The standard requirement for all levels of license is 15 hours of approved instruction made up of

- at least 3 clock-hours of local, state, and federal legislative and regulatory updates;
- 1.5 hours dealing with fair housing;

TABLE   1.3

Continuing Education Requirements

Subject Matter	Renewal until Oct. 1, 2008	Renewal on or after Oct. 2, 2008
Legislative Update	3 hrs	3 hrs
Fair Housing (Licensees performing only commercial transactions may substitute Federal Americans with Disabilities Act)	1.5 hrs	1.5 hrs
Ethics, Flipping, and Predatory Lending	3 hrs	3 hrs
Other Approved Courses	1.5 hrs	7.5 hrs
Total Hours Required	9 hrs	15 hrs

- 3 clock-hours of ethics, including the Maryland Real Estate Commission Code of Ethics, as well as discussion of flipping properties and predatory lending; and
- 7.5 hours in other approved courses.

Until October 1, 2008, licensees who have held a Maryland real estate license for ten years or more will be required to complete only 9 clock hours (3 in legislative update, 1.5 in fair housing, 3 in ethics, and 1.5 in another approved subject). On and after October 2, 2008, virtually all licensees will be required to take 15 hours of continuing education. See Table 1.3.

There are certain exceptions:

- Licensees who are qualified to practice law in the state and those who hold graduate degrees in real estate from accredited colleges or universities need complete only 7.5 hours (legislative update, fair housing, and ethics).
- Licensees who perform only nonresidential brokerage may substitute 1.5 hours of instruction in the Americans with Disabilities Act for the fair housing requirement, but they still must complete a total of 15 hours.
- Holders of reciprocal licenses of any level are not required to complete any Maryland-approved hours of instruction when renewing their licenses.

In the Brokers Act, **nonresidential property** is defined in detail as

(1) real property improved by five or more single-family units; (2) improved and unimproved real property zoned for commercial, industrial, or nonresidential use by the local zoning authority of the county or municipality in which the property is located; and (3) unimproved real property zoned for improvement as multifamily units by the local zoning authority of the county or municipality in which the property is located, [but does not include]: (1) property zoned for agricultural use; or (2) single-family units, including a condominium or co-op unit, for sale or for lease, or otherwise conveyed or to be conveyed on a single basis.

Renewals must be accomplished before licenses expire. Those renewing in a timely manner must pay to the Commission the required renewal fees and affirm that they have completed the required number of hours of continuing education. Those who have not completed the required number of hours and renewed their licenses are then not properly licensed to provide brokerage services. Activities they perform during such a lapse in proper licensure may earn no compensation for them or their firms. A person whose license has expired may apply for reinstatement of that license at any time within four years after its expiration date.

There are several (letter) categories of subject matter approved for continuing education courses:

A. Federal, State, or local legislative and regulatory changes
B. Antitrust law
C. Fair housing law
D. Real estate ethics or professional standards
E. Disclosure
F. Professional enhancement for practicing licensees
G. Technology relating to real estate brokerage services (not more than three hours per renewal)

To be approved by the Commission, all continuing education course subject matter must relate to real estate.

Approved courses may be presented by the Maryland Association of REALTORS® or its member boards, the Real Estate Brokers of Baltimore City Inc., or any similar professional association or by an educational institution approved by the State Board of Higher Education. These courses must be taught by qualified instructors who are experienced in the real estate industry. The Commission's guidelines require that continuing education instructors have experience and expertise in the area or activity about which they are teaching.

When licensees complete each unit of study, the training institution that conducted the course issues certificates of completion to each student stating the

- number of clock hours,
- name and date of the course taken,
- code letter of the subject category, and
- names of the teacher and/or the organization presenting the training.

The education provider also reports these data to the Commission.

When investigators discover that licensees have falsely represented completion of the continuing education required for renewal, the offending licensees are subject to reprimands and various fines depending upon the circumstances surrounding their misrepresentations. The Commission employs outside firms that sample each year's renewals and report licensees who made false claims. In doing this sampling, the actual certificates of completion of each course claimed must be sent to the Commission. Obviously, licensees should keep all their course completion certificates.

The Commission may waive continuing education requirements for licensees who show good cause for being unable to meet the requirement.

Inactive Status
[§17-316]

The Commission will place the licenses of associate real estate brokers and real estate salespersons into inactive status when they are no longer affiliated with licensed real estate brokers and their license certificates and pocket cards are returned to the Commission.

up to   4 years
(maximum)

A licensee whose license is on inactive status may not provide real estate brokerage services through that license. This prohibition includes accepting fees for referrals. An inactive licensee is not affiliated with any broker and may not be compensated for any act of real estate brokerage. Individuals with inactive licenses may not be paid by a "referral company."

The placement of a license on inactive status does not affect the power of the Commission to suspend or revoke the license or to take any other disciplinary action against the licensee.

Unless an inactive license is reactivated, it expires four years after the date it is placed on inactive status. Renewal while on inactive status does not constitute reactivation. Subject to the four-year limitation, a license may be renewed while it is on inactive status without complying with the continuing education requirements. However, before reactivation, all continuing education requirements not previously satisfied must be completed.

The Commission will reactivate the license of real estate brokers on inactive status and reissue license certificates and pocket cards to them if they request reactivation and pay to the Commission the $10 reissuance fee. They must also meet the continuing education requirements that would have been necessary for renewal of licenses had they not been on inactive status. Salespersons and associate brokers returning from inactive status must meet the same requirements and must also submit an affiliation commitment, contingent on their reactivation, from a broker. While on inactive status, a salesperson or an associate broker has no broker.

Display of Certificates; Loss or Destruction [§17-317]

Licensed real estate brokers are required at all times to display their own license certificates in conspicuous places in their offices. The license certificates of licensees who are affiliated with a real estate broker must be displayed at the office location out of which each of them usually works.

The Commission must immediately be notified of the loss or destruction of a license certificate or pocket card. Upon receipt of an affidavit of loss or destruction and payment of the required fee ($5 for a lost or destroyed pocket card or license certificate), the Commission will issue appropriate duplicates.

Change of Name [§17-318]

When a licensee or a firm takes a new name, then upon receipt of the required application fee ($5), the old certificate, pocket card, and any required documentation, the Commission issues the licensee a new license certificate and pocket card that reflect the change.

Licensure and the Deceased Broker [§17-319]

On the death of a licensed real estate broker, any adult member of the family may carry on the brokerage firm for up to six months to close and terminate the business. To do this, the certificate and pocket card of the deceased broker must be surrendered to the Commission. Any information required by the Commission must also be submitted.

Before the end of the six-month period for carrying on the business of a deceased real estate broker, an individual may qualify for and receive from the Commission the license of the deceased broker, if that individual

- is a member of the immediate family of the decedent,
- has been continuously licensed as a real estate salesperson for the immediately preceding three years,
- passes the real estate broker examination required by this subtitle, and
- surrenders his real estate salesperson license certificate and pocket card to the Commission.

There must also have been compliance with the conditions for carrying on the business as stated in the first paragraph of this section.

A person receiving the reissued license of a deceased real estate broker may hold and use that license for as long as four years without meeting the 135-hour educational requirement. However, if the requirement has not been met within four years, the license automatically expires.

Return of Licenses; Terminating Affiliation [COMAR 09.11.01.08]

The license certificates and pocket cards of an affiliate must be returned to the Commission by the affiliate's broker

- on the request of an affiliate, that being a real estate salesperson or associate real estate broker,
- on the death of an affiliate, or
- after a hearing before the Commission and on a finding that the license of an affiliate is to be suspended or revoked.

Real estate brokers are required to surrender to the Commission, promptly on demand, any such person's license that may be in their possession or control. Failure to do so is grounds for disciplinary action.

In the event of an affiliate's termination (discharge) a broker must

- immediately mail to the licensee, at the last known address of that individual, notice of such termination;
- submit written notice to the Commission, including a copy of the notice mailed to the licensee; and
- return the license certificate of the licensee to the Commission.

Licensing Out-of-State Applicants [§17-514]

The Commission will issue licenses only to nonresident applicants who file with the Commission a signed statement of irrevocable consent. By submitting this statement, applicants agree that suits and actions may be commenced against them without their actually being served papers notifying them of forthcoming legal actions. They are also consenting that official delivery of papers to the executive director of the Commission shall bind them in any action, suit, or proceeding brought against them in any county in which the cause of action arose or the complaining party resides.

When serving process on the executive director of the Commission, persons filing must immediately send a copy of the filing, by certified mail, to the principal office of the person against whom the action is directed.

Note: The signature block on license examination applications contains these words: "If the address of this registration is not within the State of Maryland, I do hereby irrevocably consent that suits and actions may be commenced against me in the proper courts of the State of Maryland as required by the Maryland Annotated Code."

Maryland law states that if any nonresident real estate broker, associate broker, or salesperson participates in any real estate transaction, divides a fee, and/or holds deposits from any such transaction in Maryland, that very act is construed (considered) as giving irrevocable consent.

■ PROCESSING COMPLAINTS

The Commission's Web site provides a downloadable form on which complaints against licensees may be submitted. Upon receiving a properly completed complaint form, the Commission sends a copy of it to the broker of the company involved together with a letter from the Commission's executive director, stating that the broker must respond in writing with a full explanation of the allegations and what action the broker recommends. A broker's failure to respond to this inquiry may be considered grounds for disciplinary action. A chart indicating the steps in handling a complaint against a licensee is found in Appendix C of this book.

A copy of the executive director's letter is also sent to the complainant. Later, when the broker's answer is received, the Commission sends its own reply together with a copy of the broker's response to the complainant.

The Commission may commence proceedings on a complaint made by a Commission member or by other persons (who must make such complaints under oath). Complaints must be in writing and state specifically the facts on which the complaint is based, and they may be accompanied by documentary or other evidence.

After reviewing the content of the complaint, the Commission may refer it for investigation, if it appears an infraction has occurred. A complaint not referred for investigation is considered dismissed. Within 30 days of such dismissal, any member of the Commission may file an exception disagreeing with the dismissal. If such exception is taken, the full Commission will hold a hearing to consider proceeding with an investigation.

If an exception is not filed, the dismissal is considered a final decision of the Commission. "Final decision" means that any party aggrieved by the decision may then appeal to the appropriate court; decisions may not be appealed until they are final. *Only final decisions may be appealed.*

If the Commission or its designee, based on an investigation report, determines that grounds exist for disciplinary action, the matter is referred for a hearing. Complaints not referred for a hearing after investigation must be dismissed. This has the same effect as a final decision: any party aggrieved by that dismissal may make judicial appeal.

Hearings and Notices

Except as otherwise provided in the State Government Article (e.g., situations where summary action is needed), before the Commission takes any final action, it gives the individual against whom the action is contemplated an opportunity for a hearing before the Commission or a hearing board.

At least ten days before the hearing, the hearing notice is served personally on the individuals against whom complaints have been made, or it is sent by certified mail to their last known addresses. If the individuals are licensees other than brokers, at least ten days before the hearing, the Commission shall serve notice of the hearing to each real estate broker with whom the licensees are affiliated.

The individuals may have attorneys represent them at hearings. This does *not* mean that they can fail to appear and merely send their attorneys. It means that they can bring attorneys to represent them in their hearings. If the individuals against whom action is contemplated fail or refuse to appear, the Commission may proceed to hear and determine the matter without their presence. Unlike the meetings of panels to hear complaints and examine reports of investigators, these final meetings of panels are open to the public.

Real Estate Hearing Board [§17-324]

The Commission establishes two or three real estate hearing boards—often called *panels*—each consisting of three Commission members. At least one member of each panel must be a professional member, and at least one must be a consumer member. From among each hearing board's members, the Commission designates a chairperson.

Referral of Cases

The Commission (or one of its hearing panels) may order a final public hearing on any complaint that has been filed with the Commission or on any other matter for which a hearing may be required.

Before deciding to hold hearings, a panel will meet *privately* to

- review complaints and consider whether they provide a reasonable basis for disciplinary hearings, and
- review claims against the Guaranty Fund to determine what further action to take.

Panels meet *publicly* to

- hear licensees' responses to and defenses against complaints; and then
- decide whether to authorize punitive actions against them.

Hearing boards exercise the same powers as, and conduct hearings for, the Commission. They report their decisions and actions to the Commission. Panels specifically advise the Commission of any action they take against licensees involved in monetary loss, misappropriation of funds, or fraud.

Hearing Regulations [COMAR 09.11.03]

COMAR—the Code of Maryland Regulations—provides for four types of hearings:

1. Judicial hearings
2. Applications for licensure
3. Revocation or suspension of licenses
4. Claims against the Guaranty Fund

Hearings are conducted under several levels of overlapping hearing regulations.

On dismissal of a complaint, the complainant and the licensee are notified in writing. The dismissal of a complaint after investigation is not reviewable further. Other complaints substantially based on the same facts are usually similarly dismissed.

Summary Actions [§17-328]

Summary actions are those taken *before* holding hearings to protect the public quickly against imminent loss. They are then *followed by* hearings for which formal, timely notices are given.

Revocation after Actions of Other Agencies [§17-327]

The Commission may summarily order the revocation of the license of any licensee after a licensee is convicted in a court of law of a violation of this title, the conviction is final, and the period for appeal has expired.

The license of any nonresident licensee may be revoked if the real estate regulatory agency of the state where the licensee is a resident revokes the license issued by that state and certifies its order of revocation to the Commission.

When the Commission orders summary revocations under this section, it gives licensees written notice of the revocations and the findings on which they were based. After the revocations are effective, the Commission grants the licensees whose licenses have been revoked an opportunity to be heard promptly, either before the Commission or before a hearing board.

Rather than summarily order revocations of licenses under this section, the Commission may elect not to revoke the licenses until after the licensees are given opportunity for hearings. If the Commission elects to give the licensees opportunity for hearings before revoking the license, the Commission gives notice and holds those hearings in the manner required for other hearings.

In any hearings held because of convictions or revocations by other agencies, the Commission considers only evidence of whether or not the alleged convictions or revocations in fact occurred. However, in such hearings, licensees may present matters in mitigation of the offenses charged.

Summary Suspension for Trust Fund and Other Violations [§17-328]

The Commission may summarily order the suspension of a license who

- fails to account promptly for any funds held in trust;
- on demand, fails to display to the Commission all records, books, and accounts of any funds held in trust;
- has been convicted of a crime as defined in §17–322(B)(24) (i.e., a felony; a misdemeanor that is directly related to the fitness and qualification of the applicant or licensee to provide real state brokerage services; or a crime that constitutes a violation of any provision of the Brokers Act); or
- fails, within ten days after the conviction or within ten days following release from incarceration as a result of the conviction, whichever is later, to disclose to the Commission that the licensee has been convicted of a crime as defined above.

The Commission gives the licensee notice and supporting reasons for its action and offers the opportunity to be heard later.

TABLE 1.4	Process	Occasion
License Activation Processes	Renewal	Extends a license for another two-year term. Inactive licenses also require renewal. A license that is not renewed expires.
	Reissuance (Reactivation)	Licensee returns to active status and affiliates with a broker.
	Reinstatement	Revives license that expired for lack of renewal or restores license after suspension or revocation.

A summary suspension may start immediately or at any later date set by the order, and it shall continue until the licensee complies with the conditions set forth by the Commission in its order or until the Commission orders a different disposition after a hearing held under this section.

Judicial Review [§17-329]

A party who strongly disagrees with a final decision of the Commission may appeal to a circuit court. Upon appeal, that court may set a bond not to exceed $50,000 and stay (delay) the suspension or revocation. The bond money would be for the use and benefit of any member of the public who might suffer financial loss because of any violations of the Brokers Act by the plaintiff licensees.

Notice of Revocation or Suspension [§17-330]

Whenever a licensee's license is revoked or suspended and a stay is not ordered by the Commission or a court, the Commission notifies

- the licensee,
- the real estate broker with whom the licensee is affiliated,
- the Maryland Association of REALTORS®, and
- the local Board or Association of REALTORS® and the Realtist organization in the area of the licensee's office.

If the Commission revokes or suspends the license of a nonresident licensee, the Commission also notifies the Real Estate Commission or other licensing authority in the state where the licensee is a resident, reporting the cause for the revocation or suspension of the license. Table 1.4 clarifies some often-confused terms used in license activation.

■ REAL ESTATE GUARANTY FUND (TITLE 17, SUBTITLE IV)

The Guaranty Fund exists to reimburse members of the public for actual financial losses at the hands of real estate licensees and their unlicensed employees. The maximum reimbursement for any claim is $25,000. *Higher go to circuit count*

Use of Monies Collected

The Commission deposits all money collected for the Guaranty Fund with the State treasurer, who invests it, with the investment earnings credited to the Fund.

Initial Assessment for Fund

Kerw #'s

Before granting initial licenses to applicants, the Commission requires that they pay $20 assessments that are credited to the Guaranty Fund. Regardless of how many times an individual applies to the Commission for licenses, the Commission makes only one such assessment. However, if the amount in the Guaranty Fund falls below $250,000, the Commission assesses all the individuals then holding licenses a fee—typically payable at renewal—sufficient to return the Guaranty Fund to that minimum level. At the beginning of 2008, the fund contained almost $2 million dollars.

Claims Against the Fund

Evidence

A person may recover compensation from the Guaranty Fund only for actual financial losses. Claims must be based on acts or omissions that occurred in the provision of real estate brokerage services by licensees or unlicensed employees of a licensed real estate broker. Claims must involve transactions that relate to real estate located in the State and be based on acts or omissions in which money or property is obtained from a person by theft, embezzlement, false pretenses, forgery, or an act that constitutes fraud or misrepresentation.

A claim against the Guaranty Fund must

- be in writing and under oath,
- state the amount of loss claimed,
- state the facts on which the claim is based, and
- be accompanied by documentation or other evidence that supports the claim.

At any claim hearing, the burden of proof shall be on the claimant to establish the validity of the claim.

A person may not recover from the Guaranty Fund any loss that relates to

- the purchase of any interest in a limited partnership that invests in real estate,
- a joint venture that is promoted by a real estate licensee for the purpose of investment in real estate, or
- the purchase of commercial paper secured by real estate.

A claim under the Guaranty Fund may not be filed by the spouse or by the personal representative of the spouse of the individual alleged to be responsible for the act or omission giving rise to the claim. Any claim must be filed with the Commission *within three years* of the loss or discovery of the loss.

Notice to Buyer

Real estate brokers must include in each sales contract a written notice that buyers are protected by the Guaranty Fund in an amount not exceeding $25,000. Although only buyers are mentioned in this notice, sellers may also submit claims.

Action by Commission on a Claim

The Commission must act promptly upon receiving claims by

- forwarding copies to licensees and/or unlicensed employees alleged to be responsible and to their brokers;
- requiring a written response, within 10 days, from each of those individuals concerning the allegations set forth in the claim (this 10-day period is shorter than the 20 days required for response to other inquiries from the Commission);

- reviewing the claim and any responses to the claim; and
- conducting an investigation.

On the basis of its review of a claim and any investigation it conducts, the Commission either schedules a hearing or dismisses the claim.

Special Disposition of Smaller Claims

If the claim is $3,000 or less, the Commission, through a designated staff member, such as its executive director, may issue a proposed order either to pay or to deny the claim. Both the claimant and the licensee receive a copy of this proposed order.

Within 30 days, either the claimant or licensee may request a hearing or file written exceptions to the order. If either happens, the Commission must schedule a hearing on the claim. If no hearing is requested and no exceptions taken, the proposed order becomes a final order of the Commission.

Other Claims

The Commission gives notice of the hearing and opportunity to appear before the Commission to both the claimants and the licensees or unlicensed employees alleged to be responsible. The Commission must send the required notices to every party involved before conducting the hearing.

When the persons alleged to be responsible are licensees, the Commission may combine this hearing with disciplinary proceedings against licensees arising from the same facts alleged in a claim. A claimant may be *party* to that portion of the proceedings about the claim but may be a *witness* only in the disciplinary portion.

The misdemeanor penalty for knowingly making a false statement or material misstatement of fact about a Guaranty Fund matter is a fine and/or imprisonment. This procedure would have to be in a court of law; the Commission has no power to impose a sentence of imprisonment.

Payments by the Guaranty Fund

If a claim proves valid, the Commission orders its payment by the Guaranty Fund. The amount of compensation recoverable from the Guaranty Fund is limited to the actual monetary loss incurred by the claimant. The payout may never be more than $25,000 for any one claim. The amount paid may not include

- losses other than those from the original transaction,
- commissions owed to a licensee acting as either a principal or an agent in a real estate transaction, or
- any attorney's fees incurred in seeking money from the Fund.

Payment is not made until either the time for seeking judicial review is over or any judicial stay has expired. The Commission orders payment of claims in the order in which they were awarded.

Reimbursement of Guaranty Fund

When payments are made from the Fund, the Commission immediately and without further proceedings suspends the licenses of the offending licensees. Licensees suspended in this way are not reinstated until they repay to the Fund the full amounts owed, plus interest, and make formal application for reinstatement. Reimbursement of the Fund does not affect any disciplinary actions imposed on licensees.

After payments of claims by the Guaranty Fund, licensees responsible are required to reimburse the Fund in full for the amounts paid and for interest of at least 10 percent. (General Regulation .23 presently sets the rate at 12 percent.) The licensees responsible for an individual claim are **jointly and severally liable.** That is, each does not bear a proportionate share; rather, each is responsible for the entire amount until that entire amount is paid.

If licensees do not reimburse the Guaranty Fund as provided, the Commission may have the State Collections Unit sue them for the amount that has not been reimbursed and seek liens against their real property.

■ PROHIBITED ACTS [§17-322]

After giving proper notice, conducting any needed investigation, holding the required hearing, and reaching its conclusions, the Commission is empowered to deny a license to any applicant, to reprimand licensees, and to suspend or revoke the licenses of any licensees who

- fraudulently obtain or attempt to obtain licenses for themselves or others;
- fraudulently use licenses;
- directly or through other persons willfully make misrepresentations or knowingly make false promises;
- intentionally or negligently fail to disclose to any person with whom they deal material facts that they know or should know that relate to properties with which they deal;
- as affiliates, provide or attempt to provide real estate brokerage services on behalf of real estate brokers without informing in writing any other real estate broker under whom the affiliates are licensed;
- fail to follow the law concerning the conduct of dual agency;
- retain or attempt to retain the services of any unlicensed individuals (in such a way as to evade the law prohibiting payment of a commission to an unlicensed individual);
- guarantee, authorize, or permit other persons to guarantee future profits from the resale of real property;
- solicit, sell, or offer to sell real property so as to influence or attempt to influence a prospective party to the sale of real property by offering prizes or free lots, conducting a lottery or contest, or advertising "free appraisals" unless prepared to appraise real estate free of charge for any person and for any purpose;
- accept a listing contract to sell real property that fails to provide a definite termination date that is effective automatically, not requiring require further notice from the either the buyer or the seller;
- accept a listing contract to sell real property that provides for a "net" return to a seller and leaves the licensees free to sell the real property at any price higher than the "net" price;
- knowingly solicit a party to an exclusive listing contract with another licensee to terminate that contract and enter a new contract with the licensees making the solicitation;
- solicit a party to a sales contract, lease, or agreement that was negotiated by other licensees to breach that contract, lease, or agreement for the purpose

of substituting a new contract, lease, or agreement, either for the benefit of the licensees making the solicitation or for their firm;

- for any transactions in which the licensees have served either as brokers or affiliates of brokers, fail to furnish promptly to each party to the transactions copies of the listing contracts to sell or rent real property, the contracts of sale, or the lease agreements;

- for any transactions in which the licensees have served as or on behalf of a real estate broker, fail to keep copies of all executed listing contracts to sell or rent real property, contracts of sale, or lease agreements;

- whether or not acting for monetary gain, knowingly induce or attempt to induce persons to transfer real estate or discourage or attempt to discourage persons from buying real estate by making representations about the existing or potential proximity of real property owned or used by individuals of a particular race, color, religion, sex, handicap, familial status, or national origin or by representing that the existing or potential proximity of real property owned or used by individuals of a particular race, color, religion, national origin, etc., will or may result in the lowering of property values; a change in the racial, religious, or ethnic character of a block, neighborhood, or area; an increase in criminal or antisocial behavior in the area; or a decline in the quality of the schools serving the area;

- use any of the following material if it includes the name of an organization or association of which the licensees are not members: contract forms for the listing of real property for sale, rent, or exchange; contract forms for the sale, rent, or exchange of real property; or any advertising matter;

- as real estate brokers or affiliates, advertise the sale or rent of or an offer to buy real property while failing to disclose in the advertisement the names of the licensee advertisers and the fact that the advertisers are indeed real estate licensees;

- advertise in any misleading or untruthful manner;

- as affiliates, advertise the sale or rent of or an offer to buy real property in their own names while failing to disclose in the advertisement the designated name of the real estate broker on whose behalf the affiliates are acting;

- for real estate brokerage services provided by associate real estate brokers or real estate salespersons, accept commissions or other valuable considerations from persons other than the real estate brokers with whom they are affiliated;

- fail to account for or to remit promptly any money that comes into their possession;

- pay or receive a rebate, profit, compensation, or commission in violation of any provision of this act;

- under the laws of the United States or of any state, are convicted in a court of law of felonies or misdemeanors that are directly related to their fitness and qualification to provide real estate brokerage services or of a crime that constitutes a violation of any provision of the Brokers Act;

- engage in conduct that demonstrates bad faith, incompetence, or untrustworthiness or that constitutes dishonest, fraudulent, or improper dealings;

- with actual knowledge of their violations, associate with licensees in transactions or practices that violate any provision of the Brokers Act;

- fail as real estate brokers to exercise reasonable and adequate supervision over the provision of real estate brokerage services by other individuals on their behalf;

- provide to any parties contracts that do not contain a notice of a buyer's right of selection, as required by the Brokers Act;
- require a buyer to employ a particular title insurance company, settlement company, escrow company, or title lawyer in violation of this act;
- fail to make the disclosure of representation as required by §17-528;
- violate any trust accounts provision of this act that relates to trust money;
- violate any other provision of this act;
- violate any regulation adopted under this act or any provision of the Code of Ethics; or
- violate §17-320(d) by failing as branch office managers to exercise reasonable and adequate supervision over the brokerage work of sales agents or associate brokers registered with their offices.

Instead of, or in addition to, suspension or revocation, for any violation of the Brokers Act (Title 17), the Commission may impose a penalty not exceeding $5,000 for a first violation, $15,000 for a second, and $25,000 for a third or subsequent violation. To determine the amount of the penalty imposed, the Commission considers

- the seriousness of the violation,
- the harm caused by the violation,
- the good faith of the licensee, and
- any history of previous violations by the licensee.

The Commission pays any penalty collected into the General Fund of the State.

The Commission considers several facts when granting, denying, renewing, suspending, or revoking licenses or reprimanding licensees, when the individuals concerned have been convicted of certain crimes. In the case of felonies and misdemeanors, they consider

- the nature of the crime, and
- the relationship of the crime to the activities authorized by the license.

In the case of felonies, they consider

- the relevance of the conviction to the fitness and qualification of the applicants or licensees to provide real estate brokerage services,
- the length of time since the conviction, and
- the behavior and activities of the applicants or licensees before and after their convictions.

The Drug Enforcement Act of 1990 authorizes the Commission to impose sanctions upon licensees for a controlled substance offense.

A Maryland statute, Child Support—Enforcement Procedures, subjects licensees to having their licenses suspended and renewals denied if they are overdue in the payment of child support awarded by Maryland or any other state.

■ PROHIBITED ACTS PUNISHABLE BY IMPRISONMENT

There are real estate–related criminal offenses for which imprisonment of an individual is a possible penalty. Note that the term *person* includes licensees, nonlicensees, individuals, and business entities such as corporations, partnerships, limited liability companies, and so forth. Although the Commission is empowered to pursue all violators of these provisions, including nonlicensees, and to impose monetary penalties of as much as $25,000, only a court of law can try, convict, and sentence an individual to prison.

In addition to being reprimanded, suspended, revoked, and fined by action of the Commission, the Brokers Act also provides for imposition by a court of law of fines not to exceed $5,000 and/or imprisonment not to exceed one year for a first offense, $15,000 and two years for a second, and $25,000 and three years for third or subsequent violations that involve the following sections of the Brokers Act:

§17–502	Proper handling of trust money
§17–525	Discriminatory real estate practices in Baltimore City
§17–526	Discriminatory real estate practices in Montgomery County
§17–527	Mass solicitation of listings that violates Baltimore City and Baltimore County laws
§17–530	Failure to Disclose Agency Relationship to opposing parties or their agents
§17–532	Duties to Client, including performance of dual agency and presentation of Property Condition Disclosure/Disclaimer Statement
§17–601	License generally required for performance of brokerage
§17–602	Forbidden misrepresentation by affiliates' holding themselves out to be brokers
§17–603	Broker's use of unauthorized individuals; lending license certificates
§17–604	Payment of prohibited compensation
§17–605	Payment to nonlicensed lawyers simply for referrals; certain mass solicitation
§17–606	Requirements for advertisements placed upon property subject to ground rent
§17–607	Requiring use of any particular title insurance, settlement, escrow company, mortgage lender, financial institution, or title lawyer
§17–608	Discriminatory representations to encourage sales or discourage purchases
§17–609	Solicitation intended to change racial composition of neighborhood
§17–610	Misstatement of facts in Guaranty Fund complaints
§17–611	Violation of suspension order in designated real estate conservation areas

Maryland courts are required to report to the Commission, for appropriate action, all convictions of licensees for violation of this act with respect to blockbusting and discriminatory real estate practices in Baltimore City or Montgomery County. The Commission enforces the provisions of the sections concerning Montgomery County. For this purpose it receives complaints, conducts investigations, issues subpoenas, and holds hearings.

REAL ESTATE BROKERAGE PRACTICE IN BALTIMORE CITY

Although Baltimore City does not issue or require a separate real estate license to perform real estate activities there, local law does regulate the activities of licensees who practice in that city. Many of the prohibited acts are similar, if not identical, to State law. The Baltimore City real estate license law is found in §132 of Article 19 of the Baltimore City Code under the title "Real Estate Practices."

MARYLAND SECURITIES ACT

The Maryland Securities Act requires licensing of persons engaged in the offer and sale of real estate–related securities, including limited partnership interests in real property. The Maryland Securities Commission regulates all activities construed to be securities-related business. To inquire if certain activities could be construed as securities-related business, contact the Maryland Securities Commissioner.

REAL ESTATE APPRAISERS AND HOME INSPECTORS ACT

Title 16 of the *Business Occupations and Professions* Article of the Annotated Code of Maryland establishes licensing and certification procedures for real estate appraisers as well as for home inspectors. Title 16 creates a nine-member State Commission of Real Estate Appraisers and Home Inspectors within the Department of Labor, Licensing, and Regulation to administer that act.

Individuals who are licensed to provide real estate brokerage services do not also need to be licensed as real estate appraisers when merely recommending a listing price or a purchase price for real estate, provided that the opinion is *not* called an appraisal. A competitive market analysis (CMA) is not an appraisal, and its preparation for a seller or purchaser does not require an appraisal license or certificate.

To receive a real estate appraiser's license or certification, an individual must complete mandated educational requirements, pass an examination developed by the State Commission of Real Estate Appraisers, have accumulated 2,000 hours of acceptable appraisal work as a licensed real estate appraisal trainee, and complete 75 hours of classroom instruction. To be a Licensed Appraiser, an applicant must complete 150 hours of "tested" classroom instruction, 15 of which are in the Uniform Standards of Professional Appraisal Practice. To be licensed as a Certified Residential Real Estate Appraiser, an individual must complete 200 hours of classroom study and have an associate's degree or 21 hours in specified collegiate courses. The requirements for Certified General Real Estate Appraiser include 300 classroom hours and a bachelor's degree or 30 specified collegiate courses. Each level of appraisal license authorizes prescribed levels of appraisal activity.

Real estate brokerage licensees who hold either appraisal or home inspection certifications must avoid conflicts of interest by not performing any appraisals or home inspections for real estate brokerage transactions from which they or any family members or business associates might benefit. However, brokerage licensees may perform competitive market analyses (CMAs).

Requirements for Preparing a CMA [COMAR 09.11.02.02.F]

The Real Estate Commission's Code of Ethics imposes specific requirements for licensees preparing a CMA for a prospect, customer, or client. For instance, the notice that follows must appear conspicuously on the first page of the CMA:

COMPETITIVE MARKET ANALYSIS DISCLOSURE
This analysis is not an appraisal. It is intended only for the purpose of assisting buyers or sellers or prospective buyers or sellers in deciding the listing, offering, or sale price of the real property.

In preparing CMAs, licensees must disclose to clients, prospective clients, or customers their use of any comparables in which they have any present or contemplated interest.

■ BUILDING INSPECTIONS

Licensees are not required to be experts in building construction, but they should be alert to red flags that exist in a property with which they are dealing. **Red flags** are physical indications that there may be a defect in the property not readily apparent to a layperson or an inexperienced home purchaser. Red flags often suggest the presence of latent defects. **Latent defects** are material facts that are not discoverable by ordinary inspection. When known by any party, they must be brought to the attention of all parties entering into a transaction. Parties should be strongly advised to seek the expert advice of a licensed home inspector or a licensed structural engineer.

Title 16 of the *Business Occupations and Professions* Article requires individuals who provide home inspections to be licensed by the State Commission of Real Estate Appraisers and Home Inspectors. It is unlawful to provide such inspections for consideration without this license. For doing so, there are both civil and criminal penalties, including a fine of not more than $5,000 per violation. Exempt from this requirement are state and local government inspectors and building code enforcement officials acting within the scope of their employment, as well as licensed construction professionals acting within the scope of their licenses when their services may be required in the building or remodeling of real property as long as they are not claiming to be licensed home inspectors.

For licensure as home inspectors, applicants must be high school graduates, have completed 48 hours of "off-site" training approved by a national inspection organization or by the Appraiser/Home Inspector Commission, carry $50,000 liability insurance, make application for licenses, and pay an *application* fee of $50. When granted, each *license* fee is $400.

■ CHANGES IN THE LICENSE LAW AND REGULATIONS

From time to time, changes are made in the Brokers Act and the regulations of the Commission. The material included in this chapter is current as of the date of publication. However, readers are cautioned to ascertain whether changes have been made since publication of this book.

Before the Commission adopts, amends, or repeals regulations, it publishes notice of the proposed action in the *Maryland Register* together with an estimate of economic impact, a notice of opportunity for public comment on the proposal, and the text of the proposed changes. After 45 days, the Commission may take final action on the proposal. At that time, a report of its final action is published in the *Maryland Register*. The Commission's final action takes effect ten days after that notice appears, unless the Commission specifies a later date.

While the Commission can make changes in its own *regulations* and *code of ethics* (both found in COMAR), only the General Assembly can make changes in the *statute*, the Brokers Act (Title 17). Some significant recent changes by the Maryland Legislature to Title 17, The Brokers Act, and other statutes are found in Appendix F.

QUESTIONS

1. Licensed salespersons may represent
   1. owners who employ them directly.
   2. not more than one owner at one time.
   3. only brokers under whom they are licensed.
   4. any broker who is duly licensed.

2. License certificates issued for salespersons MUST be
   1. carried by them when they are performing acts of brokerage.
   2. displayed by their brokers in their company offices.
   3. retained by the Commission.
   4. displayed by them in their homes.

3. Brokers need NOT notify the Commission when
   1. salespersons resign.
   2. changes occur in the locations any of their offices.
   3. changes occur in the names of their firms.
   4. changes occur in commission sharing.

4. As a licensed salesperson, you receive a lead from a friend who is not a real estate licensee. As previously agreed upon, you split the commission with your friend.
   1. This is a violation of the license law.
   2. This is not a violation of the license law.
   3. This is a violation of the license law only if the seller is NOT informed.
   4. This is not a violation of the license law if your broker has given you written permission.

5. To be recognized by the IRS as "qualified real estate agents" and thus to receive the advantages of "self-employed" status, licensees must do all the following EXCEPT
   1. have a written employment contract with their brokers agreeing to this status.
   2. be free from their broker's control of how their work is done.
   3. earn substantially all the income coming from their brokerage firms in the form of commissions.
   4. hold a real estate license.

6. Which of the following fees is paid biennially?
   1. Initial Guaranty Fund fee
   2. Brokers' and salespersons' original license fee
   3. Brokers' and salespersons' license renewal fee
   4. Guaranty Fund reassessment

7. In Maryland, the act of "blockbusting" is
   1. unethical but not prohibited by law.
   2. a felony.
   3. a misdemeanor.
   4. a legitimate listing technique.

8. Individuals found guilty of operating in the real estate business without a license may be fined by
   1. the district attorney.
   2. the Commission.
   3. the state or local Association of REALTORS®.
   4. the attorney general.

9. An unlicensed person improperly collecting a real estate commission is guilty of
   1. duress.
   2. a felony.
   3. a misdemeanor.
   4. fraud.

10. The Commission may discipline any licensee who is found guilty of
    1. slandering competitors.
    2. intemperance.
    3. bad faith.
    4. puffing.

11. The maximum penalty possible for filing false statements with the Commission in reference to a Guaranty Fund claim is a fine of
    1. $5,000.
    2. $10,000.
    3. $10,000 and imprisonment for two years.
    4. $25,000 and imprisonment for three years.

12. Standard licenses to provide Maryland residential real estate brokerage services can be issued only to
    1. corporations.
    2. limited liability companies (LLCs).
    3. partnerships.
    4. individuals.

13. Members of the Maryland Real Estate Commission are appointed by the
    1. Maryland Senate.
    2. Governor.
    3. House of Delegates.
    4. Executive Director of the Commission.

14. A salesperson license issued by the Commission on November 1 will expire
    1. one year from the date of issue.
    2. two years from the date of issue.
    3. April 30 of the next even-numbered year.
    4. March 1 of the next even-numbered year.

15. The main purpose of the Brokers Act is to
    1. raise revenue.
    2. protect the public interest.
    3. control salespersons.
    4. restrict competition.

16. The executive director of the Commission is
    1. appointed by the Governor.
    2. confirmed by the State Senate.
    3. appointed by the Secretary of Labor, Licensing, and Regulation.
    4. selected from the Maryland State Employees Classified System.

17. Ads placed by licensees seeking buyers for a property listed in their firm must show the
    1. name and address of the property owner.
    2. name of the listing salesperson.
    3. designated name of the broker.
    4. general location of the property.

18. The Guaranty Fund must be maintained with a minimum balance of
    1. $250,000.
    2. $25,000.
    3. $2,000.
    4. $200,000.

19. The Commission's Code of Ethics addresses relations with three groups. Which of the following is NOT one of those groups?
    1. Members of the public
    2. The Real Estate Commission
    3. Clients
    4. Fellow licensees

20. The Maryland Real Estate Commission is composed of
    1. five members.
    2. four persons who are not engaged in the real estate business and five licensed persons.
    3. four professional and five consumer members.
    4. representative brokers from real estate boards or associations throughout Maryland.

21. The Commission may refuse to issue a broker license to a Maryland resident who has filed a proper application and met the legal requirements
    1. after holding a hearing on the matter.
    2. if the applicant has been convicted of a traffic violation within the past year.
    3. without offering to hold a hearing on the matter.
    4. if the applicant has not reached the age of 21 years.

22. According to statute, authority to set license fees is held by
    1. the Commission.
    2. associations and boards of licensees.
    3. the Secretary of the Department of Labor, Licensing, and Regulation.
    4. the General Assembly.

23. In which of the following situations does an act of real estate brokerage require a real estate brokerage license?
    1. A mortgage lender sells real estate acquired through foreclosure.
    2. A person charges a modest consulting fee to guide his friend in the sale of a home.
    3. An attorney at law handling a divorce action charges 3 percent to help sell a house the couple owns.
    4. A property owner subdivides his land and sells five lots in one calendar year.

24. Fees paid for licenses finally go to the
    1. Maryland General Fund.
    2. Guaranty Fund.
    3. Real Estate Board or Association active in the area.
    4. State Real Estate Commission Fund.

25. Employees of the Commission
    1. include an executive director and field inspectors.
    2. must be licensed as brokers or salespeople while employed by the Commission.
    3. must have been licensed to get their position.
    4. are permitted to perform acts of brokerage for which a license is required.

26. Licenses of salespersons who are released by their brokers are to be
    1. returned to the Commission by the brokers.
    2. returned to the Commission by the salespersons.
    3. removed from display but retained by the brokers.
    4. returned to the salespersons.

27. The Guaranty Fund protects a buyer for certain financial losses up to
    1. $250,000.
    2. $25,000.
    3. $2,500.
    4. an unlimited amount.

28. Which of the following statements pertaining to licenses held by Maryland real estate brokerage licensees is NOT correct?
    1. Their holders are regulated by authority of the Business Occupations and Professions Article of the Maryland Annotated Code.
    2. They are issued and administered by the Maryland Real Estate Commission.
    3. They are not issued to corporations or associations.
    4. They are required for every person who sells real estate for consideration.

29. To deliver real estate brokerage services, licensed real estate salespersons MUST
    1. be affiliated with any licensed real estate associate broker.
    2. perform real estate acts only on behalf of the broker under whom they are licensed.
    3. be associated with a REALTOR®.
    4. operate a real estate business under their own name or designated name.

30. Which of these people requires a valid real estate license to perform the acts shown in return for consideration?
    1. An attorney-at-law who advertises real estate services and agrees to serve as a prospect's buyer broker
    2. A person who serves as a real estate salesperson for a homebuilder
    3. Attorneys-in-fact who use powers of attorney to earn commissions for the sale of real estate
    4. Trustees who sell properties upon which their lender has foreclosed

CHAPTER 2

Real Estate Agency

■ KEY TERMS

adverse	cooperating agents	full client treatment
affirmative	customers	implied agency
assist	disclosure	intra-company agents
brokerage	dual agents	(ICAs)
buyer's agent by written agreement	exclusive-buyer-agency company	presumed buyer's agent
buyer's agents	exclusive-seller-agency company	represent
clients		seller's agents
confidential information	fiduciary duties	single-agency company

■ OVERVIEW

While most of this chapter emphasizes Maryland real estate law and practice, some general terms are also clarified here. On occasion, a brief restatement (in parentheses) may follow a technical term.

Topics addressed include the application of agency law to real estate brokerage; consumer confusion about various kinds of possible agency relationships; presumed buyer representation; various consent and disclosure forms; and the organization and management of brokerage firms, including advertising and handling of trust funds.

■ BROKERAGE AND AGENCY: NOT ALWAYS THE SAME

In general, **brokerage** involves bringing parties together and helping them negotiate agreements in return for a fee. Many kinds of brokers—commodity brokers, for instance—often do not represent either buyers or sellers. Instead, they merely *facilitate* transactions. The student should understand that performing certain kinds of brokerage does not always and everywhere require a broker to represent—be an agent of—either party. This book, however, deals with brokerage based upon agency.

■ AGENCY

**Agency Duties
[§17-528–§17-535]**

Maryland law sets forth almost all the agency duties of real estate licensees in the Maryland Real Estate Brokers Act. This statute—referred to throughout this book as the *Brokers Act*—is found at Title 17 of the *Business Occupations and Professions* Article of the Annotated Code of Maryland.

Detailed applications of the statute are found in the Code of Maryland Regulations (COMAR) in Sections 1 to 8 of Title 9, Subsection 11. COMAR is published in loose-leaf form and is updated periodically. It is available in many public libraries.

Both the statute and the regulations are available for study and downloading from the Web site of the Maryland Real Estate Commission: *www.dllr.state.md.us/ license/occprof/recomm.html* at the link "Law & Regulation and Legislation."

Students preparing for the salesperson or broker license exam may wish to download each part of Sections 1 and 2 entitled "General Regulations" and "Code of Ethics," respectively, paragraph by paragraph, and consolidate them into a single document for study.

Agency Relationships

Maryland real estate licensees, when acting as agents, owe their **clients** (the persons they represent) **fiduciary duties** as described in the principles text: Care, Obedience, Loyalty, Disclosure, Accounting, and Confidentiality (COLDAC). Although these duties are few in number, they are in addition to the list of duties owed to **customers** (third parties). Licensees owe *customers* and other *third parties* honesty and fair dealing, reasonable care, prompt presentation of all offers and counteroffers, honest answers to all questions (except those that are properly declared to be confidential by a client or are otherwise forbidden by law), and **affirmative** (voluntary) **disclosure** of material facts. See Table 2.1.

Distinctly Different Terms: Assist and Represent

Virtually all real estate brokerage companies in Maryland are willing to *assist* purchasers as *customers* in finding properties to purchase without representing them as *clients*. They will, however, readily offer purchasers client-level representation when engaged to do so. Licensed brokerage firms may also *represent* owners as *clients* in the sale of properties. Understanding the difference between *client-level service* and *customer-level service* is fundamental to effective and lawful provision of real estate brokerage services. Licensees **represent** clients. They **assist** customers.

<table>
<tr><th rowspan="2" style="text-align:left">TABLE 2.1

An Agent's Duties and
Services to Customers
and Clients</th><th style="text-align:left">Duty or Service</th><th>Owed to
Principals
(Clients)</th><th>Owed to
Third Parties
(Customers)</th></tr>
<tr><td>Care</td><td>X</td><td></td></tr>
</table>

Duty or Service	Owed to Principals (Clients)	Owed to Third Parties (Customers)
Care	X	
Obedience	X	
Loyalty	X	
Accounting	X	
Confidentiality	X	
Magisterial Acts: Offering Expert Guidance and Judgment	X	
Affirmative Disclosure of Material Facts	X	X
Honesty and Fair Dealing	X	X
Reasonable Care and Skill in Performance	X	X
Prompt Presentation of All Written Offers and Counteroffers	X	X
Ministerial Acts: Actions of Service Not Requiring Exercise of Judgment or Giving Expert Guidance	X	X

[Handwritten annotations in left margin: "Judgment — yes —" pointing to Magisterial Acts row; "Not —" pointing to Ministerial Acts row]

◼ THE CHALLENGE OF DUAL AGENCY

Origins of Buyer Representation

Until the early 1980s, Maryland residential real estate brokers typically represented seller-clients. Although buyers were usually regarded by law as third parties, they often—sometimes to their harm—regarded the salespeople assisting them as *their* agents.

Since then, consumers have become better informed. Today, they typically demand that the licensee working with them actually serve as *their* agents—be on their team and deliver client-level service. They want knowledgeable professionals who will be loyal to them and will not only help them locate property to purchase but also protect their interests, keep their confidence, and coach them in negotiations about price and many other negotiable matters throughout the transaction.

The Industry's Response to the Demand

Today, most firms throughout Maryland, responding to this consumer demand, offer representation to buyers—client-level service. Most of the firms were already providing—and continue to provide—representation for client-sellers who list their properties with them.

The first example below illustrates a simple case of buyer representation; the second, a more complex one.

◼ **EXAMPLE 1** Broker Norman, formally representing buyer Elizabeth, shows her a property listed by broker Eugene. Arturo is the owner/seller of that property and is, therefore, Eugene's client; he is receiving client-level service from Eugene's company, and Elizabeth is receiving client-level service from Norman's. Both brokerage firms in this case are providing single-agency service: each broker is the agent of one party to this transaction.

■ **EXAMPLE 2** Client-buyer Rebecca asks salesperson Brian to show her a property, owned by seller John, which is listed with Brian's broker, Yvonne. John is obviously already a client of Yvonne's company. So at this moment, her company is being asked to represent parties on opposite sides of the same possible transaction. How can it provide client service to both seller John and buyer Rebecca?

No individual (natural person) can possibly give total loyalty to opposing parties. That is the situation Yvonne's company is facing. Yvonne definitely wants both to sell her company's listing and to earn a fee for representing buyer-client Rebecca.

The Maryland Solution: Intra-Company Agents (ICAs) [§17-530]

The situation described in Example 2 above has such potential for conflict of interest that in the late 1990s, Maryland wrote into the Brokers Act certain actions that Brian's broker Yvonne is required to take if she wishes to earn commissions from both Rebecca and John as clients. The firm must first get the written consent of all parties to this *dual agency*. Then the firm appoints two of its licensed affiliates to serve as **intra-company agents (ICAs)**. (The term *intra* means *within*, as in *intramural* games—those played *within* the *walls* of an institution.) So Broker Yvonne appoints two affiliates, Viola and Brian, as ICAs of John and of Rebecca respectively. (Since she is the firm's broker, Yvonne is prevented by law from appointing herself as one of those ICAs.) The firm—if it has the informed consent of both buyer and seller—may now serve as agent of both parties in the contemplated transaction.

To maintain each side's confidentiality, the broker backs away from the transaction personally and lets the ICAs handle their respective clients. Each ICA will give that ICA's party **full client treatment,** which includes care, obedience, loyalty, disclosure, accounting, and confidentiality.

If Yvonne's company were very small and had only its broker and one other licensee, it could not perform the dual agency allowed by Maryland law. The law requires that the broker appoint two persons *other* than the broker to be ICAs. In a multioffice company, office managers, appointed by their brokers and acting in the place of their brokers, may *appoint* ICAs but not *serve as* ICAs.

On a *Buyer Representation Agreement* form, buyers are asked, among other things, to indicate whether they are willing to consider any property that will involve dual agency. Dual agency would arise if they, as client-purchasers, were shown a property listed with their buyer broker's firm.

Buyer Prospects' Consent to Dual Agency

In addition, the company can show a client-buyer only those company listings whose owners also have consented to the possibility of dual agency when those properties were listed. The seller's consent must be reconfirmed when a specific situation involving dual agency arises; a Consent for Dual Agency form confirming their assent must indicate the specific property to be shown and the name of the specific prospect(s).

Buyers' consent to dual agency with respect to a specific property is made later, on their own Consent for Dual Agency form (Figure 2.1). This form will identify the buyers, the property, and the seller-owners by name.

FIGURE 2.1

Commission's Consent for Dual Agency

January 1, 1999

**STATE OF MARYLAND
REAL ESTATE COMMISSION**

Consent For Dual Agency

(In this form, the word "seller" includes "landlord", "buyer" includes "tenant", and "purchase" or "sale" includes "lease.")

When Dual Agency May Occur

The possibility of dual agency arises when:

> ➤ The buyer is interested in a property listed by a real estate company; and

> ➤ The seller's agent and the buyer's agent work for that same real estate company.

Before the buyer and seller can proceed to be represented by a dual agent, they must both sign a Consent For Dual Agency. If they have previously signed a Consent For Dual Agency, they must affirm their consent for the sale of a particular property to a particular buyer.

Important Considerations Before Making a Decision About Dual Agency

☞ A dual agent does not exclusively represent either the seller or buyer and there may be a conflict of interest because the interests of the seller and buyer may be different or adverse.

☞ As a dual agent, the real estate company does not owe undivided loyalty to either the seller or buyer.

Your Choices Concerning Dual Agency

When a dual agency situation in fact arises, the buyer and seller have the following options:

1. **Consent in writing to dual agency.** If all parties consent in writing, the real estate company (the "dual agent") will assign one real estate agent from the company to represent the seller or landlord (the seller's "intra-company agent") and another agent from the company to represent the buyer or tenant (the buyer's "intra-company agent"). Intra-company agents may provide the same services to their clients as an exclusive seller's or buyer's agent, including advising their clients as to price and negotiation strategy.

2. **Do not consent to dual agency.** If either the buyer or the seller, or landlord or tenant, refuses to consent in writing to dual agency, the real estate company must terminate the agency agreement for that particular property with either the buyer or the seller, or both. If the seller's agreement is terminated, the seller must then either represent him or herself or arrange to be represented by an agent from another real estate company. If the buyer's agreement is terminated, the buyer or tenant may choose to enter into a written buyer agency agreement with an agent from a different company. Alternatively, the buyer or tenant may choose not be represented by an agent of his or her own but simply to receive assistance from the seller's agent, from another agent in that company, or from a cooperating agent from another company.

■ A FIRM'S AGENCY OPTIONS IN REPRESENTATION

Licensed real estate brokers in Maryland, as in other states, may choose to operate as either *single-agency* or *dual-agency* companies. Those operating as single-agency companies typically choose to act as one of the following:

- A **single-agency company** offering to represent either buyers or sellers, but not both, in any given transaction
- An **exclusive-seller-agency company,** offering to represent only sellers in all transactions
- An **exclusive-buyer-agency company,** offering to represent only buyers in all transactions

Single-agency companies offer to represent sellers while treating prospective buyers as customers (not clients) of that brokerage. They also represent sellers when customers are brought to them by *cooperating* agents, as described in "Categories of Representation" below.

The same single-agency companies may also offer to represent buyers in dealing with properties listed with other companies. What they do *not* do is represent buyers and sellers *in the same property transaction.*

It is essential that each company decide which agency service or services it will offer and present that policy and its associated procedures to everyone in the organization. All persons affiliated with the company should be trained in the proper performance of these services. It is the responsibility of licensees who manage offices to ensure that these services are being performed according to the detailed requirements of the Brokers Act.

■ CATEGORIES OF REPRESENTATION [§17-530]

The Brokers Act and the form Understanding Whom Real Estate Agents Represent, the Maryland Real Estate Commission's relationship information form (Figure 2.2), present six roles played by licensees in Maryland real estate brokerage: seller's agent, cooperating agent, buyer's agent, presumed buyer's agent, dual agent, and intra-company agent.

- **Seller's agents** are licensees who are affiliated with or acting as listing brokers for properties. They *represent* a seller and *assist* prospective buyers (their *customers*) in buying real estate.
- **Cooperating agents** are a subtype of seller's agent. They are not affiliated with or acting as listing brokers for properties. Rather, they function as *subagents of the seller, representing* the seller through and under the seller's listing broker. They *assist* prospective buyers (their customers) in acquiring real estate. For many decades, this was the typical arrangement in transactions that involved a listing brokerage firm and a selling brokerage firm assisting a customer. This practice, which involves *subagency,* is no longer favored and is becoming increasingly rare.

    Licensees need to understand that *cobrokering* does not necessarily involve cooperating agents. Cobrokering can occur between a listing firm

F I G U R E   2.2

Commission's Representation Information Form

STATE OF MARYLAND

REAL ESTATE COMMISSION

Understanding Whom Real Estate Agents Represent

Before you decide to sell or buy or rent a home you need to consider the following information:

Agents Who Represent the Seller

Seller's Agent: A seller's agent works for the real estate company that lists and markets the property for the sellers, or landlords, and exclusively represents the sellers or landlords. That means that he or she may assist the buyer or tenant in purchasing or renting the property, but his or her duty of loyalty is only to the sellers or landlords. The seller pays the seller's agent's fee as specified in a written listing agreement.

Cooperating Agent: A cooperating agent works for a real estate company different from the company for which the seller's agent works. The cooperating agent can assist a buyer or tenant in purchasing or renting a property, but his or her duty of loyalty is only to the sellers or landlords. The cooperating agent's fee is paid by the sellers or landlords through the seller's agent's company.

Agents Who Represent the Buyer *outside an open House*

Presumed Buyer's Agent (no written agreement): When a person goes to a real estate agent for assistance in finding a home to buy or rent, the agent is presumed to be representing the buyer and can show the buyer properties that are *not* listed by the agent's real estate company. A presumed buyer's agent may *not* make or prepare an offer or negotiate a sale for the buyer. The buyer does *not* have an obligation to pay anything to the presumed agent.

If for any reason the buyer does not want the agent to represent him or her as a presumed agent, either *initially* or *at any time,* the buyer can decline or terminate a presumed agency relationship simply by saying so.

Buyer's Agent (by written agreement): A buyer or tenant may enter into a written contract with a real estate agent which provides that the agent will represent the buyer or tenant in locating a property to buy or rent. The agent is then known as the buyer's agent. That agent assists the buyer in evaluating properties and preparing offers, and negotiates in the best interests of the buyer or tenant. The agent's fee is paid according to the written agreement between the agent and the buyer or tenant. If you as a buyer or tenant wish to have an agent represent you exclusively, you must enter into a written buyer agency agreement

Dual Agents

The possibility of **dual agency** arises when the buyer's agent and the seller's agent both work for the same real estate company, and the buyer is interested in property listed by that company. The real estate company, or broker, is called the "dual agent." Dual agents do not act exclusively in the interests of either the seller or buyer, or landlord or tenant, and therefore cannot give undivided loyalty to either party. There may be a conflict of interest because the interests of the seller and buyer may be different or adverse.

If both seller and buyer, or landlord and tenant, agree to dual agency by signing a Consent For Dual Agency form, then the real estate company (the "dual agent") will assign one agent to represent the seller or landlord (the seller's "intra-company agent") and another agent to represent the buyer or tenant (the buyer's "intra-company agent"). Intra-company agents may provide the same services to their clients as exclusive seller's or buyer's agents, including advising their clients as to price and negotiation strategy, provided the clients have both consented to be represented by dual agency.

Provided by the Maryland Real Estate Commission

F I G U R E   2.2 (CONTINUED)

Commission's Representation Information Form

If either party does not agree to dual agency, the real estate company may withdraw the agency agreement for that particular property with either the buyer or seller, or both. If the seller's agreement is terminated, the seller must then either represent him or herself or arrange to be represented by an agent from another real estate company. If the buyer's agreement is terminated, the buyer or tenant may choose to enter into a written buyer agency agreement with an agent from a different company. Alternatively, the buyer or tenant may choose not to be represented by an agent of his or her own but simply to receive assistance from the seller's agent,   from another agent in that company, or from a cooperating agent from another company.

No matter what type of agent you choose to work with, you have the following rights and responsibilities in selling or buying or renting property:

>Real estate agents are obligated by law to treat all parties to a real estate transaction honestly and fairly. They must exercise reasonable care and diligence and maintain the confidentiality of clients. They must not discriminate in the offering of properties; they must promptly present each written offer or counteroffer to   the other party; and they must answer questions truthfully.

>Real estate agents must disclose all material facts that they know or should know relating to a property. An agent's duty to maintain confidentiality does not apply to the disclosure of material facts about a property.

>All agreements with real estate agents should be in writing and should explain the duties and obligations of the agent. The agreement should explain how the agent will be paid and any fee-sharing agreements with other agents.

>You have the responsibility to protect your own interests. You should carefully read all agreements to make sure they accurately reflect your understanding. A real estate agent is qualified to advise you on real estate matters only. If you need legal or tax advice, it is your responsibility to consult a licensed attorney or accountant.

Any complaints about a real estate agent may be filed with the Real Estate Commission at 500 North Calvert Street, Baltimore, MD 21202. (410) 230-6200.

This notice is information required by law and is NOT A CONTRACT.

We, the ☐ Sellers/Landlord   ☐ Buyers/Tenants acknowledge receipt of a copy of this disclosure and

that _____(firm name)

and _____(salesperson) are working as:

☐ seller/landlord's agent
☐ cooperating agent
☐ buyer's agent
☐ dual agent (See Consent for Dual
  Agency form)
(You may check more than one box)

_____   _____
Signature   (Date)   Signature   (Date)

I certify that on this date I made the required agency disclosure to the individuals identified below and they were **unable or unwilling** to acknowledge receipt of a copy of this disclosure statement

_____   _____
Agent's Signature   (Date)

Name of Individual to whom disclosure made   Name of Individual to whom disclosure made and either a subagent firm or a buyer-broker firm. "Cooperating agent" is now a title reserved by statute to refer only to a subagent.

■ **Buyer's agents** are licensees who *represent* prospective buyers (their *clients*) in the acquisition of real estate. When representing buyers in acquiring a property listed with another company, *buyer's agents are not subagents of the owner-seller*. They are *not* cooperating agents, as described in the paragraphs above; they represent the buyer.

There are two classes of buyer's agents:

1. The **presumed buyer's agent**, who has no express agreement to represent a prospect, still owes the prospect fiduciary duties yet has no right to claim any payment for this representation.
2. The **buyer's agent by written agreement** owes fiduciary responsibilities for tasks set forth in a written (buyer representation) agreement and may earn compensation for such performance.

■ **Dual agents** are *firms* (not individuals) that represent not only sellers but also prospective purchasers in the same property transaction. All parties must sign the Consent for Dual Agency form, presented in Figure 2.1, if dual agency is to proceed.

■ Intra-company agents are a subtype under dual agents. They are pairs of licensees affiliated with a broker and assigned by their broker (or by an office manager) to deliver client-level service (one to the seller and one to the buyer) in the sale of a specific parcel of real estate listed with their company. They are acting on behalf of their firm, which is the dual agent. Both buyer and seller must agree to this arrangement for it to go forward.

■ PRESUMED BUYER'S AGENCY RELATIONSHIP DISCLOSURE FORM [§17-533]

Since January 1, 1999, the Brokers Act has declared that a licensee who shows prospects real estate to purchase—and is neither affiliated with nor acting as the broker of the listing company for the properties shown—is *presumed by law* to be representing those prospects. The licensee represents the prospects in this way unless or until either the prospects or the licensee should decline the presumed representation. At the earliest time feasible, the licensee should present the Commission's form describing the various kinds of agents to the prospects. The Brokers Act requires that the form (Understanding Whom Agents Represent) be presented *not later than* "the first scheduled face-to-face meeting" with prospects. The REALTOR® Code of Ethics, in contrast, requires that disclosure of agency representation be presented "at first contact." Prudence dictates that it be presented by licensees as early as possible—not waiting for a "scheduled" meeting. It is extremely important to remember that *presenting the agency disclosure form does not create a buyer-broker relationship for which compensation may be claimed, and it does not bring to an end presumed representation.* Until presumed buyer representation is ended, the licensee still owes much to the prospect (the presumed client), but the prospect owes nothing to the licensee.

Affiliates acting under presumed buyer representation (PBR) may lawfully show prospects properties listed with other firms. But because the prospects have not agreed to *written, contractual* buyer representation, they are free to walk away and later buy through another firm any or all property they have been shown by the first firm. These *presumed clients* may walk away as long as the licensee continues in the role of *presumed buyer representative*. They have all the freedom of customer-prospects combined with the right to expect client-level service—all without any financial responsibility to the firm that is serving them. Of course, prospects being assisted *as customers* also are free to walk away from the company that has been assisting them, but they have had no claim to fiduciary duties—to client-level service.

A licensee can end this undesirable situation with prospects simply by telling them "I do not perform presumed buyer representation," or "Our firm does not perform presumed buyer representation." A good time to say this is while presenting and explaining the Commission's Agency Disclosure at the paragraphs entitled "Presumed Buyer's Agent." Firms should establish a policy as to when and how to do this.

Before 1999, custom and practice regarded prospects simply as customers. The more recent statutory reversal of such situations has caused considerable confusion among long-time agents.

Why was this change made? It was intended to protect the average, poorly informed prospect. In the past, most prospective buyers or tenants thought (or felt) that the salesperson working with them was their agent and was "on their team." After all, wasn't the salesperson polite and helpful and seemingly knowledgeable? So they told "their agent" all their secrets—such things as their urgency to find a property and their bargaining strategies. The Brokers Act now places the salesperson "on the prospect's team" until either the prospect or the licensee expressly declines to continue this presumed relationship. This law now makes it harder for licensees to pick prospects' brains—learning their bargaining strategy and degree of urgency to find a property—and then use that information against them by telling these things to a client-seller and so giving that seller a considerable bargaining advantage. Such information is now considered *confidential* (fiduciary duties to the presumed client include confidentiality), and that confidentiality continues even after the presumed agency ends. This is true even if the presumed clients (buyer prospects) walk away and never come back. It is also true if the presumed clients later refuse both presumed representation and contractual, formal representation. It continues if the prospects turn into customers—and even if the presumed clients die.

Any facts learned from prospects during the period of presumed buyer representation must be kept confidential by the licensee and not be used to the clients' disadvantage in any later negotiations.

To avoid this potential conflict-of-interest problem, some firms make it their policy for affiliates to decline presumed buyer representation very early in their contacts with prospects. This refusal to engage in presumed buyer representation can be made orally or in writing. Other firms leave the decision of whether to engage in presumed representation up to each affiliate.

Ending Presumed Representation

Other than by entering into a formal written buyer representation agreement, presumed agency representation of buyers ends, by action of law, when any one of the following occurs:

- The licensee or the prospects reject the presumed relationship. (This can be done orally.)
- The buyers either want to begin negotiations or wish to draw up an offer for the purchase of a specific property listed with another firm.
- The buyers wish to be shown a property listed with the licensee's own company.

The first instance may occur at any time before either the second or third. When presumed buyer representation (PBR) is refused either by the licensee or the prospects, the prospects become *customers*, unless they subsequently enter into a formal, written representation agreement. Without such a written representation agreement, they are owed only customer-level duties.

■ AGENCY DISCLOSURE: UNDERSTANDING WHOM REAL ESTATE AGENTS REPRESENT

Timing of Presentation [§17-530]

The Brokers Act requires that all licensees who are representing sellers disclose to buyers, or to the agents of the buyers, the fact that they (the licensees) are representing sellers. When they represent buyers, they are similarly required to disclose that fact to sellers or sellers' agents. This latter disclosure may be made orally.

Again, the form that the Commission requires *all* licensees to use in disclosure of representation to buyers is shown in Figure 2.2.

This form is not a contract; it is an information piece on which signatures of prospects and licensee are requested. However, the prospects' signatures are *not required* for the presentation of the form to be effective. If the prospect will not sign it, the law allows the licensee alone to sign it, stating that the prospects could not or would not sign. Dates recorded on the form show that the disclosure was made in a timely way so as to satisfy the law. Prospects are to be given a copy of the completed form even if they have refused to sign it.

What This Form Doesn't Do

There are two things that presenting this form does *not* do. It does not end presumed buyer representation, and it does not create a formal buyer-representation contract. Though many licensees think that the form does one or both of those two things, it does neither.

Contents of Form

On this form, the buyers can see checked (□) which of the four types of agent their salesperson is acting as in dealing with them. It is basically an information form about how real estate agents in general may work and how this salesperson, in particular, is working.

Decisions at Presentation

Buyers who receive this form may simply read it and, possibly, sign it. If they do not expressly reject presumed buyer representation at this point, the presumed representation continues. Buyers are free to refuse both presumed and formal written representation. If they do so, they continue as *customers* to be assisted in seeking a property to buy. They will then, of course, receive customer-level service.

If the buyers want *formal* buyer representation, with client-level service, they must enter into a written agreement with the licensee's firm to represent them as purchasers. Buyer representation agreements are discussed in Chapter 4.

■ THE CLIENT'S RIGHT OF CONFIDENTIALITY [§17-532]

Whatever **confidential information** a licensee learns from individuals while representing them—either under a formal representation agreement or as a presumed buyer representative—such as information about their personal finances, bargaining strategy, and motivations to buy or to sell, must of course be kept confidential throughout the entire transaction. In addition, the confidentiality continues after the agency ends, after a transaction is completed, and even after a written agency agreement expires. Information that was previously confidential may only be disclosed with the written permission of the former client or when the information has become public knowledge by the former client's publication of it.

Agents are forbidden, for example, to reveal confidential information to other clients whom they may later represent—or to other agents in their own company who may represent parties negotiating with the previous clients—or to use such "inside information" to the disadvantage of the previous clients. When licensees later represent new clients in a transaction involving the former client, they must disclose to the new clients that they cannot reveal to them confidential matters about the old client.

The subject of confidentiality is so important that it deserves repeated explanation and clarification in a company's regular training sessions for sales personnel. Awareness of the need for greater confidentiality should reduce or even end casual office conversation about cases, clients, and customers.

Brokerage offices that practice dual agency should provide locked files or other security arrangements so that confidential information about buyers or sellers in the same transaction is kept segregated and does not fall into the hands of the intra-company agent representing an **adverse** (opposite) party. The broker—who is actually the dual agent—has full access to all this information but is forbidden by law to share it with adverse parties in any transaction, unless mandated by court order or by the requirement to disclose newly discovered material facts. Of course, material facts should *never* be treated as confidential, because they must be revealed to all parties in every case.

■ AGENCY RELATIONSHIP NOT DETERMINED BY WHICH PARTY PAYS [§17-534]

Maryland law now clearly states that agency relationships and responsibilities are *not* determined by which party pays for brokerage services. Before 1998, when this principle was spelled out in the Brokers Act, it was already part of the common law but unknown to most licensees.

Application of This Principle

For example, when sellers pay—or agree to pay—a brokerage fee charged by a buyer's broker, this payment does *not* make that broker the sellers' agent. This prevents a claim by the seller in this example that the licensee representing the buyer should have worked in that seller's best interest. It also prevents buyers from claiming that the licensee engaged to represent them was really under the control of the seller. Before the statute clarified this issue, such claims had been used (however improperly) to attack and seek rescission of sales agreements on the basis of "undisclosed dual agency."

This matter is counterintuitive—that is, it goes against conventional wisdom and also against what many students have actually heard in previous classes. Pay particular attention to it.

> *The payment or promise of payment of compensation to a licensed real estate broker by a seller, lessor, buyer, or lessee, or by a licensee acting for a seller, lessor, buyer, or lessee: (1) is not determinative of whether a brokerage relationship has been created or exists; and (2) does not create or determine the existence of a brokerage relationship between a broker and a seller, lessor, buyer, lessee, or licensee. [§17-534(d)]*

Even more counterintuitive is the fact that it is *not* necessary for a brokerage fee to be promised or paid to *create* an agency relationship with a licensee. Certain behaviors and statements of a licensee may properly be construed (interpreted) by a member of the public—and later by a court—to indicate that the licensee is indeed that person's agent, even without a formal agreement.

Consider this example: A licensee who says to a customer, "Trust me; I'll get you a great deal," is asking the customer to regard her as trustworthy and loyal—that is, as the customer's agent. If this occurs while the licensee is already serving as agent or subagent for the sellers, an undisclosed (probably unintended but certainly unlawful) dual agency is created, which may later prove to be the basis for rescission of sales contract, loss of commission, suit for damages, and disciplinary action by the Commission.

Last, but unfortunately not least, the person to whom the licensee owes loyalty (because of a careless remark) owes the licensee nothing for his trouble! This **implied agency,** like presumed representation, can amount to all work and no pay.

Remember: No individual licensee can *directly* and *personally* represent both parties to a Maryland residential transaction. When a brokerage firm is properly involved in a dual agency situation, its broker *is* the dual agent but does not directly and personally deal with the parties; instead, the broker appoints two intra-company agents to do so.

■ DISCLOSURE AND FAIRNESS [COMAR 09.11.02.02 A]

According to the Code of Ethics of the Commission, the obligation of absolute fidelity to the client's interest is primary, but it does not relieve licensees from the statutory obligation to deal fairly with all parties to a transaction and to reveal material facts.

Statutory attempts to guarantee fairness by requiring disclosures often miss their mark. This is because members of the public often receive so many lengthy, technical disclosures that they end up with little or no understanding of what is being communicated! Hurrying prospects through the signing of disclosure forms and perhaps saying, "These are merely formalities required by law," makes it even more likely that the disclosures will not disclose anything. Such behavior should be avoided.

QUESTIONS

1. Real estate brokers' principals are their
   1. managers.
   2. clients.
   3. prospects.
   4. customers.

2. In handling a transaction involving the purchase and sale of residential real property, a real estate broker
   1. is the agent of the owner of the property being sold.
   2. may *NOT* act as the agent of the buyer.
   3. may *NOT* represent both buyer and seller in the same transaction without designating two intra-company agents.
   4. may personally represent both *BOTH* buyer and seller if both parties agree.

3. Arthur has been assigned by his broker, Bettina, to work with Carlos to provide buyer representation for the purchase of a property listed by Dorene, a salesperson with Bettina's company. Bettina has named Dorene to represent the seller. In this situation, which of the following is *TRUE?*
   1. Carlos is a prospect; Arthur is his intra-company agent; Bettina is a single-agency broker; and Dorene is the intra-company agent for the seller.
   2. Carlos is a client; Arthur is his intra-company agent; Bettina is a disclosed dual agent; and Dorene is the intra-company agent of the purchaser.
   3. Carlos is a customer; Arthur is his salesperson; Bettina is an intra-company agent; and Dorene represents the seller.
   4. Carlos is a client; Arthur is his intra-company agent; Bettina is not a single-agency broker; and Dorene is the intra-company agent for the seller.

4. Brokers who represent buyers of real estate
   1. are regarded by the law as dual agents in such transactions.
   2. must disclose this agency relationship to sellers.
   3. are in violation of the Brokers Act.
   4. will not be compensated.

5. Which of the following statements is *TRUE* concerning presumed buyer representation?
   1. Presumed buyer representation begins when a licensee shows a prospective purchaser a property listed by another brokerage firm.
   2. Presumed buyer representation ends when a licensee shows a prospective purchaser a property listed with another brokerage firm.
   3. A prospective purchaser who declines to enter into a buyer representation agreement is no longer owed confidentiality for matters discussed with the licensee who had been providing presumed buyer representation up to that point.
   4. A licensee is no longer the presumed buyer representative of a purchaser who makes an offer on a property.

6. Which statement concerning agency is *TRUE?*
   1. The broker is the agent of the party who is paying for the broker's services.
   2. The broker is allowed to be a dual agent in a transaction if no harm is done.
   3. The salesperson may personally act as dual agent if both buyer and seller agree in writing.
   4. The broker who represents both buyer and seller in the same transaction must appoint two intra-company agents.

7. Agents' duties to their principals do *NOT* include
   1. disclosure of all facts.
   2. loyalty.
   3. timely presentation of all written offers and counteroffers.
   4. reporting to a client-buyer that one of the seller's family members had AIDS.

8. Under the Brokers Act, licensees who are representing sellers must disclose this fact to buyers or to the agents of the buyers

   1. at first contact.
   2. when an offer is made.
   3. not later than the first scheduled face-to-face meeting.
   4. when the buyer or agent of the buyer asks.

9. Which of the following does a licensee NOT owe to a customer?

   1. Due care
   2. Disclosure of material facts
   3. Obedience
   4. Honesty

10. Which of the following statements about agency is TRUE in Maryland?

   1. Maryland does not allow a brokerage firm to represent both buyer and seller in the same transaction.
   2. Dual agency in a transaction is permitted only in brokerage firms consisting of three or more licensees.
   3. Licensee Mary's performance of ministerial duties for a customer justifies the claim by that customer that Mary ". . . acted in a way that indicated she was my agent."
   4. The broker of a firm may act as one of the two intra-company agents required for dual agency.

CHAPTER

3

Real Estate Brokerage

■ KEY TERMS

beneficial owner   independent contractors   trust money
branch office managers   real estate brokerage   unlicensed person
designated name   supervision

■ OVERVIEW

In this chapter, you will be introduced to many requirements for the proper conduct of real estate brokerage operations. They include forms of business organization through which services may be delivered, supervisory responsibilities of brokers and branch managers, evidences of reasonable and adequate supervision, the role of teams in a real estate brokerage firm, activities in which personal assistants may and may not engage, representing developers in the sale of their real estate, how affiliates relate to the brokerage firm, and requirements for disclosing licensee identity in advertising. This information is not only basic to passing the state licensing examination but is fundamental to proper conduct of real estate brokerage.

■ BROKERAGE [§17-101]

As mentioned in Chapter 1, the Brokers Act defines **real estate brokerage** as performing certain services *for another person in return for consideration*. These services are

- selling, buying, exchanging, or leasing real estate;
- collecting rent for the use of any real estate;
- giving assistance in locating or obtaining any residential real estate for purchase;
- regularly dealing in real estate or in leases or options on real estate;
- promoting the sale of real estate by listing it in a publication issued primarily for promoting real estate sales;
- subdividing land and selling the divided lots; and
- acting as consultant in any of these activities.

Title 09 of the Code of Maryland Regulations (COMAR) recites numerous specific ways in which the Brokers Act governs every aspect of providing brokerage services. Until 2000, relevant sections of COMAR were published in a booklet *together* with the Brokers Act. However, the statute and the regulations come from different sources.

COMAR includes the General Regulations of the Real Estate Commission with the guidance of the Department of Labor, Licensing, and Regulation under the authority of the Brokers Act. For licensees, these regulations have the *force of law* despite being "only" regulations.

ORGANIZATION OF BROKERAGE FIRMS [§17-321]

The Role of the Broker   The broker doesn't have to be a partner in the partnership that owns a brokerage firm, nor must the broker be an officer, board member, or stockholder of the firm or officer of a limited liability company (LLC). Neither must the broker be the owner of a sole proprietorship to be the firm's broker. Brokers may provide real estate brokerage services through any of the forms of business organization if they are employed by or have another contractual relationship with that firm and have been designated by the firm as its broker, personally responsible for the provision of real estate brokerage services. Only one individual serves as broker in every Maryland real estate firm, no matter how many branch offices and agents are in the organization.

Prior to delivering brokerage services through any one of the organizational forms, brokers must submit notice to the Real Estate Commission of their intention to do so. The notice must include

- the name of the real estate broker submitting the notice,
- a statement that the named individual has been designated as the broker of the firm,
- the address of the firm's principal place of business and of each proposed branch office,
- any designated name that the firm intends to use in conducting its business,
- a list of all the licensed associate real estate brokers and licensed real estate salespersons who will be affiliated with the broker of the firm, and
- any other information that the Commission may require by regulation.

The Commission maintains current information regarding every corporation, partnership, LLC, and sole proprietorship through which Maryland real estate brokerage services are provided. Any other individual who participates in providing brokerage services for a firm while associated with the firm as a partner, officer, shareholder, or in any other capacity must hold either a salesperson's or an associate broker's license. However, company officers, shareholders, corporate board members, and so forth who do not personally involve themselves in providing brokerage services do not need to be licensed.

A brokerage firm—whether corporation, partnership, or LLC—that provides real estate brokerage services is not relieved from responsibility for the acts or omissions of its officers, partners, employees, or agents. The form of its organization does not shield it from such accountability.

Similarly, individuals who provide real estate brokerage services through—or on behalf of—corporations, partnerships, and so forth, are not relieved of individual responsibility for their actions in providing those services because of the way they are affiliated with the firm, either as employees or nonemployees.

Limitation on Affiliates' Interests [§17-511]

Not more than 50 percent of the ownership control in any form of business organization providing real estate brokerage services may be held directly or indirectly by salespersons or associate brokers or any combination thereof. Otherwise, affiliates might become able to control their principal, the broker, rather than the other way around. Whenever affiliates apply for new licenses or renewals, they must disclose to the Commission the percentage of control they hold in the firm. This percentage must include other percentages held by immediate family members who are not themselves licensees in that firm. Immediate family members who *are* licensees will report their own percentages of ownership on their license applications.

Affiliation Arrangements [§17-321]

Brokers may provide brokerage services personally and/or through real estate salespersons and associate brokers licensed under them. Such affiliates typically are statutory nonemployees ("IRS-qualified" real estate agents, as explained in Chapter 1), but employee status is also a possibility. Such "qualified real estate agents" (nonemployee affiliates) are often referred to as **independent contractors,** though, in fact, independent contractor status, as defined by common law, is a very elusive status to describe or to demonstrate. "Qualified" agent status, on the other hand, is easy both to define and prove, as shown in Chapter 1. Any individual, including a licensed associate real estate broker, who provides real estate services on behalf of a real estate broker is considered a real estate salesperson with respect to the provision of those services. Except when serving as branch managers, licensed associate brokers have no more authority than salespersons and only perform the duties of salespersons.

■ SUPERVISION [§17-320 AND COMAR 09.11.05]

Supervision means direction and review of professional real estate activities. Commission General Regulation .05 requires that brokers supervise all licensees affiliated with them, whether those affiliates are employees or qualified real estate agents—self-employed so-called "independent contractors." Affiliates may not operate unsupervised no matter how they are related to the firm.

There is a misunderstanding of this matter among many affiliates and some brokers, who dwell on the word *independent* in "independent contractor." Affiliates are not in any way independent from their broker or from the broker's supervision and control. Brokers can tell their affiliates not only what to do but how to do it. After all, the broker is responsible both to the Commission and to the courts for the conduct of their agents (affiliates). Salespersons and associate brokers are general agents of their broker; their broker is their principal.

A general legal rule is that principals are responsible for the actions of their agents in the agents' performance of their duties. It follows that because brokers are responsible for the actions of their agents, they must have authority to control them. Moreover, a broker cannot escape the duty to supervise by claiming "My salespersons are independent contractors, so I can't tell them how to conduct their brokerage activities," or "I can't be watching my agents all the time."

Brokers are also to direct and review the supervisory activities of each branch office manager. These **branch office managers** (who must be licensees, generally with at least three years' active brokerage experience) are charged with responsibility to supervise the professional real estate activities of associate brokers and salespersons registered to their offices. Brokers do not supervise affiliates in branch offices personally but through their branch office managers. The supervisory duty of the branch manager is *in addition to*, rather than *in place of*, supervision by the firm's broker.

Factors to be considered in determining reasonable and adequate supervision include, but are not limited to, providing

- regular training or education sessions held at least once every two months;
- experienced supervisory personnel to review and discuss contract provisions, brokerage agreement provisions, and advertising;
- written procedures that give clear guidance for handling deposit monies and other funds;
- mechanisms to ensure compliance with all fair housing laws and regulations;
- clear advertising requirements for real estate transactions;
- review of all contracts that have been signed by all parties;
- procedures for, and limitations on, the use of unlicensed personal assistants;
- emphasis on disclosure of agency relationships by licensees in real estate transactions;
- emphasis on the obligation of all licensees to comply with the Broker Act, the Commission's Regulations and Code of Ethics, as well as all applicable local, State, and federal laws and regulations;
- restrictions on the sale or lease of a licensee's real property and the purchase or leasing of real property by licensees for their personal use; and
- prohibitions on unauthorized practice of law by a licensee.

In addition, the broker or office manager wishing to prove reasonable and adequate supervision would produce evidence of

- affiliates' attendance at sales and training meetings,
- review of all executed contracts,
- review of all advertisements placed by any affiliate,

■ compliance with the firm's written procedures and policies distributed to its affiliates, and

■ procedures for informing affiliates of new or changed real estate laws and regulations.

These examples of "reasonable and adequate" supervision impose a substantial burden on brokers to maintain a paper trail of many events and actions. When brokers charged with failure to provide supervision cannot show sufficient evidence of meeting most of these requirements, they are presumed to have failed to supervise, and the burden of proof of supervision falls on them.

■ PERSONAL ASSISTANTS

Some salespersons and associate brokers use personal assistants to help them in the conduct of their work. Some of these assistants hold real estate licenses, while others do not. Neither the Brokers Act nor COMAR makes specific mention of personal assistants. But "Guidelines for the Use of Unlicensed Employees" from the Office of the Maryland Attorney General, posted on the Real Estate Commission's Web site, lists what unlicensed employees in a brokerage firm may and may not lawfully do. Notice that an individual working in a brokerage firm who holds a license, but not under that firm's broker, is considered to be unlicensed for the purposes of those guidelines.

Actions of Unlicensed Persons

The Commission's guidelines specify what such **unlicensed persons** may and may not do.

Unlicensed persons *may* do the following:

■ Answer the telephone and forward calls to a licensee
■ Submit listings and changes to a multiple listing service
■ Follow up on loan commitments after a contract has been negotiated
■ Assemble documents for closing
■ Secure documents (public information) from courthouses, public utilities, and so forth
■ Have keys made for company listings
■ Write and place ads subject to the review and approval of the (employing) licensee and supervising broker
■ Type contract forms at the direction of and for approval by licensee and supervising broker
■ Compute commission checks
■ Place signs on property
■ Arrange the date and time of home, termite, and well/septic inspection; mortgage application; presettlement walk-through; and settlement
■ Prepare flyers and promotional information for approval by licensee and supervising broker
■ Act as courier service to deliver documents, pick up keys, etc.
■ Schedule an open house
■ Schedule appointments for licensee to show listed property
■ Accompany a licensee to an open house or showing for security purposes or to hand out preprinted materials

Unlicensed persons *may not* do the following:

- Prepare promotional materials or ads without the review and approval of the licensee and supervising broker
- Show property
- Answer any questions on listings, title, financing, closing, and so forth
- Discuss or explain a contract, listing, lease, agreement, or other real estate document with anyone outside the brokerage
- Be paid on the basis of real estate activity, such as a percentage of commission, or any amount based on listings, sales, and so forth
- Negotiate or agree to any commission, commission split, management fee, or referral fee on behalf of a licensee
- Discuss the attributes or amenities of a property, under any circumstances, with a prospective purchaser or lessee
- Discuss the terms and conditions of the real property offered for sale or lease with the owner of real property
- Collect, receive, or hold deposit monies, rent, other monies, or anything else of value received from the owner or lessor of the real property or from a prospective purchaser or lessee
- Provide owners of real property or prospective purchasers or lessees with any advice, recommendations, or suggestions as to the sale, purchase, exchange, or leasing of real property to be listed or real property presently available for sale or for lease
- Hold themselves out in any manner, orally or in writing, as being licensed or affiliated with a particular company or real estate broker as a licensee
- Contact the public concerning the availability of real estate brokerage services, unless an inquiry about a specific property is immediately referred to a licensee

Under the Internal Revenue Code, the IRS will likely consider unlicensed persons whom affiliates hire to assist them to be employees of those licensees. As employers, licensees would be liable for complying with all IRS requirements on record keeping and payroll deductions, as well as being responsible for carrying workers' compensation insurance on their employees, withholding employees' portions of Social Security and Medicare contributions, and paying employers' portions of each.

■ REAL ESTATE "TEAMS"

As is the case with "personal assistants," the Brokers Act makes no mention of "teams." The basic entity recognized in the law is the brokerage firm; the only licenses are those of brokers, associate brokers, and salespersons. Recently, groups of salespersons and associate brokers have appeared in many real estate firms throughout the State, bringing together persons having a variety of talents into cohesive units. Their purpose, presumably, is to facilitate service to the public and thus to maximize income to their members. They are typically composed of licensees from one office and usually have a "team leader."

Responsibility for Supervision

A memorandum from the Commission, dated November 2007, points out that the supervision of licensees required by statute is the responsibility of brokers through their branch managers and that "a team [or] group leader is not a supervisor, unless that person is the branch office manager or the broker." Legal responsibility for supervision of team members (and everyone else in offices) remains the responsibility of their brokers and branch managers.

Forms of Organization

As permitted by §17-512 of the Brokers Act, with their brokers' permission, salespersons and associate brokers may organize themselves into limited liability companies (LLCs) or into professional service companies (PSCs). If they are so organized, the statute authorizes individual licensees within a group to direct the broker to pay commissions they earn to the LLC or PSC. Brokers are not authorized to be part of either such LLCs or PSCs.

The Brokers Act clearly requires every shareholder in an LLC and every member of a PSC to be licensed either as a real estate salesperson or an associate real estate broker. This is best interpreted to mean *under the broker of that firm*, because the Commission regards a person working in Firm A but licensed only in Firm B as an unlicensed person when acting in Firm B.

Teams may not operate out of any office that is not a branch office registered to the team members' broker's firm.

Because Title 17 does not address the subject of "teams" or "groups," there is no language preventing those "teams" that are not organized either as LLCs or PSCs from being made up of a combination of licensees and nonlicensees. Nonlicensees who are part of a team must conduct themselves according the Commission's memo on what unlicensed persons may and may not do, quoted earlier in this chapter.

Advertising by Teams

The designated name of the broker (the firm name) must be meaningfully and conspicuously displayed in all advertising; of course, this includes advertising by teams! When any telephone number is shown in advertising, the telephone number of the broker or branch office manager must also be shown.

If a broker has a designated (trade) name, it must appear in all the broker's advertising, including all signs. Teams may have names (e.g., The Alpha Group), but they do *not* have designated names recognized by the Commission. Lawful team advertising is done only under the authority, supervision, and approval of the firm's broker or the broker's designee.

> *An associate broker or salesperson [and, presumably, any combination of those licensees, such as a "team"] may not use an individual telephone number or e-mail address in any advertisement unless the identified telephone number of the broker or branch office manager (identified as such) also appears in the advertisement. (Paraphrased from the Commission's Code of Ethics, 01.G[2])*

For the protection of the public, teams must *not* present themselves in advertising as if they were brokerage firms.

Dual Agency

The Brokers Act requires that *dual agency* must only occur under clearly defined conditions. The broker or a designee of the broker must obtain the written informed consent of all parties for the broker to act as the dual agent. The broker or the broker's designee then assigns one licensee to act as the intra-company agent for one party and a second licensee to act as the intra-company agent for the other party. An intra-company agent must be either an associate broker or a salesperson of the firm. Brokers may not act as intra-company agents; they are already the dual agents.

If the broker, either personally or through a designee, appoints two members of the same team to be intra-company agents for the parties, those individuals must exercise great care in ensuring that disclosure of confidential information does not take place among or between team members.

It is conceivable that a broker might designate a team leader (who could be either a salesperson or associate broker) as the individual who could then appoint intra-company agents within that individual's team. This practice almost invites the charge of unethical behavior should any dispute about proper performance of fiduciary duties in the course of a transaction arise.

Bonuses

§17-514(d)(1)(30) of the Brokers Act states:

> *If a real estate broker offers any financial bonuses to licensees affiliated with the broker for the sale or lease of real property listed with the real estate broker, the real estate broker shall provide to each party to a real estate transaction a statement that discloses that financial bonuses are offered.*

The Commission's memo of November 2007 concerning teams adds, "If there are similar financial incentives offered within the team, those must also be disclosed."

Trust Money [17-502 (b) (1)]

> *A real estate broker promptly, but not more than 7 business days after the acceptance of a contract of sale by both parties, shall deposit trust money in an account that is maintained by the real estate broker:*
> (i) *separately from the real estate broker's own accounts; and*
> (ii) *solely for trust money.*

All trust money must be promptly submitted to the broker for deposit in the broker's escrow account, unless a written contract provision calls for a different disposition. The Brokers Act makes no provision for any account, other than the broker's account, for trust monies. Surely a broker would not authorize a team to use a modified contract in which the parties agree to hold deposit money in a team's account, thus circumventing the protection the statute intends for the public.

■ LICENSEE SALES COMMISSION DISPUTES

The licensing law does not authorize the Real Estate Commission to arbitrate any disputes between brokers or between brokers and salespersons over distribution of commissions. Such disputes may be submitted for arbitration to the respective Board or Association of REALTORS®, if the parties to the dispute are members of the same board, or to the Maryland Association of REALTORS®, if the parties to the dispute are members of different boards or associations. Arbitration may also be pursued through other agencies. To prevent commission disputes, the percentage and distribution of commissions should be agreed to in writing, especially those setting forth the agreement between brokers and their salespersons. Division of compensation between brokerage firms, however, is usually based on information in the published multiple listing and, typically, confirmed orally.

■ PLACES OF BUSINESS: OFFICES [§17-517]

Each licensed real estate broker who is not a resident of Maryland shall also maintain an office in Maryland, if the state in which the nonresident broker resides requires that a resident of Maryland who is licensed in the other state maintain an office in that state.

The place of business in Maryland required by the Brokers Act for all broker licensees must be an office or headquarters where they and their employees and/or affiliates regularly transact real estate business. The Commission does not recognize mobile (rolling) offices. The broker's office is to have a specific street address where investigators can readily find financial and other records. Records of the firm's transactions, including the records of the broker's escrow account, must be kept in a secured location at this stationary office. Commercial answering services, mechanical recording devices, or mail drops, singly or in combination, do not satisfy the requirement for an office. Brokers must display in their main offices their own licenses and the licenses of all their affiliates registered with the Commission as working at that location.

The federal *Americans with Disabilities Act* requires that places of public accommodation make reasonable modifications to meet the needs of persons with disabilities. Real estate offices are such places. Access for the public should be barrier-free, and employees should be alerted to assist any physically challenged persons who visit an office. Moreover, every firm with 15 or more employees in each of 20 weeks per year—and this number includes affiliates—must make reasonable accommodation to the needs of any person with a disability who works for the firm.

Workplace Discrimination [Human Relations (49B) Sections 11; 11A; 11B; 11C; 11D]

Amendments to the Human Relations Commission Article, effective in 2007, increase the avenues of redress for employees and associates who charge their employer with workplace discrimination. They may now, under certain circumstances, individually sue the employer themselves or seek the aid of the Human Relations Commissions in such a suit. Alternatively, they may make a civil complaint in which the presiding administrative law judge may make awards of $50,000, $100,000, $200,000, or $300,000, based on the number of employees of the firm. In addition to compensatory damages, back pay and attorney's fees may be awarded in these actions. Although a firm with 14 or fewer employees is not mentioned in that scale of awards, it is now vulnerable to private law suits.

Privacy of Customers' Personal Information [Commercial Law §14-3501–§14-3506]

Effective January 1, 2008, the Maryland Personal Information Protection Act made it an unfair or deceptive trade practice for a business to fail to protect the personal information of customers—persons seeking to purchase or lease a product or to obtain a service. Personal information is defined as an individual's Social Security number, driver's license number, financial account or credit card number, or taxpayer ID number. This includes information in hard copy or unencrypted digital form that, retrieved, could easily be read. After investigation of any security breach, businesses must provide notice to those individuals that a breach has occurred that is reasonably likely to result in misuse of individuals' personal information. This is a major challenge for brokerage firms with countless documents and data to secure.

Maintenance of Records [§17-508]

Effective October 1, 2008, the Brokers Act requires all real estate licensees to keep copies of listings and any other documents obtained in connection with a transaction involving brokerage services for five years starting from the date of closing, the date of listing, or the date of the end of a property management agreement. This limits the time over which the costly, strategic storage and security plan—involving encryption of data and/or other means of secure storage—must be maintained. Before this legislation, there had been no time limit on the requirement to keep records.

Office Signs [§17-519]

A real estate broker must display a sign clearly visible to the public at each office and branch office that the real estate broker maintains. The sign must include the words *Realty*, *Real Estate*, or, where authorized by the respective trade associations, REALTOR® or *Realtist*.

Changes in Office Location [§17-520]

Within ten days of changing the location of any office, a real estate broker must submit

- written notice on a form provided by the Commission of such change in the address of the principal office and any branch office of the broker;
- the license certificate and pocket card of the broker or, for the branch office, its certificate; and
- the required fee.

Upon receipt of these things, the Commission issues a new certificate and card to the broker for the unexpired period of the broker's license or branch office certificate. If a real estate broker changes the address of the principal office or a branch office and fails to submit the required notice, the license of the broker is *automatically suspended* until the broker submits the required notice.

Branch Offices [§17-518]

Licensed real estate brokers may maintain branch offices in the State. They must appoint managers for each branch office who are either associate brokers or salespersons (generally) with three years of active experience. A recent provision of the law allowing salespersons with shorter periods of licensure history to be appointed branch managers requires such applicants to have completed the 135 hours of broker prelicense education and have passed the state broker licensing exam. In the two years since this possibility was provided, not one applicant has taken advantage of it.

Managers must exercise reasonable and adequate supervision over the provision of real estate brokerage services by all affiliates working out of their branch offices. This responsibility is in addition to, not in lieu of, the responsibility of the broker. Licenses of all licensees registered with a branch office are displayed in that branch office together with a branch office certificate that shows, among other things, the name of the broker, as registered with the Commission, and the address of the main office.

Newly issued branch office certificates and their renewals are for two-year periods. There is a $5 fee for each certificate. Applications for branch office certificates must identify the individuals appointed as managers of the branch offices and be accompanied by payment of the required fees.

■ DISCLOSURE OF LICENSEE STATUS AND OF TEAM RELATIONSHIPS

As previously discussed, licensees within a company sometimes work with one another and with nonlicensee support staff and call themselves a "group" or "team." Licensees may not acquire an interest in or purchase property listed with them or their firm—for themselves personally or for any member of their immediate family, their firm, any member of their firm, *any unlicensed member of a brokerage group or team of which they are part,* or any entity in which they have an ownership interest—without making their true position known to the owner of the listed property.

Additionally, when selling or leasing property in which licensees, their firm, or any member either of their immediate family, their firm, or any brokerage group or team of which they are a part have an ownership interest, licensees shall reveal that interest in writing to all parties to the transaction.

Moreover, when a licensee who is part of a group or team signs real estate documents in the course of performing brokerage activities, that signature must be the licensee's own name and not the name of a brokerage group or team.

■ ADVERTISING

Definition [§17-527.2]

Advertisement includes any

- correspondence,
- mailings,
- newsletters and brochures,
- business cards,
- sale or lease sign riders,
- promotional items,
- automobile signage,
- telephone directory listings,
- radio and television announcements,
- telephone solicitations, and
- Internet voice-overs.

Regulation .19 B states, "*Advertising* means all oral, written, and visual advertising done by the licensee or by others on behalf of the licensee including telephone solicitation by individuals or by machine. The Commission's standards apply to all advertising."

Use of Designated Names in Advertising [§17-527.1, §17-527.2, §17-527.3]

A **designated name** is the name that appears on the license certificate of a licensee. Whenever brokers or affiliates, or individuals acting on their behalf, advertise in any medium, the advertisement must *meaningfully and conspicuously* present the designated name of that broker licensee (i.e., the firm's name) as identified to the Commission. A franchise logo or a company logo, although it may appear in an advertisement, does *not* satisfy the requirement to identify the broker's firm. When an affiliate publishes his own name in an advertisement, it must be exactly as shown on his pocket card and license certificate. The ad must *also* meaningfully and conspicuously display the designated name of the firm with which he is affiliated.

Telephone Numbers and E-mail Addresses

Associate brokers and salespersons may not use their individual telephone numbers or e-mail addresses in advertisements, unless the identified telephone number of their broker or branch office manager also appears in the advertisement. There is renewed emphasis on and active enforcement of these requirements.

The memorandum below, from the Commission's Web site, addresses this issue:

> *The Commission is concerned that members of the public may be unaware of how to register any questions or concerns that may arise in their dealings with a particular associate broker or salesperson. The Commissioners believe that many issues can be resolved with the assistance of the broker or branch office manager, and that this requirement will make it easier for that assistance to be obtained.*

To address this concern, it is generally agreed that when an office phone number is provided in advertising, any person or automatic answering service responding to that number must give the caller at least the choice of speaking with the broker or the branch office manager or with the licensee mentioned in the advertisement.

Both the Brokers Act and COMAR require that all licensees show in all advertising the fact that they are licensees. This disclosure must be made even when the licensees are selling their own real property. Licensees may not advertise the listings held by other brokerage firms without prior approval by those firms.

Broker licensees using a franchise name in any advertising are required to include, clearly and unmistakably, their own name or their firm's designated name as registered with the Commission. Both brokers and their affiliates must make clear the designated name of the brokerage in every encounter—whether face-to-face or by radio, telephone, e-mail, or any other means.

Licensees having their own Web sites must be certain to present the designated name of their firm, clearly and conspicuously, at least on home pages. They must also show more than a franchisor name or a franchise logo to identify their particular firm. Each franchisee has a distinct name; that name should be conspicuously presented. It is not enough, for example, to show "Century Executives" (a fictional franchise name) and/or some image of an airship. Instead, "Century Executives 4000" (the fictional designated name of one of Century Executive's franchisees) must be shown. It would also be well to display, if not as prominently, the firm's designated name on every page of the Web site. The Commission is concerned that affiliates are naming only themselves on Web sites and so giving the impression to the public that they are brokers or that a team is a licensed brokerage firm.

Signs on Ground Rent Properties [§17-606]

Licensee For Sale signs displayed on property subject to ground rent must state the amount of the annual ground rent and the full cost of capitalization if the price of the property is shown. The lettering showing the ground rent and capitalization must be at least as large as the lettering showing the property sale price. *Capitalization* is the sum for which the land could be redeemed—purchased in fee—from its leasehold owner. Maryland ground rents are discussed in Chapter 13 of this book.

COMAR requires that a licensee obtain an owner's permission before placing signs on a property. Licensees should check local laws regarding the use of sale, directional, and open house signs on public property. They should also honor any restrictions imposed by cooperatives, condominiums, and homeowner associations. Licensees should familiarize themselves with HUD guidelines and rules concerning the use of the Equal Housing Opportunity logo or slogan in every display ad to avoid giving even the appearance of discriminatory intent.

■ TELEMARKETING AND "BROADCAST" FAX SOLICITATION

Since 2003, the Federal Trade Commission has maintained a National Do Not Call Registry to which millions of Americans have added their home telephone numbers to avoid being disturbed. Certain categories of callers are exempt from the prohibition on calling these listed numbers: charities, surveys, political organizations, and companies with which the recipient has done business during the last 18 months. However, each business is required to have its own registry of numbers for persons who have specifically asked it (one by one) to stop calling. Maryland has passed similar legislation. To solicit—live or by machine—a licensee must access the federal, state, and company do-not-call lists to avoid violating the restriction. The federal penalty for a pattern of violations is $11,000 per call. It is a firm's duty to inform its affiliates of the firm's policies and data resources so as to honor the law and to avoid expensive violations.

There is no "do-not-fax" list. However, faxed advertising must include on each fax page the name of the sender and the sender's phone number to call to prevent receiving more faxes from that sender. Under the Junk Fax Prevention Act of 2005, the sender of an unsolicited advertisement sent to an individual's fax machine is liable for a minimum of $500 per page; damages may also be trebled at the court's discretion upon a finding that the violation was deliberate. Since 2005, the amended law has allowed unsolicited fax advertising if the sender has an established business relationship (EBR) with the recipient and the recipient has given the fax number to the sender with permission to use it. The fax must still contain a no-cost opt-out number to call, available 24/7.

Maryland Prohibition on Commercial Fax Solicitation [Commercial Law §14–1313]

A person may not intentionally make an electronic or telephonic transmission to a facsimile device for the purpose of commercial solicitation. *Commercial solicitation* means the unsolicited electronic or telephonic transmission in the State to a facsimile device to encourage a person to purchase goods, *real property*, or services.

There is a maximum penalty of $1,000 for each such solicitation. Commercial solicitation, however, does not include a transmission made in the course of continuing prior negotiations or one made in the course of continuing a pre-existing business relationship with the person receiving the transmission.

■ FUNDS OF OTHERS HELD IN TRUST (TITLE 17, SUBTITLE V, PART I)

Trust money is defined as a deposit, payment, or other money that a person entrusts to a real estate broker to hold for the benefit of the owner or beneficial owner of that money and for a purpose that relates to a transaction involving real estate in this State.

The **beneficial owner** of funds in a trust account is that person—other than the owner of the trust money—for whose benefit a licensee holds the money. In summary, the *owner* of an earnest money deposit is the *purchaser*, while the *beneficial owner* is the *seller*.

Management of Trust Money [§17-504]

The Brokers Act requires that when brokers receive trust money, such as earnest money deposits, and are not directed in writing to the contrary by the money's owner and beneficial owner, they must *promptly* deposit those funds in a non-interest-bearing checking account, a non-interest-bearing savings account, or any combination of these accounts that they maintain for that purpose in authorized financial institutions in Maryland. The account must be exclusively for the funds of others and contain none of the broker's or firm's funds (no "commingling"). Real estate brokers may not use trust money for any purpose other than that for which it is entrusted to them (no "conversion").

Brokers are required to report the bank's name and the account numbers to the Commission as soon as they start depositing trust monies there. If a licensee establishes another non-interest-bearing or special escrow account, changes an escrow account number, or transfers the account to another bank, the broker must notify the Commission in writing within ten days of such action. Trust monies from multiple transactions may be deposited in a single trust money account.

Associate real estate brokers or real estate salespersons who receive trust monies while providing real estate brokerage services shall immediately submit such money to their brokers.

Earnest monies must be deposited promptly but in no event later than seven business days after acceptance of the contract by both parties. *Promptly* should be interpreted to mean "at the earliest opportunity." Earnest money deposit checks that accompany offers to purchase are usually not transacted (deposited in the firm's trust account) until the negotiation to purchase is completed. At any time prior to that completion, the broker is not only free, but obliged, to return the deposit to the offeror-buyer upon that offeror's request. If the broker has deposited the offeror's check, no refund is usually made until the check clears.

Authorized Financial Institutions [§17-503]

Except when directed to the contrary in the fully signed purchase agreement, brokers must deposit all trust money in an escrow account in a financial institution located in the State whose deposits are insured by the Federal Deposit Insurance Corporation, the Federal Savings and Loan Insurance Corporation, the National Credit Union Administration, the State of Maryland Deposit Insurance Fund Corporation, or the Maryland Credit Union Insurance Corporation.

Disposition of Trust Money [§17-505]

The Brokers Act sets forth several options under which a broker may release earnest money held in trust. These choices address both situations in which the transaction goes smoothly to settlement and those where one or both parties dispute the distribution of the deposit when the transaction has collapsed.

The Brokers Act requires that real estate brokers maintain trust money in an authorized account until one of four things happens:

1. The real estate transaction is consummated or terminated, and the money paid out as intended.
2. The real estate broker receives proper written instructions from the owner and beneficial owner, agreeing on withdrawal or other disposition of the trust money.
3. A court directs disposition of funds after a broker's filing of an action of interpleader.
4. When the owner or beneficial owner of the trust money fails to complete the real estate transaction for which the trust money was entrusted, prior to distributing the trust money, the real estate broker shall notify both the owner and the beneficial owner (from here on, referred to as the buyer and the seller, respectively) of the broker's intention to distribute the trust money to the party who, in the broker's good-faith opinion, is entitled to receive it in accordance with the terms of the real estate contract. This notice must be delivered either in person or by a combination of certified mail, return receipt requested, and regular mail. It shall state whether the trust money will be paid to the buyer or the seller and tell both that either of them may prevent distribution of the trust money by submitting a formal, written, similarly delivered protest within 30 days. If neither party submits a protest within that time, the trust money is to be distributed in accordance with the real estate broker's notice. Brokers who receive a letter of protest may distribute the trust money in accordance with one of the other three alternatives or simply leave it in the firm's trust account indefinitely.

Brokers may not be held liable for exercising (or not exercising) the fourth alternative. Authority to make good-faith disbursement of funds must be granted *in the purchase agreement* that entrusted the funds to the broker at the time of offer and acceptance. Without such authority, the broker may not use that process to disburse the funds.

When the duty of real estate brokers to maintain trust money in an account terminates—typically at closing—they must promptly account for all trust money. Real estate brokers may invest trust money as the owners (the buyers) and beneficial owners (the sellers) of the trust money instruct in writing or as the real estate brokers, owners, and beneficial owners have set down in a written agreement.

Records to Be Kept Secure [§17-507]

Brokers must keep, in a secured area within their office, all records of trust money. They are also required to keep copies of all real estate transaction documents formed in the course of their brokerage activities. The records of trust money activity are to be available to the Commission on demand. On reasonable notice, a licensee must allow a representative of the Commission access to other required records in the licensee's place of business during business hours.

Authority to Sign Trust Account Checks [COMAR 09.11.01.20]

The firm's real estate broker must be the signer, or at least one of the signers, on checks drawn on escrow accounts that the broker is required to maintain. The broker may designate an alternate signer to sign checks. This designated alternate signer, however, must be a licensee. A nonlicensee may be a required cosigner on the broker's escrow account, provided all checks are also signed by a licensee designated by the broker. At least one licensee must sign every check.

QUESTIONS

1. Any outdoor sign or advertisement displayed on property for sale subject to ground rent
   1. must, if price is shown, also show the annual ground rent but need not show any other details until inquiry is made by a prospective purchaser.
   2. must, if price is shown, show ground rent and cost of capitalization in lettering no smaller than the lettering used for the price.
   3. need show only leasehold price.
   4. need show only leasehold price and the phrase *plus* GR.

2. When licensees advertise real property they have listed for sale,
   1. the name of the salesperson need not be included in the advertisement, but the designated name of the broker must be shown.
   2. only the broker's name is permitted in advertisements.
   3. the price of the property must be included in all advertisements.
   4. members of multiple listing services may advertise any of the services' listings.

3. The requirement that a broker maintain an office is satisfied by having a
   1. telephone answering service.
   2. post office box.
   3. mechanical answering machine.
   4. definite place of business.

4. A real estate brokerage firm performing activities for which a real estate license is required may be operated by
   1. real estate salespersons.
   2. an associate broker.
   3. any person holding a valid real estate license issued by the State Real Estate Commission.
   4. a licensed real estate broker.

5. Advertising by a broker *MUST* include the
   1. designated name of that broker as registered with the Commission.
   2. name of the broker's REALTOR® board or association or Realtist organization.
   3. name of the licensed real estate broker.
   4. name of the licensee who listed the property.

6. In Maryland, the person primarily responsible for the real estate brokerage services provided through a corporation is the
   1. president of the corporation.
   2. licensed real estate broker of the firm.
   3. chairperson of the board.
   4. majority stockholder of the corporation.

7. Salespersons may use their own names and phone numbers in advertising listed property if
   1. the designated name of their firm is clearly and meaningfully shown, as well as the firm's phone number.
   2. their office manager's name is shown in letters at least half the size of the salesperson's.
   3. different colors for the broker's and salesperson's names are used.
   4. the broker gives permission.

8. When there are no instructions to the contrary from their owner and beneficial owner, the Brokers Act states that earnest money deposits
   1. may be commingled with the broker's funds.
   2. must be deposited in an insured and approved financial institution in Maryland.
   3. are to be placed in an interest-bearing account.
   4. may be withdrawn at any time prior to settlement, as long as a licensee's signature appears on the escrow check.

9. A check drawn on a brokerage firm's escrow (trust) account
    1. must be signed by the associate broker of the firm using her designated name.
    2. must be signed by at least two licensees in the firm.
    3. may be cosigned by an appointed nonlicensee, if signed by a nonappointed licensee.
    4. does not necessarily need a second signature, if signed by the broker of the firm.

10. Unlicensed persons working in a brokerage firm may do all the following EXCEPT
    1. compute commission checks.
    2. submit listings and changes to a multiple listing service.
    3. conduct an open house.
    4. schedule appointments for a licensee to show listed property.

yellow bk chp 6

Listing Agreements and Buyer Representation Agreements

■ KEY TERMS

automatic renewal
provisions

buyer representation
agreements

completed disclosure
form

latent defects

listings

material fact

ministerial acts

net listing agreements

owner in severalty

subagents

■ OVERVIEW

Maryland recognizes representation agreements between real estate brokers and sellers and those between real estate brokers and buyers. (References to *buyers* and *sellers* should be understood, in this book, to apply to *tenants* and *landlords* whenever possible.)

Listings are contracts that create agency relationships in which brokers agree to help sellers sell realty and sellers agree to compensate them for their service. These agreements may be either *exclusive-right-to-sell*, *exclusive-agency*, or *open* listings as these terms are explained in the students' principles text.

The process of persuading a property owner to enter into such an agreement with a broker is called *listing a property*. It is typically done by affiliates (salespersons and associate brokers) on behalf of brokers. Although this procedure may later result in compensation for affiliates, only their brokers and the client-seller are parties to the agreement. Moreover, the listing contracts belong to the brokers.

Buyer representation agreements are contracts that create an agency relationship under which, for compensation, brokers agree to help buyers find property. They may be *exclusive buyer agency*, *exclusive-agency buyer agency*, or *open buyer agency* agreements. These agreements are also typically arranged by affiliates but are contracts between their brokers and the client-buyers and belong to their brokers.

■ RESIDENTIAL BROKERAGE AGREEMENTS

No "Standard" Form

Realty industry boards and associations provide listing and buyer representation agreement forms for their members' use, but no standard form is provided by either statute or regulation for either listing (seller representation) agreements or buyer representation agreements. The law does, however, have some specific requirements and prohibitions for whatever forms are used.

Required Provisions [§17-534]

All residential agency agreements—representing buyers or sellers, open or exclusive—must be in writing and signed by the parties to those agreements. Copies are to be given to all signers before agreements are acted on by a firm.

With respect to Maryland real estate, each agreement must state the duties and authority of the agent, the compensation to be paid to the agent, the performance that will call for such payment, and when payment is to be made. It also must state a definite date on which the agreement will end without further notice from either party and any provisions for possible early termination. This makes it unlawful to include **automatic renewal provisions** in the agreement that would require a client to take any action to terminate representation at the end of its original term. Agency contracts may be extended only by signed, written extension agreements.

The agreement must set forth whether the listing firm is authorized to receive compensation from persons other than its client. Also, it must state whether the agent is authorized to cooperate with other brokers and share compensation with them. The agreement should either approve or refuse to approve compensation for cooperating agents (**subagents**) and/or for buyer brokers. In addition, it must reveal the amount (usually expressed as a percentage) of the shared compensation with which other brokers will be compensated. Clients in agency agreements may not waive any of the above protective requirements in their contracts.

In agency agreements (listings), seller-principals have choices to make with respect to dealing with buyer agents, subagents, and dual agents. These choices are indicated on the completed listing forms together with such routine issues as offering ("asking") price, date of availability, acceptable forms of financing, and possible help with purchasers' closing costs.

Net Listing Forbidden [§17-322(b) and COMAR 09.11.01.01(b)]

Listings may not take the form of **net listing agreements** in which brokers retain all sale proceeds in excess of some minimum sales proceeds agreed to by sellers.

Additional Offers: One Effect of Silence [§17-532(c)]

The Brokers Act states that when there is no express agreement to the contrary—that is, when there is *silence* about these matters—in the brokerage agreement, listing brokers

- *are not* required to seek additional offers for a listed property that becomes subject to a contract of sale, but
- *are* required, absent client instructions to the contrary, to present additional written offers and counteroffers on a property that is "under contract" that come to the broker's firm.

Most listing agreements provided by associations in the industry do address these choices directly in the preprinted listing form, usually in a way that imposes the least burden on the brokerage firm. These forms typically do not require further showing and mandate no presentation of later offers.

■ OTHER PROVISIONS

Ministerial Acts [§17-528, §17-532]

Ministerial acts are acts performed by a licensee that do not involve discretion or the exercise of judgment by that licensee. They may be performed both on behalf of clients and of third parties (nonclients) before, during, and after the writing of a contract agreement. When agency agreements authorize agents to perform ministerial acts on behalf of third parties, those acts cannot be construed (interpreted) to violate the agents' duty of loyalty to their clients. Neither may they be construed to indicate an agency agreement between the nonclient and the licensee performing those acts.

Copies of Agency Agreements [§17-322(b) 15,16; COMAR 09.11.01.12]

Licensees must give copies of agency agreements to seller-clients before beginning to carry out the tasks assigned in the agreements. Licensees must also keep copies of all such agency agreements for five years either from the date they are signed or from the scheduled date of any settlement called for by a sales contract entered into during the listing. Copies of documents creating buyer representation should also be kept for the five-year period.

Disclosure and Disclaimer Statement [§17-322(e); and COMAR 09.11.02.02(J)]

At the time of listing a residential property for sale, brokers or their affiliates are to present the Commission's Residential Property Disclosure and Disclaimer Statement to sellers for their completion and signature. They should warn sellers that neither disclosure nor disclaimer relieves sellers of the legal requirement to make voluntary disclosure to purchasers of all material property defects. Failure by either a buyer's or seller's broker to present this form—properly completed—to the prospective buyer before presentation of the buyer's written offer opens the offending licensee to disciplinary action because that failure could result in a contract's becoming void or voidable. When they are being asked to complete this form, sellers must be warned that whether they choose to "disclose" or "disclaim," **latent defects** must always be made known to prospective purchasers. Latent defects are defined later in this chapter under "Seller Disclosure."

Licensee Responsibilities for Disclosure [§17-530(b) and §17-533(i)]

Licensees already representing either a seller or a buyer, not later than their first scheduled face-to-face meeting with the other party, must disclose in writing their existing agency relationship, using the Relationship Information Form "Understanding Whom Agents Represent," mandated by the Commission. (See Figure 2.2 in Chapter 2 of this book.) A licensee serving in the capacity of presumed buyer-agent must orally disclose that fact to any seller or the seller's agent.

Note: An exact photocopy of a completed buyer's form shall not subsequently be used to disclose agency representation to sellers. Sellers receiving "Understanding Whom Agents Represent" must get their own forms calling for their own personal signatures. To give a copy that does not apply amounts to failure to make the required disclosure.

An offer to purchase should never be presented until the purchasers have received a properly completed Maryland Residential Property Disclosure and Disclaimer Statement for the property that is the subject of the offer. (See Figure 4.1.) Many listing agents leave multiple copies of a completed form on a table in a for-sale property. However, delivery of this form must be evidenced by a properly dated receipt for it from the buyer. A licensee representing a seller is responsible to see that this form is presented in a timely manner and to keep proof of that presentation.

Licensees must also provide to buyers, on behalf of client-sellers, the federal lead-paint disclosure form for any properties that buyers are considering that was built before January 1, 1978 (i.e., in 1977 or earlier). If the buyers are clients and the sellers are not represented by any licensee, it is then the responsibility of the buyer's agent to procure any required lead-paint disclosure form and present it to the buyer before presenting any offer from that buyer.

There is one form for property being rented and a different one for property being purchased. It is vitally important to use the correct one. Use of the wrong one is regarded by federal law as utter failure to meet the disclosure requirement. That failure is subject to penalties of as much as $10,000 each for repeated, deliberate violation. Moreover, a disclosure form with any item not completed is also held to be no disclosure at all.

In addition to the appropriate form, prospective purchasers and tenants must be given the government booklet *Protect Your Family From Lead in Your Home*.

■ LISTING AGREEMENT PROPERTY INFORMATION

In agency agreements for the sale of a property, the age of the house, area of the lot, zoning of the property, taxes, and other detailed property information should appear in the portion of listing agreements that will be published. If accurate data are not available from the owner, the listing licensee should obtain correct data from public records or personal inspection. Estimates of such information and "educated guesses" are totally unacceptable when facts are required.

Listing licensees should also examine any existing house location survey of the property, note what information it shows regarding property lines and improvements, and attempt to determine if it is thorough and up-to-date. Accurate information, responsibly presented in the listing, reduces chances for confusion and uncertainty when the property is shown and a contract offer prepared.

When describing the condition of the property in remarks distributed through the multiple listing service (MLS), licensees must be careful not to say anything that buyers may later consider misrepresentation. Licensees must also take care

FIGURE 4.1

Property Disclosure and Disclaimer Statement

MARYLAND RESIDENTIAL PROPERTY DISCLOSURE AND DISCLAIMER STATEMENT

Property Address: _____

Legal Description: _____

NOTICE TO SELLER AND PURCHASER

Section 10-702 of the Real Property Article, *Annotated Code of Maryland*, requires the owner of certain residential real property to furnish to the purchaser either (a) a RESIDENTIAL PROPERTY DISCLAIMER STATEMENT stating that the owner is selling the property "as is" and makes no representations or warranties as to the condition of the property or any improvements on the real property, except as otherwise provided in the contract of sale, or in a listing of latent defects; or (b) a RESIDENTIAL PROPERTY DISCLOSURE STATEMENT disclosing defects or other information about the condition of the real property actually known by the owner. Certain transfers of residential property are excluded from this requirement (see the exemptions listed below).

10-702. EXEMPTIONS. The following are specifically excluded from the provisions of §10-702:
1. The initial sale of single family residential real property:
    A. that has never been occupied; or
    B. for which a certificate of occupancy has been issued within 1 year before the seller and buyer enter into a contract of sale;
2. A transfer that is exempt from the transfer tax under §13-207 of the Tax-Property Article, except land installment contracts of sales under §13-207(a) (11) of the Tax-Property Article and options to purchase real property under §13-207(a)(12) of the Tax-Property Article;
3. A sale by a lender or an affiliate or subsidiary of a lender that acquired the real property by foreclosure or deed in lieu of foreclosure;
4. A sheriff's sale, tax sale, or sale by foreclosure, partition, or by court appointed trustee;
5. A transfer by a fiduciary in the course of the administration of a decedent's estate, guardianship, conservatorship, or trust;
6. A transfer of single family residential real property to be converted by the buyer into use other than residential use or to be demolished; or
7. A sale of unimproved real property.

Section 10-702 also requires the owner to disclose information about latent defects in the property that the owner has actual knowledge of. The owner must provide this information even if selling the property "as is." "Latent defects" are defined as: Material defects in real property or an improvement to real property that:
(1) A purchaser would not reasonably be expected to ascertain or observe by a careful visual inspection of the real property; and
(2) Would pose a direct threat to the health or safety of:
(i) the purchaser; or
(ii) an occupant of the real property, including a tenant or invitee of the purchaser.

MARYLAND RESIDENTIAL PROPERTY DISCLOSURE STATEMENT

NOTICE TO OWNERS: Complete and sign this statement only if you elect to disclose defects, including latent defects, or other information about the condition of the property actually known by you; otherwise, sign the Residential Property Disclaimer Statement. You may wish to obtain professional advice or inspections of the property; however, you are not required to undertake or provide any independent investigation or inspection of the property in order to make the disclosure set forth below. The disclosure is based on your personal knowledge of the condition of the property at the time of the signing of this statement.

NOTICE TO PURCHASERS: The information provided is the representation of the Owners and is based upon the actual knowledge of Owners as of the date noted. Disclosure by the Owners is not a substitute for an inspection by an independent home inspection company, and you may wish to obtain such an inspection. The information contained in this statement is not a warranty by the Owners as to the condition of the property of which the Owners have no knowledge or other conditions of which the Owners have no actual knowledge.

How long have you owned the property? _____

Property System: Water, Sewage, Heating & Air Conditioning (Answer all that apply)

Water Supply	❏ Public	❏ Well	❏ Other _____	
Sewage Disposal	❏ Public	❏ Septic System approved for _____(# bedrooms)		
Garbage Disposal	❏ Yes	❏ No		
Dishwasher	❏ Yes	❏No		
Heating	❏ Oil ❏ Natural Gas	❏ Electric	❏ Heat Pump Age ____	❏ Other _____
Air Conditioning	❏ Oil ❏ Natural Gas	❏Electric	❏ Heat Pump Age ____	❏ Other _____
Hot Water	❏ Oil ❏ Natural Gas	❏Electric Capacity _____ Age____	❏ Other _____	

Property Disclosure and Disclaimer Statement

Please indicate your actual knowledge with respect to the following:

1. Foundation: Any settlement or other problems?   ❑ Yes   ❑ No   ❑ Unknown
Comments:_____

2. Basement: Any leaks or evidence of moisture?   ❑ Yes   ❑ No   ❑ Unknown   ❑ Does Not Apply
Comments:_____

3. Roof: Any leaks or evidence of moisture?   ❑ Yes   ❑ No   ❑ Unknown
        Type of Roof:_____Age_____
Comments:_____
        Is there any existing fire retardant treated plywood?   ❑ Yes   ❑ No   ❑ Unknown
Comments:_____

4. Other Structural Systems, including exterior walls and floors:
Comments:_____
        Any defects (structural or otherwise)?   ❑ Yes   ❑ No   ❑ Unknown
Comments:_____

5. Plumbing system: Is the system in operating condition?   ❑ Yes   ❑ No   ❑ Unknown
Comments:_____

6. Heating Systems: Is heat supplied to all finished rooms?   ❑ Yes   ❑ No   ❑ Unknown
Comments:_____
        Is the system in operating condition?   ❑ Yes   ❑ No   ❑ Unknown
Comments:_____

7. Air Conditioning System: Is cooling supplied to all finished rooms? ❑Yes ❑ No ❑ Unknown ❑ Does Not Apply
Comments:_____
        Is the system in operating condition? ❑ Yes   ❑ No   ❑ Unknown   ❑ Does Not Apply
Comments:_____

8. Electric Systems: Are there any problems with electrical fuses, circuit breakers, outlets or wiring?
        ❑ Yes   ❑ No.   ❑ Unknown
Comments:_____
        Will the smoke detectors provide an alarm in the event of a power outage? ❑Yes   ❑ No   ❑ Does Not Apply
Comments:_____

9. Septic Systems: Is the septic system functioning properly?   ❑ Yes   ❑ No   ❑ Unknown   ❑ Does Not Apply
        When was the system last pumped?   Date_____   ❑ Unknown
Comments:_____

10. Water Supply: Any problem with water supply?   ❑ Yes   ❑ No   ❑ Unknown
Comments:_____
        Home water treatment system: ❑ Yes   ❑ No   ❑ Unknown
Comments:_____
        Fire sprinkler system: ❑ Yes   ❑ No   ❑ Unknown   ❑ Does Not Apply
Comments:_____
        Are the systems in operating condition?   ❑ Yes   ❑ No   ❑ Unknown
Comments:_____

11. Insulation:
        In exterior walls?   ❑ Yes   ❑ No   ❑Unknown
        In ceiling/attic?   ❑ Yes   ❑ No   ❑ Unknown
        In any other areas?   ❑ Yes   ❑ No   Where?_____
Comments:_____

12. Exterior Drainage: Does water stand on the property for more than 24 hours after a heavy rain?
        ❑ Yes   ❑ No   ❑ Unknown
Comments_____
        Are gutters and downspouts in good repair?   ❑ Yes   ❑ No   ❑ Unknown
Comments:_____

F I G U R E   4.1 (CONTINUED)

Property Disclosure and Disclaimer Statement

13. Wood-destroying insects: Any infestation and/or prior damage? ❏ Yes   ❏ No   ❏ Unknown
Comments:_____

        Any treatments or repairs? ❏ Yes   ❏ No   ❏ Unknown
        Any warranties?   ❏ Yes   ❏ No   ❏ Unknown
Comments:_____

14. Are there any hazardous or regulated materials (including, but not limited to, licensed landfills, asbestos, radon gas, lead-based paint, underground storage tanks, or other contamination) on the property?
        ❏ Yes ❏ No   ❏ Unknown
If yes, specify below
Comments:_____

15. If the property relies on the combustion of a fossil fuel for heat, ventilation, hot water, or clothes dryer operation, is a carbon monoxide alarm installed in the property?
        o Yes   o No   0 Unknown
Comments:_____

16. Are there any zoning violations, nonconforming uses, violation of building restrictions or setback requirements or any recorded or unrecorded easement, except for utilities, on or affecting the property?
        ❏ Yes ❏ No ❏ Unknown
If yes, specify below
Comments:_____

17. Is the property located in a flood zone, conservation area, wetland area, Chesapeake Bay critical area or Designated Historic District?
        ❏ Yes   ❏ No   ❏ Unknown   If yes, specify below
Comments:_____

18. Is the property subject to any restriction imposed by a Home Owners Association or any other type of community association?
        ❏ Yes   ❏ No   ❏ Unknown   If yes, specify below
Comments:_____

19. Are there any other material defects, including latent defects, affecting the physical condition of the property?
        ❏ Yes   ❏ No   ❏ Unknown
Comments:_____

NOTE: Owner(s) may wish to disclose the condition of other buildings on the property on a separate RESIDENTIAL PROPERTY DISCLOSURE STATEMENT.

The owner(s) acknowledge having carefully examined this statement, including any comments, and verify that it is complete and accurate as of the date signed. The owner(s) further acknowledge that they have been informed of their rights and obligations under §10-702 of the Maryland Real Property Article.

Owner _____   Date _____

Owner _____   Date _____

The purchaser(s) acknowledge receipt of a copy of this disclosure statement and further acknowledge that they have been informed of their rights and obligations under §10-702 of the Maryland Real Property Article.

Purchaser _____   Date_____

Purchaser_____   Date_____

Property Disclosure and Disclaimer Statement

MARYLAND RESIDENTIAL PROPERTY DISCLAIMER STATEMENT

NOTICE TO OWNER(S): Sign this statement only if you elect to sell the property without representations and warranties as to its condition, except as otherwise provided in the contract of sale and in the listing of latent defects set forth below; otherwise, complete and sign the RESIDENTIAL PROPERTY DISCLOSURE STATEMENT.

Except for the latent defects listed below, the undersigned owner(s) of the real property make no representations or warranties as to the condition of the real property or any improvements thereon, and the purchaser will be receiving the real property "as is" with all defects, including latent defects, which may exist, except as otherwise provided in the real estate contract of sale. The owner(s) acknowledge having carefully examined this statement and further acknowledge that they have been informed of their rights and obligations under §10-702 of the Maryland Real Property Article.

The owner(s) has actual knowledge of the following latent defects: _____

_____

_____

Owner _____   Date_____

Owner_____   Date_____

The purchaser(s) acknowledge receipt of a copy of this disclaimer statement and further acknowledge that they have been informed of their rights and obligations under §10-702 of the Maryland Real Property Article.

Purchaser _____   Date_____

Purchaser _____   Date_____

Page 4 of 4

FORM: DLLR/REC/P/10-1-01Rev
Rev 10-1-07

not to insert information into the MLS that betrays sellers' confidentiality. This obligation of confidentiality does *not* extend to material facts.

Material Facts [§17-322(b)4 and COMAR 09.11.02.01(d)]

To prevent error and misrepresentation, the Commission's Code of Ethics requires that licensees make reasonable efforts to discover all material facts about each property they list. A **material fact** includes any negative information about a property that is not readily visible to or discoverable by a prudent purchaser and that might tend to discourage a purchaser from going forward with the purchase. The Brokers Act requires that licensees disclose material facts that they know, *or should know*, to each prospective buyer. This is a demanding requirement.

Stigmatized Property [§17-322.1]

A licensee may not be held personally liable for failure to disclose that an owner or occupant of the property is, was, or is suspected of being infected with human immunodeficiency virus (HIV) or diagnosed with acquired immunodeficiency syndrome (AIDS). In fact, it is a violation of federal and state law to communicate information about the alleged presence of such diseases, even when asked.

In addition, Maryland statutes declare that the occurrence of a homicide, suicide, natural death, accidental death, or felony on a property is *not* a material fact that licensees are required to disclose. For failure to disclose such events, the statute exempts licensees, not sellers. Therefore, failure to disclose them is *not* a basis for disciplinary action against the licensee by the Commission or for a civil suit against that agent (by a surprised buyer).

Some licensees also consider it prudent to get their client-sellers' approval to *disclose affirmatively*—that is, voluntarily and without being asked—certain facts, such as the reported history of homicide, suicide, natural death, accidental death, or felony on the subject property. They do this to prevent buyers, who often learn these facts on their own between contract and settlement, from then trying to escape their contracts.

Notice that even when sellers give permission to answer questions about these matters, under the Brokers Act, their agents are not required to *volunteer* the information as they would in the case of material facts. But to meet the requirement of truthfulness, they must answer prospects' questions about these matters when sellers have given permission.

■ RESIDENTIAL PROPERTY DISCLOSURE AND DISCLAIMER FORM [REAL PROPERTY ARTICLE §10-702]

Seller Disclosure

The Brokers Act directs the Commission to provide a Residential Property Disclosure and Disclaimer Statement (Figure 4.1) and require its use in residential transactions by all brokerage firms in Maryland. There are occasional additions and other modifications to the form, the most recent of which is a new item #15, which asks,

> If the property relies on the combustion of a fossil fuel for heat, ventilation, hot water, or clothes dryer operation, is a carbon monoxide alarm installed in the property?

This simple inquiry has a hidden dimension. The phrase "alarm installed" has a technical definition buried in its statutory source at *Real Property* Article §10-702.

To be "installed," the alarm must be hardwired with battery backup mounted according to certain building standards and about 15 feet from each sleeping area. Although homeowners complete this form without help or suggestions from their listing agents, the listing agents should urge homeowners to take special care in answering this question.

Licensees are urged always to use the most current version of this Maryland Residential Property Condition Disclosure and Disclaimer Statement. Failure to do so will likely expose seller-clients to the risk of rescission of sales contracts. Incidentally, sellers, even when marketing their own residential property without broker assistance, are still required to present this form to purchasers before the offer to purchase is submitted.

A revised form (dated 10/1/07) calls for the homeowner to list any latent defect in the subject property. It defines *latent defects* as

> *material defects in real property or an improvement to real property that: (1) A purchaser would not reasonably be expected to ascertain or observe by a careful visual inspection of the real property; and (2) Would pose a direct threat to the health or safety of: (i) the purchaser; or (ii) an occupant of the real property, including a tenant or invitee of the purchaser.*

This definition seems to make latent defects a subtype of material facts: a subtype that is not easy to notice and that poses a direct health or safety threat. It remains to be seen if this sharpening of the definition will serve to reduce or to increase seller liability in the long run.

At the time a listing agreement is prepared and executed, this important document is to be completed by the sellers. This instrument affects all parties to a sales transaction. On this form, sellers choose whether *or not* to disclose the condition of a large number of physical features of the listed property. If they choose to make such disclosure, they should complete the disclosure form.

A **"completed" disclosure form** is one in which sellers respond to *every* inquiry, even if only to say "unknown" or "not applicable." By leaving even one response completely blank (or by giving contradictory answers), the sellers fail to meet the obligations imposed by Maryland law. Such failure also enables the buyers to rescind the contract in the same way as if they had not been given the Disclosure and Disclaimer Statement at all.

Disclaimer: "As Is"

If sellers choose not to disclose, they must complete the Disclaimer portion of the form, the one that makes this refusal and states that they are selling the property "as is" except as otherwise provided in the sales contract.

A copy of this four-page form—whichever portion is completed—once signed and dated by the purchasers is attached to and moves forward with the contract offer. Contrary to popular belief, use of the term *as is* does not free the sellers or their agents from the required affirmative (voluntary) disclosure of material facts and latent defects.

Either disclosing or disclaiming may be the more appropriate choice under certain economic conditions—such as a buyers' market or a sellers' market—but licensees should not coach sellers in this choice. They should certainly not suggest use of the disclaimer as a means of withholding material facts. Nor should they guide the sellers' answer to any question in the Disclosure portion.

If sellers need guidance in these decisions and answers, they should turn to competent legal counsel and/or other technical experts. The responses are to be the representations of the owners, not of a licensee.

Listing agents should obtain from sellers the completed Maryland Residential Property Disclosure and Disclaimer Statements at the time of taking listings. Listing licensees must inform sellers of their rights and obligations arising from this form. Completion of this form is required in all sales of residential properties containing four or fewer single-family units. (There are seven situations in which the sale of single-family properties does not require the use of the form. These limited situations are listed in the preprinted Disclosure and Disclaimer Statement in its introductory paragraphs.)

Duty to Provide Purchasers with Statement

Maryland statutes make it the duty of sellers, even when selling their single-family residential real property For Sale by Owner (FSBO), to complete and deliver to each purchaser, upon or before entering into a contract of sale, a Disclosure and Disclaimer Statement of which either the Disclosure or the Disclaimer portion is completed. Both portions must be submitted, even the blank one. When sellers are represented by a licensee, it becomes the duty of that licensee to provide them with the form and explain to them their obligation to complete it for delivery to each buyer-prospect.

It is then the duty of a licensee representing client-buyers to explain *their* rights and obligations with respect to this form. If the buyer is not represented by a licensee, this duty falls on the licensee representing the owner-seller. The rights and obligations of all parties are listed in this form.

When listing licensees learn that prospective purchasers are planning to make an offer, they must make every effort to provide those prospects with the Disclosure and Disclaimer Statement in a timely manner. This can be done personally or through the buyers' agent.

When listing agents do not know in advance that an offer is forthcoming, they should present the completed Disclosure and Disclaimer Statement to the purchasers or their agent immediately when an offer is produced. The purchasers can then reconsider their offer in the light of the Disclosure and Disclaimer Statement before releasing the offer for presentation.

Effect of a Properly Completed Statement

When purchasers do receive the Disclosure and Disclaimer Statement before or upon entering into a contract, they are prevented from later rescinding the agreement of sale based on any information revealed in the Disclosure and Disclaimer Statement.

Purchasers who do not receive this Disclosure and Disclaimer Statement before they enter into a sales contract retain the right to rescind the contract

- until five days after they finally receive the form;
- until they apply for a loan (if the loan office gives them notice that they are losing their right of rescission); or
- until settlement or occupancy, whichever is earlier.

This means that if purchasers never get a Disclosure and Disclaimer Statement and are never warned by a lender of the loss of their right to rescind, they may rescind at any time before settlement or before presettlement occupancy.

■ TERMINATION OF AGENCY AGREEMENT [§17-322(10), §17-534]

Maryland law sets no minimum or maximum time periods for agency agreements. The term of such an agreement is negotiable between client and broker. However, every listing and every buyer representation agreement must contain a definite termination date on which it will end without further notice from either party. Automatic extension provisions violate this law.

Unless the agency agreement states the contrary, licensees have no further obligations or duties to clients after termination, expiration, or completion of performance of the brokerage relationship, except to account for all trust monies and to keep confidential all personal and financial information about the clients or other matters that clients request be kept confidential.

Death of an **owner in severalty** (sole owner) would normally terminate a listing agreement by operation of law. However, death of one owner, when a married couple has held title as tenants by the entirety, may not necessarily terminate a listing. It is prudent to have the language of a listing form reviewed by a firm's legal counsel to clarify whether such an agency agreement will be binding on a deceased seller's estate. Purchasers would benefit from advice on the same matter from their own counsel.

Licensees may withdraw from representing either buyer-clients or seller-clients who refuse to consent to disclosed dual agency. The licensees may then terminate brokerage relationships with them. However, the Brokers Act states that brokers—acting as dual agents, with proper notice and appointment of an intracompany agent for each party—simply by making required disclosures of the existence of dual agency, have not thereby terminated their brokerage relationships. Persons receiving those disclosures must decide whether *they* want to terminate, based on the disclosures.

In this State, a trustee sale, foreclosure sale, tax sale, or condemnation proceeding that involves the listed property will generally terminate a listing.

■ DETERMINING AMOUNT AND DISTRIBUTION OF BROKERAGE FEES

Antitrust Compliance [Commercial Law Article §11-204]

Brokers (typically working through licensees affiliated with them) negotiate their compensation (brokerage fee) with the sellers *in each transaction*. The amount or commission rate charged in a transaction is not set by any law, regulation, association, or board. Prospective clients and brokers negotiate commission rates. Even to suggest otherwise is a violation of federal and State antitrust laws and can bring severe penalties. Commission splits between and among brokers in co-brokering situations are similarly negotiable. Commission schedules within brokerage firms are established by negotiation between brokers and the affiliates licensed under them.

Agency Relationship Not Created by Payment of Fee [§17-534(d)]

The Brokers Act clearly states that payments or promises to pay compensation to licensees do not determine that brokerage (agency) relationships have been created or exist, nor do they create brokerage relationships. Contrary to a long-held notion, persons whose money goes to agents do *not* become clients of those agents just because of the payment.

When Fee Earned and When Paid [Real Property §14-105]

Maryland law indicates that, unless there is a previous agreement to the contrary, listing brokers have *earned* their commissions when sellers accept and sign (what the sellers believe to be) enforceable contracts of sale. Sellers typically *pay* brokerage commissions at settlement, using proceeds arising from the settlement. Brokers and homeowners may, however, agree at the time of listing that if settlement does not take place, no commission is due. Such a proviso, being strongly to the disadvantage of the broker, does not appear in widely used industry listing forms.

Agency Agreement Basic to Claim [§17-516]

According to the Brokers Act, brokers performing brokerage services may not maintain an action (sue) for commission unless they had authority (derived from their then current, active license) to provide those services at the times both of offering to perform and of performing the services.

Handling Dual Agency Decisions

Licensees procuring a listing should introduce the sellers to the possibility of potential buyers also being represented by their company. They should explain the concept of "intra-company agents" as outlined in the Brokers Act and seek the sellers' decision as to whether they will accept dual agency should such an opportunity present itself. The sellers' response can be reflected in the provisions of the listing agreement itself. If a dual agency situation does arise, sellers must *again* consent—this time to dual agency involving a specific *purchaser*. If there is "no deal" and other clients of the seller's broker present themselves, a new consent for dual agency form must be completed by the seller—this one identifying the new prospective purchaser.

Similarly, buyer-clients may agree to dual agency in their initial representation agreement with the broker but must also consent *again* when a specific opportunity arises—this time on a consent form identifying a specific *property*. If that situation does not result in an agreement and the buyers want to make an offer on another property listed by the buyers' broker, they must complete yet another consent for dual agency agreement, this one identifying the property that is the subject of the current effort.

Co-brokerage Among Brokers [COMAR 09.11.02.03(b)]

The Code of Ethics states that brokers shall cooperate with other brokers on property listed exclusively by their firms whenever it is in the interest of their clients. The co-brokering companies may then share commissions on a previously agreed-to basis. Negotiations concerning properties that are under exclusive listings must be carried on solely through the property owners' listing brokers.

In the listing interview, brokers (or their agents) are advised to present to sellers the Relationship Information Statement ("Understanding Whom Agents Represent") required by the Commission. (See Chapter 2.) Using the explanations contained in that form, the sellers may decide what, if any, relationship(s) they want their listing contract to permit with other real estate firms. Will it be cooperation with subagency? Will it be buyer brokerage? Will it be whichever of the two "happens"? The terms *co-broker* and *co-brokerage* are used here to distinguish other relationships from the narrow definition of *cooperating agent* given by statute and appearing in every Relationship Information Statement. The Statement describes a subagent. The term *co-brokerage* includes both subagency and buyer-broker situations.

Sellers should be helped to understand that licensees from other companies who represent a purchaser will not be "on their team." They will be representing the sellers' adversary, the buyer. Sellers should also decide if—and how—the commission they pay will be shared with another company if no subagency is involved in dealing with another brokerage. Many listing forms allow sellers to authorize their broker to work with and compensate buyer brokers by sharing part of the brokerage fee.

On the listing data form that brokers submit to the MLS, they should show how sellers have decided to choose from among their representation options. They also will show the amount of the cooperating commission in the event of co-brokering. The preponderance of residential real estate transactions has historically involved one or another form of co-brokering.

Listings Must Be Signed [COMAR 09.11.01.12]

When all relevant data have been entered on the listing form, all persons who have an ownership interest in the property must sign it. Alternatively, persons who have proper authorization from the owners—such as attorneys-in-fact, acting under a carefully drafted power of attorney—may sign the listing for them. Competent legal counsel should be consulted in approaching such situations. It is the responsibility of the listing agent to make sure that the signatures of all required parties are on a listing. A listing becomes effective on the date of the last required signature.

When separated or divorcing couples holding title as tenants by the entireties wish to list property, the author recommends consultation with the attorneys representing the parties. Even divorced parties may each retain an interest, likely making both their signatures necessary for an enforceable listing.

When sellers are corporations, trustees, guardians of minors, or personal representatives, documentation of the authority of persons signing the listing is often required. Such documents as corporate bylaws and minutes of the meeting of the board authorizing a property to be put on the market are among usual requirements. Licensees faced with such complex situations are urged to seek competent legal guidance.

Common Source Information Companies [§17-535]

The Brokers Act states that licensees who make use of common source information companies, such as MLSs, are not considered to be agents of those services or companies simply by virtue of their use of data from them. So licensees who participate in sale of multiple-listed properties are not thereby construed (considered) to be the agents or subagents of any client of another broker by reason of their participation. These information services may not restrict access to their services to licensees based on the level of their licenses.

Industry Forms [§17-312(17)]

The word REALTOR® and its related logo appear in the printed portion of many MLS listings and areawide contract forms and many addenda. Licensees who use any form that bears the name of an organization of which they are not members violate the Brokers Act.

Several boards and associations of REALTORS® offer MLSs serving sometimes specific and sometimes overlapping geographic areas. Listing contract forms and numerous addenda are available from local real estate boards, associations, and MLSs for the exclusive use of their members. There are often special forms for different types of property: residential for sale or lease, commercial/industrial for sale or lease, income property, farms, commercial office rental, residential lots, unimproved land, condominiums, cooperatives, and businesses. Although the brokerage industry has produced forms for statewide use and regional use within the State, licensees should be alert to differences that still exist among those forms and between those forms and the forms unique to certain other brokerage firms. It is misleading, incorrect, and careless to refer to an areawide form as a "standard" form—a term that, to many consumers, implies government approval and, therefore, safety.

LOCAL REQUIREMENTS

Licensees should familiarize themselves with and conform to all relevant county and municipal requirements in areas where they provide real estate services. For instance, Baltimore County zoning regulations require "development plan notice and conveyances" to be provided to any purchaser of a home in any area covered by an approved development plan. In other counties, air traffic patterns are part of the information that prospective purchasers must receive. From time to time, counties severely restrict the use of signs. One county has established special licensing requirements for persons who wish to post any signs in residential areas within that jurisdiction. Client-sellers should be made aware of such requirements that will affect their transaction.

■ OUT-OF-STATE LISTINGS

Maryland licensees are not authorized to show out-of-state property, even though it is properly listed and advertised in Maryland, unless they also have valid licenses issued in the state where the property is located and comply with all laws of that state.

QUESTIONS

1. Broker use of which type of residential listing agreement is illegal in Maryland?
   1. Net
   2. Exclusive agency
   3. Open
   4. Exclusive right to sell

2. When using a broker to market their house, sellers complete the Residential Property Disclosure and Disclaimer Statement
   1. at settlement.
   2. when an offer is received.
   3. when the property is being listed.
   4. after a sales contract has been signed.

3. When purchasers receive no Residential Property Disclosure and Disclaimer Statement either before, at, or after entering into a purchase agreement, the
   1. contract is void by action of law after three days.
   2. purchasers may rescind the contract before they apply for a mortgage loan.
   3. contract is voidable by the purchaser for five days.
   4. lender has five days to tell the purchaser of the right to void the agreement.

4. Sellers must receive a copy of their listing agreement
   1. if they request it.
   2. before the broker advertises the property or offers it for sale.
   3. within 15 days after acceptance by the broker.
   4. only when a buyer is found.

5. To show a property located in Virginia that is multiple-listed with a Maryland brokerage, a Maryland licensee MUST
   1. hold a Virginia real estate license.
   2. be a member of Maryland's multiple listing service.
   3. be a Maryland broker licensee.
   4. hold a multiple-state license certificate.

6. A listing agreement form published by a multiple listing service may be used by any
   1. broker or salesperson licensed by the Commission.
   2. member of any board or association of REALTORS®.
   3. licensed member of the organization that operates that listing system.
   4. licensee.

7. A listing on Maryland residential property
   1. may contain an automatic renewal provision.
   2. may be parol.
   3. must be in writing and signed by all parties.
   4. may leave the commission fee to be negotiated at the time an offer is made.

8. Purchasers who receive the Residential Property Disclosure and Disclaimer Statement before signing their contract offer may
   1. rescind the contract at any time up to three days after signing.
   2. rescind the contract at any time up to five days after signing.
   3. rescind at any time prior to settlement or to taking occupancy.
   4. not rescind the contract based on any facts the statement discloses.

9. The amount or rate of commission on a real estate sale
   1. must be stated in the listing agreement.
   2. is established by the Commission.
   3. is established by the local real estate board or association of REALTORS®.
   4. is established by law.

10. In Maryland, a residential listing agreement
    1. does not create an agency.
    2. may be oral.
    3. must be in writing.
    4. need not contain a definite termination date.

CHAPTER

5

Chp 7

Interests in Real Estate

■ KEY TERMS

adverse possession easement by prescription high-water mark

■ OVERVIEW

Freehold estates, such as fee simple absolute, fee determinable, fee conditional, and life estates—as well as future interests, such as remainder and reversion—are recognized in Maryland. Leasehold estates for years, from period to period, at will, and at sufferance are also recognized. In addition, the ground rent system, as described in Chapter 13 of this book, is found in several areas.

The legal life estates dower and curtesy have been abolished, and there is no homestead exemption in Maryland.

■ EASEMENT BY PRESCRIPTION AND ADVERSE POSSESSION

An **easement by prescription** may be acquired in Maryland when an adverse user makes use of another's land for the required period—20 years. Notice that the term *prescriptive* comes from what is *prescribed* by statute. **Adverse possession** for a similar, prescribed period can also ripen into a claim for ownership. However, it must be not only open, hostile, continuous, and notorious occupancy but also under *claim of right* or *color of title*.

By requiring such claim or color, Maryland rejects *squatters' rights*. Squatters acquire no claim to land merely by squatting on it; they are trespassers. Claim of right or color of title arises in a situation where an innocent buyer is deeded property by a person thought to be its owner but later proved not to be. Such an innocent buyer is said to be a *bona fide purchaser* (BFP) for value. Consult competent legal counsel in cases involving prescriptive easements and adverse possession.

■ RIPARIAN RIGHTS

Owners of real estate bordering a navigable body of water in Maryland have the common-law right to make a landing, wharf, or pier for their own use or for the use of the public. The right to make such an improvement is also subject to state and federal rules and regulations. The owner who makes such improvement owns the pier over the water but not the water beneath it.

Title to land beyond the mean (average) high-water mark of navigable waters, as well as to the waters themselves, belongs to the public. Regardless of the property descriptions in owners' deeds, they legally own their riparian property as far as the mean high-water mark. **High-water mark** is the highest elevation of water in the usual, regular, periodic ebb and flow of the tide, not including storms or floods.

■ AGRICULTURAL LAND PRESERVATION EASEMENT

The Maryland Agricultural Land Preservation Foundation exists to purchase easements on land in certain areas for the purpose of restricting land to agricultural use. Details are contained in the *Agriculture* Article of the Annotated Code of Maryland. The State is actively purchasing development rights and seeking to slow residential subdivision of agricultural land. The State's purchases of these easements are funded in large part by the revenues produced by the real estate transfer tax. Further discussion is found in Chapter 14 of this book.

Since 2007, a purchaser has the right, under certain conditions, to rescind a contract purchasing Maryland real estate found to be encumbered by one or more conservation easements or other restrictions held by certain entities. Sales contracts and other notice of such easements are required to control such rescission. This is described more fully in Chapter 9.

QUESTIONS

1. Easements to restrict land to agricultural use may be purchased by the
   1. Maryland Land Development Corporation.
   2. Maryland Department of Assessments and Taxation.
   3. Maryland Agricultural Land Preservation Foundation.
   4. Maryland Environmental Department.

2. Which of the following would meet or exceed the requirement for prescriptive easement in Maryland?
   1. 15 years' continuous use.
   2. 15 years' intermittent use.
   3. 25 years' intermittent use.
   4. 25 years' continuous use.

3. Which of the following is recognized in Maryland?
   1. Dower
   2. Homestead exemption
   3. Curtesy
   4. Easement by prescription

4. Jefferson Thomas owns several acres of Maryland land located on both sides of a navigable waterway. Thomas has the right to
   1. build a pier on one of the riverbanks, subject to State and federal laws.
   2. construct a dam across the river to divert the waters into an artificial lake on his property.
   3. construct a wharf without State approval.
   4. make use only of the dry land.

5. Funds to purchase agricultural easements come from
   1. general (ad valorem) tax revenues.
   2. special assessments for this specific purpose.
   3. fines on developers who overdevelop agricultural land.
   4. transfer taxes imposed at the time of real estate transfers.

CHAPTER 6

How Ownership Is Held

■ KEY TERMS

appurtenances
bylaws
common elements
condominium
council of unit owners
declaration
developer

general common
 elements
joint tenancy
limited common elements
partition proceeding
proprietary lease
real estate investment
 trust (REIT)

rules
tenancy in common
tenants by the entirety
time-share estate
time-share license
units

■ OVERVIEW

Maryland law recognizes ownership in severalty and various forms of concurrent ownership: tenancy in common, joint tenancy, tenancy by the entirety, partnership, and trust—all as described in the principles text. It also provides for condominium, time-share, and cooperative ownership.

■ FORMS OF CONCURRENT OWNERSHIP (CO-OWNERSHIP)

Tenancy in Common and Joint Tenancy

Unless the deed clearly specifies otherwise, a conveyance of Maryland real estate to two or more persons normally creates **tenancy in common.** To create a **joint tenancy,** it is necessary to use such words as "to Fred Donaldson and Sam Roberts, as joint tenants and not as tenants in common." One might also add the phrase "with right of survivorship." However, a deed to a husband and wife is presumed to create a tenancy by the entirety unless it specifies tenancy in common or joint tenancy.

Tenancy by the Entirety

In Maryland, only a legally married husband and wife can own property as **tenants by the entirety.** (Common-law marriages cannot be established in Maryland but are recognized as valid if established in other jurisdictions that recognize and permit them.) Both husband and wife must sign a deed to convey property they hold as tenants by the entirety. Neither spouse who owns Maryland real property as a tenant by the entirety may petition a court for its partition.

Tenants by the entirety may grant their property back to themselves as either tenants in common or joint tenants, or they can grant the entire property either to one spouse or the other. They can do this without having ownership pass through the hands of a third ("straw") party. They can also deed their property into a trust. Competent legal assistance is always important in such transfers.

A tenancy by the entirety is terminated by the death of either spouse, with the survivor holding the property in severalty. Notice that the term *severalty* appropriately describes the condition of being severed (separated) from others and owning by oneself.

Common is Default

Although Maryland is not a community property state, at the time of divorce, the Property Disposition in Divorce and Annulment statute has many of the same effects as the community property rules that govern in other states.

Upon divorce or other legal termination of the marriage, tenants by the entirety are considered tenants in common, by operation of law. But when divorce occurs, causing the former couple's ownership to change to tenancy in common by action of law, a court may still delay any **partition proceeding** (division of the property by one against the other's will) for a period as long as three years. Normally, a tenancy in common, like joint tenancy, can be partitioned at any time by one tenant (owner) without the agreement of the other. The ban on partition after divorce can occur if the property is to be occupied as the "family home" by the custodial spouse with minor children.

Trust

The provisions of the *Uniform Partnership Act* apply in Maryland. The statute allows a corporation (as well as an individual) to become a member of a partnership. Also, the **real estate investment trust (REIT),** a form of unincorporated trust or association, is recognized. The procedures for forming or dealing with a REIT are legally complex. Brokerage licensees involved in any way with a REIT should strongly urge their clients to employ legal counsel. The licensees themselves may be required by law to hold securities licenses to engage in such activities. The *Maryland Securities Act,* found in the State's *Corporations and Associations* Article, requires a securities license for persons engaged in selling securities that are real estate related.

■ CONDOMINIUMS [REAL PROPERTY ARTICLE, TITLE 11]

Detailed provisions of the *Maryland Condominium Act* are contained in Title 11 of the *Real Property* Article of the Annotated Code of Maryland. Any licensee involved with condominium sales or development should obtain a complete copy of the law and seek competent legal advice. The Condominium Act is enforced by the Division of Consumer Protection in the Office of the Attorney General.

Definitions

A **condominium** is a property subject to a plan of organization called a *regime*. It is governed by a **council of unit owners,** usually through a board of directors, and may be either an unincorporated body or an incorporated nonstock corporation. Persons who subject their property to a condominium regime are called *developers*. Condominium **units** are spaces described in three dimensions in the declaration and on the condominium plat.

All the parts of a condominium other than its units are **common elements. Limited common elements** are identified in the declaration or described on the condominium plat and are reserved for the exclusive use of one or more, but fewer than all, of the unit owners. **General common elements** are all the common elements except the limited common elements.

Converting Property to a Condominium

To create a condominium, the property owner must expressly declare the intention to do so by recording a declaration, bylaws, and a detailed plat of the proposed site. These documents must comply with statutory requirements. When this has been done, the property is then said to be under a condominium regime, and the owner is its **developer**. The condominium regime must be registered with the Secretary of State before a condominium unit may be sold or even offered for sale. The declaration may subsequently be amended within certain limits only by the written consent of 80 percent of the unit owners at the time of amendment.

Public Offering Statement

A contract for the *initial* sale of a residential condominium unit to a member of the general public is not enforceable by the seller until the purchaser is given a copy of the Public Offering Statement registered with the Secretary of State. This Statement contains the proposed contract for purchase of units; the declaration, bylaws, rules, and regulations; proposed property management agreements; insurance policies; maintenance agreements; and a proposed budget and financial reports. Many other items make this a very difficult package for purchasers to read, study, and understand.

Whether they read the Statement or not, buyers may make written rescission of a purchase contract, without stating any reason, within 15 days after they receive it. Buyers who rescind within this time limit are entitled to prompt return of all deposits.

Buyers who proceed to settlement lose their rights to terminate. A purchaser's right to rescind or cancel under the Condominium Act may not be waived in the contract of sale.

Conversion of Residential Rental Facility

Before a residential rental facility can be converted to condominium ownership, tenants must be given notice in the form prescribed by law. This notice is also registered with the Secretary of State at the same time as the Public Offering Statement. A tenant may not be required to vacate the premises prior to the expiration of 180 days from the giving of notice, except for breach of the lease. However, the tenant may terminate the lease, without penalty for termination, by providing at least 30 days' written notice to the landlord after receiving proper notice of conversion. Many other statutory requirements protect tenants during conversion of a rental property to condominium.

Ownership of Units and Interests in Common Elements

In addition to exclusive ownership of a condominium unit, each unit owner has a right to share a defined, undivided percentage interest in the common elements of the property. Unit owners' undivided interests in the common elements cannot be partitioned or separated from the unit to which each percentage is assigned. Owners of every unit in a condominium are members of the council of unit owners. That council is considered a legal entity even if it is not incorporated.

Organization: Declaration, Bylaws, and Rules and Regulations

In addition to federal, State, and local laws and ordinances, a condominium is governed according to its declaration, bylaws, and rules and regulations. The rules must conform to the bylaws, the bylaws must conform to the declaration, and the declaration is subject to the statute. In Maryland, the statute—in some states called a *horizontal property act*—is called the *Maryland Condominium Act*.

The recorded **declaration** must contain the name by which the condominium is to be identified, including or followed by the phrase "a condominium." It must also contain a description of the land and buildings, with a statement of the owner's intent to establish a condominium regime; a general description and number of each unit, its perimeter, location, and other identifying data; a general description of the common elements and the units to which their use is restricted initially; the percentage interest in common areas related to each unit; and the number of votes at meetings of the council of unit owners that go with each unit. These related common elements and voting rights are **appurtenances**—things of value that attach to a property.

At the least, the **bylaws** must express the form of administration, whether the council is to be incorporated, whether some or all of the council's duties may be delegated to a board of directors or a manager and what powers the owners have in directors' selection and removal, the council's mailing address, the procedure to be followed in council meetings, and the manner of assessing and collecting unit owners' respective shares of the common expenses. By law, the council of unit owners must be established within 60 days after the initial sale of units representing 50 percent of votes in the condominium. Bylaws of a condominium are recorded at the same time as its declaration. Unless higher percentages are required in the bylaws, they may be amended by the affirmative vote of unit owners having at least two-thirds of the votes in the council of unit owners.

In addition to rules set forth by the developer and recorded in the Public Offering Statement, the council of unit owners (or the board of directors, if so authorized in the bylaws) can pass **rules** to govern the condominium by majority vote at any properly advertised meeting held for that purpose. The bylaws specify what body originates and changes rules. They also define a quorum for the meeting at which rules are voted upon. A simple majority of those present and voting adopts rules.

Termination of Regime

Unless taken by eminent domain, a condominium regime may be terminated only by agreement of at least 80 percent of the unit owners (more if so specified in the declaration).

Common Expenses, Taxes, Assessments, and Liens

Unit owners are responsible for their percentage share of the common expenses of the council of unit owners. Assessments against each unit owner for common expenses are unrecorded liens on their units. But a lien may be foreclosed in the same manner as a mortgage or deed of trust if it is recorded and action to foreclose it is brought within three years.

Each unit is taxed as a separate and distinct entity on the county tax records. A delinquent tax on a specific unit will not affect the title to other units on which all taxes and assessments have been paid.

Under the Consumer Protection Act of the *Commercial Law* Article of the Annotated Code of Maryland, certain condominium disputes will be investigated by the Division of Consumer Protection of the Office of the Attorney General, which is authorized to administer a program of voluntary mediation of condominium disputes involving unit owners, boards of directors, and/or councils of unit owners.

Resale of Unit

A contract for the resale of a unit by a unit owner other than a developer is not enforceable unless that contract contains, in conspicuous type, a notice in the form specified in the Condominium Act (Section 11-135). The unit owner is required to furnish four things to the purchaser no fewer than 15 days prior to the closing:

1. A copy of the declaration (other than the plat)
2. The bylaws
3. The rules or regulations of the condominium
4. A certificate containing statements concerning such things as monthly expenses, proposed capital improvements, fees payable by unit owners, financial statements of the condominium, insurance coverage, and much more.

Once resale purchasers receive all these condominium documents ("condo docs"), they have seven days to give written notice rescinding their contract to purchase without stating any reason. This right is waived if they proceed to closing before the seven-day period ends.

Condominium resale contracts must contain the required clauses and disclosures to ensure compliance with the Act. Local real estate boards and associations usually offer their members a Condominium Contract of Sale and Condominium Listing Contract.

Renting a Condominium Unit in Montgomery County

In Montgomery County, before a tenant executes a lease for an initial term of 125 days or more, the owner of any residential rental property within any condominium or development is required to provide to the prospective tenant—to the extent applicable—a copy of the rules, declaration, and recorded covenants and restrictions that limit or affect the use and occupancy of the property or common areas and under which the owner and the tenant are also obligated.

The State Securities Commission requires that anyone offering part ownership or interest in condominiums must disclose the inherent risks of such an investment. Limited-use resort securities must comply with the registration and antifraud requirements of the State Securities Act.

■ TIME-SHARE OWNERSHIP

There are two principal forms of time-sharing: the right-to-use (time-share license) method and the purchase-of-fractional-interest (time-share estate) method. In the **time-share license** form, owners of interests in vacation properties, including condominiums, hotels, motels, marinas, and boats, may trade their vacation periods and facilities either directly or indirectly through space banks that are maintained by firms established to help time-sharers swap vacation facilities. In the **time-share estate**, widely used in Maryland in both the Eastern Shore and the western areas, customers buy fractional interests for designated time periods in a resort condominium, either on a rental (estate for years) or permanent (fee simple) basis. The fee simple buyer receives a deed for a share of the property.

The Maryland Real Estate Time-Sharing Act [Real Property Article, Title 11A]

The *Maryland Real Estate Time-Sharing Act* provides for the creation, sale, lease, management, and termination of time-share interests; registration of certain documents; registration of time-share developers with the Commission; and certain bonding requirements. Certain advertising and promotional practices are prohibited. Developers are required to prepare Public Offering Statements describing time-share projects and are regulated by the Secretary of State. Certain protections for purchasers are provided, such as sales contract cancellation periods and disclosures of information, warranties, and exchange programs. Any licensee involved in time-share sales or development should obtain a complete copy of the Act or seek competent legal advice. Time-share developers and persons selling time-share estates are also subject to the provisions of the Brokers Act.

Public Offering Statement.   Upon or before the signing of a sales contract, the developers must deliver to each purchaser a Public Offering Statement.

The requirements for disclosure under the Time-Sharing Act differ substantially from those required under the Condominium Act.

Conversions.   A developer who desires to convert a building more than five years old into a time-share project is required to include an engineer's report in the Public Offering Statement and to give any tenant or subtenant at least 120 days' notice of the intention to convert the building to a time-share project.

Cancellation rights.   *First purchasers* of time-shares have the right to cancel the sales contract until midnight *of the tenth calendar day* following the latest of (1) the contract date, (2) the day on which the time-share purchaser received the last of all documents required as part of the Public Offering Statement, or (3) the date on which either the time-share unit meets all building requirements and is ready for occupancy or the developer obtains a payment and performance bond and files the bond with the Commission. This right of cancellation cannot be waived.

Unlike the law concerning condominiums, no closing on a time-share can occur *until* the purchaser's cancellation period has expired. If closing is held prior to the cancellation period, the closing is voidable at the option of the purchaser for a period of one year after the expiration of the cancellation period.

Resale disclosures.   Owners selling their time-share are required to furnish to the purchaser, before execution of the contract or transfer of title or use,

■   a copy of the time-share instrument, and
■   a resale certificate containing the information required by the Time-Sharing Act.

The resale purchaser may cancel the contract to purchase at any time *within seven days after receipt of the resale certificate* without reason and without liability and is then entitled to the return of any deposits made under the contract.

Deposits.   All purchase money received by a developer from a purchaser must be deposited in an escrow account designed solely for that purpose with a financial institution whose accounts are insured by a government agency. The funds remain there until the end of the ten-day cancellation period or any later time provided for in the contract. Purchase money may then be released to the developer, provided the developer maintains a surety bond. No claim can be made against the Real Estate Guaranty Fund if a loss is covered by that bond.

Warranties.   All time-share units sold by developers have implied warranties of three years for common elements and one year for units with respect to structural components and heating and cooling systems. In addition, the developer must warrant to a purchaser of a time-share that any existing use of the time-share unit that will continue does not violate any law.

Sales contract.   The statute requires contracts for the first sale of time-shares to use specific language to disclose cancellation rights. Contracts must also show the estimated completion date of each unit and each common element as well as estimates of the time-share expenses and facility fees. All this is intended to disclose the total financial obligation being incurred by purchasers.

Exchange programs.   The Time-Sharing Act requires detailed information concerning each exchange program a developer makes available for purchasers' use.

Registration.   The Time-Sharing Act requires that developers, with certain exceptions, register with the Commission. A developer may not offer a time-share to the public until the developer has received from the Commission a certificate of registration as a time-share developer. The developer is required to file certain documents and material with the Commission. The Time-Sharing Act gives the Commission the authority to

■   issue regulations and orders consistent with the Act,
■   investigate possible violations of the act and subpoena witnesses and documents in connection with the investigations,
■   bring suit against violators,
■   order violators to correct conditions resulting from the violation, and
■   revoke the registration of any developer who is convicted of violating the Act.

In addition, the Secretary of State is authorized to adopt regulations necessary to implement and enforce the provisions of the act pertaining to Public Offering Statements. A violation of the act could provide grounds for the suspension or revocation of a broker's or salesperson's license under the Brokers Act.

Project broker. Developers are required to designate a licensed real estate broker as the project broker for each time-share project. Each time-share project is considered a separate real estate office for purposes of the Brokers Act. Any person who sells, advertises, or offers for sale any time-share must be a licensed broker, an associate broker, or a salesperson or be exempt from licensure under Title 17. An unlicensed person may be employed by a developer or project broker to contact, but not solicit, prospective buyers so long as the unlicensed person

- performs only clerical tasks,
- schedules only those appointments induced by others, or
- prepares or distributes only promotional materials.

Time-Share Regulations [COMAR 09.11.04]

Regulations governing time-shares require that records be maintained of names and addresses of all personnel retained for sale of time-share estates, including agents, employees, and licensees, whether employees or independent contractors. Records must also be made and kept of all sales transactions, of estates conveyed and encumbrances on them, and of amounts of purchase money held for such sales. The Commission may require certification of such amounts by a Certified Public Accountant. Developers must also maintain bonding in prescribed amounts for deposit monies being held.

Time-share marketing statements about the characteristics of the time-share project or estate may not be false, inaccurate, or misleading. A developer may not indicate that an improvement will be placed in a time-share project unless the developer has sufficient finances and bona fide intentions to complete the improvement. Statements used in the marketing of time-share estates located in Maryland may not induce a prospective purchaser to leave the State for the purpose of executing a contract for sale when to do so would circumvent the provisions of Maryland law. No one may advertise or represent that the Commission has approved or recommended any time-share project or estate offered for sale.

MARYLAND COOPERATIVE HOUSING CORPORATION ACT [CORPORATIONS AND ASSOCIATIONS ARTICLE, TITLES 5–6B]

The Maryland Cooperative Housing Act provides for conditions, contracts, rights, and requirements relative to the development and sale of interests in cooperatives. Detailed provisions are contained in statutes. A member of the cooperative receives a **proprietary lease,** an agreement with the cooperative housing corporation that gives the member an exclusive possessory interest in a unit and a possessory interest in common with other members in that portion of a cooperative project not constituting units. It creates a legal relationship of landlord and tenant between the corporation and the member.

MARYLAND HOMEOWNERS ASSOCIATION ACT [REAL PROPERTY ARTICLE §11B]

This act sets forth conditions, rights, and requirements regulating homeowners associations (HOAs) in the State.

For sales contracts to be binding on purchasers, sellers must make disclosure showing that the property is subject to an HOA; listing the rights, responsibilities, and obligations of purchasers; and disclosing purchasers' rights of rescission in the event that the Maryland Homeowners Association Act (MHAA) information is not provided to them by sellers in a timely manner. This information recites factual details pertaining to disclosures, which must include liability, warranties, meetings, books, and records. Time periods for rescission vary in relation to the number of lots in the HOA. The rescission period in initial sales is different from that in resales.

Any violation of the Maryland Homeowners Association Act that affects a "consumer" falls under the enforcement duties and powers of the Division of Consumer Protection of the Office of the Attorney General of the State, thus giving such homeowners associations protections similar to those afforded condominiums and cooperatives.

■ CANCELLATION PERIODS

Because it is important for real estate licensees to know the cancellation periods allowed by law for various types of condominium and time-share sales contracts, they are summarized in Table 6.1.

TABLE 6.1

Cancellation Periods in Various Sale Situations

Type of Sale	Period for Cancellation	After
Condominium by Developer	15 days	Receipt of Public Offering Statement
Condominium by Developer	5 additional days	Receipt of any later amendments to Public Offering Statement
Condominium by Resale	7 days	Receipt of Resale Certificate (This certificate must also be received no fewer than 15 days prior to closing.)
Time-Share by Developer	10 days	Contract, receipt of last required disclosure document, or receipt of occupancy permit, whichever is last. A settlement performed before the end of a cancellation period is unlawful and voidable by purchaser.
Time-Share by Resale	7 days	Receipt of Certificate
HOA	Varies by number of lots and whether original or resale	n/a

QUESTIONS

1. Which of the following forms of ownership is *NOT* usually recognized in Maryland?
   1. Tenancy in common
   2. Community property
   3. Trust
   4. Ownership in severalty

2. In Maryland, a deed that conveys ownership to "Karen and David Muñoz, husband and wife" but does *NOT* specify the form of ownership
   1. automatically creates a tenancy in common.
   2. must be redrawn before the property is sold, specifying the form of ownership.
   3. is construed to create tenancy by the entirety.
   4. is construed to create ownership in severalty.

3. Which of the following is *NOT* true? In Maryland, a tenancy by the entirety
   1. may be held only by a husband and wife.
   2. continues after the death of one of the owners.
   3. gives each individual possession of the entire estate.
   4. may not be partitioned.

4. A time-share developer is required to
   1. register with the State Real Estate Commission.
   2. register with the State Treasurer.
   3. register with the local board or association of REALTORS®.
   4. be a licensed real estate broker.

5. The bylaws of a condominium can be changed or altered by
   1. the manager of the property.
   2. affirmative vote of two-thirds of the unit owners.
   3. the council of unit owners by majority vote.
   4. a simple majority of unit owners.

6. A developer who proposes to convert a residential rental facility to a condominium regime *MUST* register with the
   1. office of the Attorney General.
   2. local Board of REALTORS®.
   3. Secretary of State.
   4. Maryland Real Estate Commission.

7. A developer selling a newly built condominium unit to original purchasers
   1. is liable for damages as a result of misleading statements for five years after the sale.
   2. is subject to the purchasers' voiding the contract if the developer fails to deliver a Public Offering Statement to them.
   3. is protected by the doctrine of caveat emptor from liability for misleading statements.
   4. must register a Public Offering Statement with the State Real Estate Commission.

8. Purchasers of time-shares from the developer
   1. have a right to cancel the contract only if the seller has misrepresented material facts.
   2. have ten days in which to cancel the sale for any reason.
   3. must close the sale within ten days after signing the sales contract.
   4. must obtain a payment and performance bond to ensure their compliance with the contract.

9. A contract for resale of a condominium by its owner (other than its developer) is *NOT* enforceable unless the owner furnishes the buyers, no later than 15 days prior to the closing,
   1. a copy of the declaration.
   2. the bylaws, rules, and regulations.
   3. a statement regarding monthly expenses, proposed capital improvements, other fees, financial statements of the condominium, and insurance details.
   4. all of the above.

10. Should a dispute develop between or among unit owners, the board of directors, and/or council of unit owners, to whom may the parties may apply for mediation?
    1. The local Board of REALTORS®
    2. The office of the county state's attorney
    3. The office of the Attorney General
    4. The local Board of Development and Planning

CHAPTER 7

chp 9

Legal Descriptions

■ KEY TERMS

boundary survey	misdemeanor	system of coordinates
location drawing	recorded plat of	
metes and bounds	subdivision	

■ OVERVIEW

Two of the methods of property description presented in the student's principal text are those in most frequent use in Maryland real estate brokerage. They are the **metes and bounds** and **recorded plat of subdivision** methods. In addition, Baltimore City has its own map coordinates system used by the city's Bureau of Plans and Surveys. Baltimore also describes property by using a system based on city blocks. Maryland has still another method—a **system of coordinates** it shares with the rest of the United States, Canada, Mexico, and nations in Central America. It is based upon precise indication of longitude, latitude, and elevation.

Maryland Coordinate System [Real Property §14-401–§14-406]

While not a part of the federal rectangular survey system, this system is based on the North American Datum (starting plane) established in 1927 and known as NAD27. Modified in 1983 as NAD83, it was adopted by the Maryland legislature, taking effect from 1987 to 1992. Based on satellite technology and observations, the 1983 data removed distortions associated with NAD27. Also, NAD83 fit the size, shape, and center-of-mass location of the earth more accurately. These data are reflected in the sometimes puzzling numbers and tick marks appearing at the edges of the street book maps so frequently used by real estate licensees. Licensees may never have to use this data but may want to be aware of their existence and purpose.

At the very least, a description that identifies land "with reasonable certainty" is required in a contract for sale of realty. Postal address alone is usually not an adequate legal description except for such short residential leaseholds as one or two years.

■ EXAMPLES OF LEGAL DESCRIPTIONS USED IN CONTRACTS

Metes and Bounds

■ **EXAMPLE 1** "Beginning at an iron pipe set on the northeast side of Annapolis Street at a point located South 38° 45' East, 200 feet from where the northeast side of Annapolis Street intersects the southeast side of Giddings Avenue—all as shown on Aldridge's Revised and Corrected Plat of West Annapolis recorded among the Land Records of Anne Arundel County in JCB Liber 4, Folio 297; and running thence and at right angles to Annapolis Street, North 51° 15' East, 150 feet to a pipe; thence South 38° 45' East 50 feet to a pipe; thence South 51° 15' West, 150 feet to a pipe on the northeast side of Annapolis Street; thence with same, North 38° 45' West, 50 feet to the place of beginning."

■ **EXAMPLE 2** "That certain parcel of real estate located in Worcester County, Maryland, being on the east side of Farm Lane, north of Jerry Road, being further known as the Arthur R. Jackson property, consisting of one acre, more or less, with the improvements thereon, previously conveyed by deed of Robert Allen, grantor, recorded in FWH Liber 29, Folio 1312, the exact boundaries and acreage to be determined by means of a survey, which has been ordered to be prepared by Johnson and Landsman, surveyors, Snow Hill."

Recorded Plat of Subdivisio

■ **EXAMPLE** "Lot #16, Block #3 of the Plat of Melville Development Corporation as surveyed by John Walmer, Catonsville, Maryland, August 15, 1968, as recorded in FWH Liber 295, Folio 1720, in the County of Ridge, State of Maryland."

■ SURVEY MARKERS

Surveyors are governed by the *Maryland Professional Land Surveyors Act.* They are licensed by the State Board for Professional Land Surveyors. The Board specifies that they use specific types of stakes, markers, monuments, or other landmarks in their work.

It is a **misdemeanor**—a crime less than a felony—intentionally to move, damage, or obliterate any markers on property belonging to another person if the marker was put in place by a civil engineer, surveyor, real estate appraiser, or members of their teams. The exception is when the marker interferes with proper use of the land. A fine of not more than $500 can be imposed upon conviction.

If there is a dispute over any boundary line or if the bounds mentioned in a document are lost, the circuit court of the county where the property is located may be petitioned to establish the boundary lines or the location of the missing bounds. These experts' fees are considered costs in the proceeding.

In 2005, the legislature reduced the time in which a person may file suit against a land surveyor for an error in a survey from 20 to 15 years after the survey or within 3 years after the discovery of the error, whichever occurs first.

■ LOCATION DRAWINGS AND BOUNDARY SURVEYS

The Office of the Secretary of Licensing and Regulation, through its Board for Professional Land Surveyors, requires that surveyors have a signed election form requesting either a location drawing or a boundary survey from the party ordering the survey. This election (choice) should be made by purchasers at the time of forming their agreement to purchase.

The **boundary survey** identifies property boundary lines and corners sufficiently well to establish the physical position and extent of the boundaries, including visible indications of rights that may arise from prescription or adverse possession. It is needed for an owner having a fence placed or other improvements erected. It reports that monuments have either been located or placed on the property.

A **location drawing** provides a plat of the property that shows the location of any improvements. It costs less than a boundary survey but is often sufficient for most residential resales and refinancing situations.

A description of each type and of its uses, limitations, and costs appears on the election form. The form electing which survey is being ordered is typically submitted by the title, settlement, or law office preparing for settlement.

■ SUBDIVISION PLATS

Subdividers must have plats of proposed subdivisions prepared by a licensed surveyor and approved and recorded by local authorities before offering them for sale. Reference to a recorded subdivision plat may be part of a sufficient legal description. No distances on a subdivision plat may be marked "more or less" except those lines that begin, terminate, or bind on a body of water.

QUESTIONS

1. In Maryland real estate contracts, lot, block, section, and similar references to a subdivision plat
   1. are permitted in individual lot descriptions when the plat was properly recorded.
   2. must be prepared by licensed real estate brokers.
   3. are not sufficient for sales agreements but are good enough for listings.
   4. are sufficient for listings but not for sales agreements.

2. A location drawing
   1. is essentially the same as a boundary survey.
   2. is appropriate for typical residential resales.
   3. costs more than a boundary survey.
   4. can properly be used for placing fences and other improvements.

3. Which of the following is MOST likely to be a sufficient legal description?
   1. 142 Pinehurst Road, Ocean Pines
   2. That lot fronting 100 feet on Pinehurst and being 250 feet deep
   3. That two acres, shown on attached plat of subdivision survey as prepared by Landsman & Co., surveyors of Catonsville, Maryland
   4. 1776B Liberty St., Snow Hill, Md., being the northern half of a duplex

4. "Beginning at the intersection of the east line of Goodrich Boulevard and the south line of Jasmine Lane and running south along the east line of Goodrich Boulevard a distance of 230 feet; thence easterly parallel to the north line of Wolf Road, a distance of 195 feet; thence northeasterly on a course of N 22°E, a distance of 135 feet; and thence northwesterly along the south line of Jasmine Lane to the point of beginning." This legal description is an example of a
   1. block description.
   2. rectangular survey.
   3. subdivision description.
   4. metes-and-bounds description.

5. Most property descriptions used in Maryland real estate transfers
   1. refer to the government rectangular survey system.
   2. consist of the street or mailing addresses of the properties.
   3. are based on recorded plats of subdivision or metes-and-bounds data.
   4. consist of the post office box numbers.

CHAPTER 8

Real Estate Taxes and Other Liens

■ KEY TERMS

first-time homebuyers
Homeowners Property Tax
  Credit Program
impact fees

mechanics' liens
notice of reassessment
phase-in provision
senior tenants

statutory period of
  redemption
triennial assessment
unperformed contracts

■ OVERVIEW

Maryland property taxes are levied by and for the support of the State, county, and city governments as well as local special taxing districts. A number of counties also impose **impact fees** on developers in addition to property taxes on owners. The impact fees are levied on new residential units to pay for additional public facilities and services for the use and benefit residents of new construction. Such fees, of course, increase the purchase price of housing, because developers pass along the cost of the fees to purchasers.

■ ASSESSMENT

Residential real property is assessed for tax purposes by the State Department of Assessments and Taxation. That department has local offices in Baltimore City and in each Maryland county.

In 2001, Maryland's general (ad valorem) tax assessment ratio was raised from 40 percent to 100 percent of the market value estimated by triennial assessment. The effect of raising the assessment ratio and lowering the tax rate was revenue-neutral and so required no increase in the dollar amount of the taxes being paid. The purpose of the change was to make property tax rates in the State appear competitive with those in surrounding jurisdictions in hopes of attracting prospective residents and employers. (See Table 8.1.)

The procedure for assessing property in Maryland, the **triennial assessment,** is based on a three-year cycle in which one-third of all properties are revalued every year for tax purposes.

Each county has been organized into three principal assessing areas to coincide with the years of the assessment cycle. The areas generally have similar density and other common characteristics and are reviewed on a rotating basis. By the end of a three-year period, all properties have been physically reviewed and valued once; then a new cycle commences.

An inspection of the exterior premises always accompanies a revaluation. If changes in zoning or use occur, or if additions or extensive improvements to property have been made, the property may be revalued out of its three-year sequence.

Real property assessment is further controlled by a **phase-in provision** that was designed to take some of the financial sting out of swiftly rising property values. For that one-third of real properties reassessed in a particular year, the first one-third of any increase in value is added for that year, and the balance is added in equal increments over the following two years. For example, a property increasing in value from $200,000 to $260,000 would be assigned a value of $220,000 the first tax year, $240,000 the second, and $260,000 the third.

Upon completion of the triennial review, if the value of a property is found to have changed, the owner is sent a **notice of reassessment** that shows the property's assessment for the next three years; no other notice is sent until the new cycle begins three years later. Taxpayers who believe that their assessments are improper may appeal within 45 days of receiving their notice of assessment.

■ PAYMENT

Taxes on residential property are paid in two equal installments. The first payment is *due* July 1 but can be *paid* as late as September 30 without penalty. The second, *due* January 1, can be *paid* as late as January 31. One of the purposes of the two-payment arrangement is to reduce the amount of ad valorem tax "set asides" to be paid by purchasers at settlement. The statute requires counties to prepare their data-processing systems for quarterly payments, which may be authorized by future legislation.

Lenders who accept responsibility to forward property taxes on the mortgaged properties accumulate the required funds in expense (escrow/trust/impound) accounts. They are required to pay those taxes within 45 days after the earlier of the following: (1) the first due date after their receipt of the tax bill or (2) after

TABLE   8.1

County Tax Rates

	2007–2008 (FISCAL 2008) COUNTY TAX RATES		
Counties and Baltimore County	***Real Property Tax Rate in Dollars per $100 of Assessment**	**†Transfer Tax is the consideration payable multiplied by this rate.**	**Recordation Tax Quoted in Dollars per $500 of Transaction Amount**
Allegany	0.9829	0.50%	0.005	3.25
Anne Arundel	0.891	1.00%	0.010	3.50
Baltimore City	2.268	1.50%	0.015	5.00
Baltimore County	1.100	1.50%	0.015	2.50
Calvert	0.892	0.00%	0.000	5.00
Caroline	0.870	0.50%	0.005	5.00
Carroll	1.048	0.00%	0.000	5.00
Cecil	0.960	0.00%	0.000	4.10
Charles	1.026	0.00%	0.000	5.00
Dorchester (first $30,000 exempt for residential)	0.896	0.75%	0.0075	5.00
Frederick	0.936	0.00%	0.000	6.00
Garrett (first $50,000 is exempt for owner-occupied)	1.000	1.00%	0.010	3.50
Harford	1.082	1.00%	0.010	3.30
Howard	1.014	1.00%	0.010	2.50
Kent	0.972	0.50%	0.005	3.30
Montgomery	0.627	1.00%	0.010	3.45
Prince George's	0.960	1.40%	0.014	2.20
Queen Anne's	0.770	0.50%	0.050	3.30
St. Mary's	0.857	1.00%	0.010	4.00
Somerset	0.940	0.00%	0.000	3.30
Talbot (first $50,000 is exempt for owner-occupied)	0.475	1.00%	0.010	3.30
Washington	0.948	0.50%	0.005	3.80
Wicomico	0.881	0.00%	0.000	3.50
Worcester	0.700	0.50%	0.050	3.30

* To this assessment, add any municipal tax.

† This is in addition to the State Transfer Tax Rate of 0.500%.

This information is found at *www.dat.state.md.us*.

funds collected by the lender are sufficient to pay the amount of taxes and interest due. Lenders who fail to forward escrowed taxes as provided above must bear any additional costs of penalties and interest.

■ PROPERTY TAX RELIEF PROGRAMS

The Homestead Tax Credit Program

This program is designed to protect owner-occupied residence assessments from the effects of rapid inflation. It automatically provides a credit against the real estate tax if the assessment on a dwelling increases over the previous year by more than a certain percentage determined by the state legislature. The credit equals the amount by which the reassessment exceeds the established percentage and applies if certain other conditions were met during the previous calendar year. Beginning in 2008, homeowners are required to submit—even if they have done so before—*a one-time tax credit application*, which is included in the 2008 Assessment Notice sent to one-third of the property owners.

Homeowners Property Tax Credit Program

Because the Homestead Tax Credit Program does not take into account homeowners' ability to pay, the State legislature created the **Homeowners Property Tax Credit Program**, popularly known as the "circuit breaker." After taking into account homeowners' net worth, gross annual income, and assessed value of their property, this program, for homeowners of all ages, sets limits on the amount of residential property tax due. Application for this relief must be made each year. Under this program, there is also a tax credit for renters who meet various income and asset requirements when the assessed value of their property does not exceed $250,000. This tax credit can be as much as $750 per year.

Property Tax Deferral

This program allows property owners, age 65 or older, to elect to defer the increase in their property tax bill. Each local government must first adopt the program. The local government then has the authority under State law to impose income restrictions and interest rate amounts. The deferred taxes become a lien on the property and must be repaid when the property is transferred. Montgomery County makes this deferral program available to homeowners of all ages who meet certain residency and income requirements.

Other Relief

Owners of unsold or unrented single-dwelling units or newly constructed or substantially rehabilitated commercial properties may be entitled to tax credits not exceeding the property taxes on the improvements. The credit applies for no more than one year immediately following construction or substantial rehabilitation.

Special provision has also been made for **senior tenants,** age 60 or older, to receive as much as $600 from the State to offset property taxes. Asset and income limits are among certain restrictions that apply.

The residential property *owned by a veteran* with a permanent, 100 percent, service-connected disability is exempt from property tax. The 100 percent disability may result from blindness or some other disabling cause. This benefit is retained by the *unremarried surviving spouse* of the deceased disabled veteran as well. Application for this benefit must be accompanied by documentation of veteran status, 100 percent disability, and ownership of the property.

Assessment on a residence owned by an individual who is *legally blind* is reduced by $15,000. The property must be the individual's legal residence and not be occupied by more than two families. The *unremarried surviving spouse* of a blind individual receives the same benefit. No individual may claim both the exemption for being blind *and* the exemption for being a disabled veteran.

■ TRANSFER AND RECORDATION TAXES

Except as discussed in the following paragraph, in every written or oral agreement for the sale or other disposition of property, it is presumed, in the absence of any contrary provision in the agreement or the law, that the parties to the agreement intended that the cost of any recordation tax or any State or local transfer tax be shared equally between the grantor and grantee. This presumption does not apply to mortgages or deeds of trust. (Refer to Table 8.1.)

First-Time Maryland Homebuyers

The law provides that **first-time homebuyers** will not pay the State transfer tax. In a transfer involving such a buyer, the State transfer tax of 0.5 percent is reduced to 0.25 percent and must be paid by the seller. Furthermore, unless the parties in such a transaction agree to the contrary, the recordation taxes and local transfer taxes are to be paid by the seller. *First-time homebuyers* are defined in the law as

purchasers who have never before owned and occupied a principal residence in this State, will occupy the property as their principal residence, and/or meet certain other requirements.

■ CORPORATE FRANCHISE TAX

Most corporations are taxed annually on their franchise, or right, to do business in the State. The annual tax becomes a general lien on the property of the corporation and can be enforced against it. When a broker files for a real estate license and the brokerage is a corporation, the Commission requires that a copy of the brokerage's Articles of Incorporation be filed also.

■ PROPERTY TAX ASSESSMENTS, AGRICULTURAL USE

Lands that are actively devoted to farm or agricultural uses are favorably assessed on the basis of those uses rather than on their, probably more intensive, highest and best use.

Agricultural Use Assessment

The State Department of Assessments and Taxation establishes criteria for the purpose of determining whether land qualifies for assessment as agricultural use. The State's purpose is to slow the conversion of farm lands into more intensive, nonfarm uses.

Agricultural Transfer Tax

The Agricultural Transfer Tax, ranging from 3 percent to 5 percent of the consideration, funds the State's Agricultural Land Preservation Program. The tax is based on multiple factors: the size of the tract, improvements that may be in place, and the value of the land reflected in the consideration. The tax is waived in a transfer in which the purchaser promises to keep the land in agricultural use for five tax years. The tax is more fully discussed in Chapter 10 of this book.

The Agricultural Transfer Tax is calculated by the Assessments Office and is payable at the time the property transfer to a nonagricultural user takes place. Negotiation about which party will pay should be reflected in the contract of sale. A full discussion of this tax is found at the Maryland State Department of Assessment and Taxation Web site: *www.dat.state.md.us/sdatweb/agtransf.html.*

■ AD VALOREM TAX DELINQUENCY AND REDEMPTION

This tax is due in two payments: one on July 1 and the other on January 1 each year. Taxes that are not paid by September 30 and by January 31 under the two-payment system are considered delinquent, bear interest as provided by law, and are subject to a real estate tax sale held by the county treasurer.

The dates and rules regarding such sales are made by each county. Tax-delinquent properties sold at a tax sale are not conveyed immediately to the buyer. During a six-month **statutory period of redemption,** the delinquent taxpayer may redeem the property by paying the county treasurer the amount of the delinquent tax plus the accumulated interest on penalties and related legal fees. The annual interest rate for redemption is established by law by various jurisdictions. In some cases, it is as high as 20 percent. If no redemption is made during the six-month period, the tax sale buyer may apply to the court for the issuance of a deed to the property. Unpaid taxes create a priority (first) lien on real property.

Ad valorem taxes on a parcel of property that remain unpaid for longer than three years, perhaps because the lien on the property did not sell at three successive tax sales, are no longer collectible. There is a three-year limitation of actions on this tax. Only the most recent three years' taxes remain a lien on any property. A number of tax program pamphlets are available in each county's Tax Assessment Office.

■ MECHANICS' LIENS

Mechanics' liens, as discussed in the main textbook, are authorized by law in many states to protect the rights of contractors, suppliers, and other persons engaged to improve real estate. In addition to mechanics and materialmen, Maryland grants architectural, engineering, land surveying, and landscaping service providers to file mechanics' liens. Work on Maryland real estate that improves a property by 15 percent of its previous value qualifies for a mechanic's lien. Contractors or suppliers have six months after completion of such work to record a notice of their lien. They then have one year from the date of recording to petition the courts to enforce the lien in the event such petition was not included when the lien was recorded.

It is unlawful for **unperformed** (executory) **contracts** between contractors and sub-contractors relating to construction, alteration, or repair of a building, structure, or improvement to contain a provision that waives or requires that the subcontractor waive the right to file a mechanic's lien.

Buyers purchasing recently constructed or improved properties should seek protection against possible outstanding mechanics' liens. In the usual purchase of real estate, the buyer's attorney has responsibility to ascertain that the property being purchased is free from unpaid taxes, mechanics' liens, or other outstanding liens. A building or the land on which the building is erected may not be subjected to a lien under this subtitle if, prior to the establishment of the lien, legal title has been granted to a bona fide purchaser for value.

Release of Lien

When a lien on real property is satisfied, lienholders are required to mail or deliver a release of the lien within seven days after receiving payment. The release may be in the form of the original note, marked "paid" or "canceled." If lienholders fail to provide such a release after demand by the payor, the payor may bring action in the circuit court. In such an action, the lienholders or their agent may be liable for delivery of the release, as well as for all costs and expenses of the action.

QUESTIONS

1. In Maryland, real estate taxes are imposed by
   1. cities.
   2. special taxing districts.
   3. counties.
   4. all of the above.

2. All residential real property in Maryland is
   1. reassessed for tax purposes each year.
   2. assessed for tax purposes at the property's full market value.
   3. reassessed for tax purposes every other year.
   4. reassessed after each resale.

3. Nyla Mack owns a contracting firm in Maryland. On February 1, Arch Chandler hired the Mack firm to construct a large addition to his five-bedroom house. Mack finished work on the project on March 15; it is now April 15, and Mack has not yet been paid. Based on this situation, which of the following is *CORRECT*? Mack has until
   1. August 1 to record a notice of lien.
   2. August 1 to enforce the mechanic's lien.
   3. September 15 to record a mechanic's lien.
   4. October 15 to enforce a mechanic's lien.

4. Pierre Andre makes semiannual real estate tax payments on the lot beneath his house. Which of the following statements is *FALSE*?
   1. Andre's payments will be due July 1 and January 1 of each tax year.
   2. Andre's first semiannual payment becomes late if not paid by September 30.
   3. Andre's second semiannual payment becomes late if not paid by January 31.
   4. Andre's second semiannual payment becomes late if not paid by March 31.

5. Ted Bolton has never before owned a principal residence in Maryland. He will settle on the purchase of a $400,000 home to occupy here in April. How will the State transfer tax (usually 0.5 percent of the consideration) be apportioned at settlement?
   1. Bolton will pay $0, and sellers will pay $1,000.
   2. Bolton will pay $1,000, and sellers will pay $1,000.
   3. Bolton will pay $0, and sellers will pay $2,000.
   4. The apportionment will be whatever Bolton and the sellers agree in the contract of sale.

Real Estate Contracts

■ KEY TERMS

attorneys-in-fact
equitable title
executory contract
installment contracts

lease purchase option
  agreement
lease with option to renew
new home warranty

option price
parol transfer
powers of attorney

■ OVERVIEW

Maryland real estate contracts are used for, among other things, sales, rentals, options, and installment sales. This chapter discusses various contract issues, including age requirements for valid contracts, the Statute of Frauds, mandatory clauses for residential resales, and limitation of actions on contract enforcement in this state. It also presents the industry-created statewide sales contract now available for REALTOR® use throughout Maryland (Figure 9.1). Students who go on to practice real estate brokerage as REALTORS® are advised always to use the latest version of such contracts and their appropriate addenda.

■ GENERAL CONTRACT RULES: COMPETENCY, STATUTE OF FRAUDS, LIMITATION OF ACTIONS

Competency

Under Maryland law, a person reaches the age of majority and has the capacity to enter into a valid real estate contract at age 18. However, minors married to persons who have reached the age of majority may enter into valid real estate contracts jointly with their spouses.

Statute of Frauds

To be legally enforceable under Maryland's Statute of Frauds, all contracts for the transfer of any interest in real property for more than one year must be in writing and signed by the parties. Any **parol** (oral) **transfer** of an interest in real property for more than one year conveys no more than a tenancy at will. While Maryland laws require a 30-day notice to vacate under a tenancy at will, various counties require longer periods.

The Maryland Statute of Frauds does not require a lease for a term of one year or less to be in writing to be enforceable. The year's term starts the date the lease is entered into, rather than the date on which occupancy begins. Regardless of this interesting fact, all licensees are required by Commission regulations to reduce to signed, written form *all agreements*—including leases of any length—that they help negotiate.

Limitation of Actions (Statute of Limitations)

Suits to enforce a simple contract must be filed within three years. For contracts signed "under seal," however, the time limit is 12 years. A statement in the body of a contract that it is made "under seal" and/or uses the phrase "witness my seal" above the signature block creates a contract under seal. Such a contract is called a *specialty* contract, and is subject to action for enforcement for 12 years.

■ CONTRACTS FOR THE SALE OF REAL ESTATE

Real estate sales contracts and other contract forms must always be drafted (drawn up "from scratch") by attorneys. Licensees are authorized only to insert required information into forms that attorneys have drafted. Licensees who draft even clauses or phrases on their own could be accused of the misdemeanor *unauthorized practice of law*. Under Maryland statutes, the maximum penalty for such "unauthorized practice" is a fine of not more than $5,000 and/or imprisonment for not more than one year.

Although licensees, unless otherwise licensed to do so, cannot act as attorneys in their brokerage activities, they should nevertheless emphasize to buyers and sellers that a signed sales contract is legally binding. Buyers and sellers should obtain legal counsel to interpret and approve the provisions of contracts. It is grossly misleading, and probably an example of the unauthorized practice of law, to give false assurance to the parties, such as, "Don't worry; there will be an attorney at settlement," or, "An attorney can always find a way to get you out of it," as if that would protect them from their own errors in judgment.

To avoid confusion that might arise from use of a variety of contract forms, the Maryland Association of REALTORS® (MAR), working with its member associations and boards throughout the State, prepares a contract form that its members may use in residential sale transactions statewide. The MAR, with the aid of its legal counsel, also provides contract language for 20 or more addenda. All these forms are copyrighted by the MAR and may not be altered or modified without the prior written express consent of that association. MAR member-brokers are free either to use the statewide forms—as long as they make no changes in their wording—or to have attorneys draft forms for each particular firm's use. Non-member-brokers may not use the MAR forms. When presenting a state- or areawide contract for approval by the parties, avoid the cliché "This is our standard contract," implying that it cannot be modified by the parties as part of their negotiations.

A sample of the MAR's Residential Sales Contract is shown in Figure 9.1.

■ INFORMATION REQUIRED IN CONTRACTS

In certain circumstances, Maryland statutes require that licensees include specific information in contracts. Other information is required in *all* contracts of sale, even when the sellers are not licensees and are simply selling their own property. Unless otherwise specifically agreed, a contract of sale is generally not made invalid by the omission of "required" disclosures such as those discussed below.

Deferred Water and Sewer Charges

All contracts for the sale of improved residential real property must disclose *the estimated cost* of any deferred water and sewer charges for which the purchaser may become liable. Violation of this disclosure requirement entitles the initial purchaser of the improved property to recover from the seller twice the amount of deferred charges the purchaser would be obligated to pay during the five years of payments following the sale.

Disclosure of Licensee Status

When they are themselves either the sellers or purchasers of real estate, licensees must notify the other party of their being licensees. This notification must be in writing and is typically made within the contract itself.

Presence of Ground Rent

A real estate sales contract must disclose *any ground rent or leasehold interest* involved in the sale. If the ground rent is presently irredeemable, this fact must be indicated. If the ground rent is to be redeemed at the time of settlement, responsibility for notice, costs of redemption, and so forth should be fixed as part of the written agreement.

A contract for the sale of real property subject to a ground rent must contain a notice of the existence of the ground rent and a warning that if ground rent is not paid on time, the reversionary owner of the ground rent may have a lien for unpaid ground rent placed on the property and then bring an action to foreclose the lien and seek possession. If these actions are successful, a ground landlord can become the fee simple owner of both the land and all improvements (houses) on it.

Allocation of Recordation Fees and Transfer Tax

The Brokers Act requires that every contract for use in the sale of residential property that is used as a dwelling place for one or two single-family units must contain the following statement in conspicuous type or handwritten:

> *Section 14-104 of the Real Property Article of the Annotated Code of Maryland provides that, unless otherwise negotiated in the contract or provided by local law, the cost of any recordation tax or any state or local transfer tax shall be shared equally between the buyer and seller.*

Notwithstanding this statement, the *First-Time Home Buyers Closing Cost Reduction Act* of 1995 reduces the State transfer tax from 0.5 percent to 0.25 percent in transactions involving first-time homebuyers, with that entire amount to be paid

FIGURE 9.1

Maryland Association of REALTORS® Residential Sales Contract

RESIDENTIAL CONTRACT OF SALE

This is a Legally Binding Contract; If Not Understood, Seek Competent Legal Advice.
THIS FORM IS DESIGNED AND INTENDED FOR THE SALE AND PURCHASE OF IMPROVED SINGLE FAMILY RESIDENTIAL REAL ESTATE LOCATED IN MARYLAND ONLY. *FOR OTHER TYPES OF PROPERTY INCLUDE APPROPRIATE ADDENDA.*

TIME IS OF THE ESSENCE. Time is of the essence of this Contract. The failure of Seller or Buyer to perform any act as provided in this Contract by a prescribed date or within a prescribed time period shall be a default under this Contract and the non-defaulting party, upon written notice to the defaulting party, may declare this Contract null and void and of no further legal force and effect. In such event, all Deposit(s) shall be disbursed in accordance with Paragraph 19 of this Contract.

1. DATE OF OFFER: _____.

2. SELLER: _____

3. BUYER: _____

4. PROPERTY: Seller does sell to Buyer and Buyer does purchase from Seller, all of the following described Property (hereinafter "Property") known as _____ located in _____ City/County, Maryland, Zip _____ , together with the improvements thereon, and all rights and appurtenances thereto belonging.

5. ESTATE: The Property is being conveyed: _____ in fee simple or _____ subject to an annual ground rent, now existing or to be created, in the amount of _____Dollars ($_____) payable semi-annually, as now or to be recorded among the Land Records of _____City/County, Maryland.

6. PURCHASE PRICE: The purchase price is _____Dollars ($_____).

7. PAYMENT TERMS: The payment of the purchase price shall be made by Buyer as follows:

(a) An initial Deposit by way of _____ in the amount of _____Dollars ($_____) at the time of this offer.
(b) An additional Deposit by way of _____ in the amount of _____ Dollars ($_____) to be paid within _____ (____) days from the Date of Contract Acceptance.
(c) All Deposits will be held in escrow by:_____.
(If not a Maryland licensed real estate broker, the parties may execute a separate escrow deposit agreement.)
(d) The purchase price less any and all Deposits shall be paid in full by Buyer in cash, wired funds, bank check, certified check or other payment acceptable to the settlement officer at settlement.
(e) Buyer and Seller instruct broker named in paragraph (c) above to place the Deposits in: **(Check One)**
 ☐ A non-interest bearing account;
OR ☐ An interest bearing account, the interest on which, in absence of default by Buyer, shall accrue to the benefit of Buyer. Broker may charge a fee for establishing an interest bearing account.

8. SETTLEMENT: Date of Settlement _____or sooner if agreed to in writing by the parties.

9. FINANCING: Buyer's obligation to purchase the Property is contingent upon Buyer obtaining a written commitment for a loan secured by the Property as follows:

(Check) ☐ Conventional Loan as follows:
 Loan Amount $ _____
 Term of Note _____ Years
 Amortization _____ Years
 Interest Rate _____ %
 Loan Program _____
 Loan Origination/Discount Fees (as a % of loan amount):
  Buyer agrees to pay _____%;
  Seller agrees to pay _____%.
 Buyer shall receive the benefit of any reduction in fees.

☐ FHA Financing Addendum
☐ Gift of Funds Contingency Addendum
☐ Owner Financing Addendum
☐ VA Financing Addendum
☐ Assumption Addendum
☐ OTHER: _____

☐ No Financing Contingency

Buyer _____/_____   Page 1 of 11   10/07   Seller _____/_____

F I G U R E   9.1 (CONTINUED)

Maryland Association of REALTORS® Residential Sales Contract

10. FINANCING APPLICATION AND COMMITMENT: Buyer agrees to make a written application for the financing as herein described within _____ (____) days from the Date of Contract Acceptance. If such written financing commitment is not obtained by Buyer within _____ (____) days from the Date of Contract Acceptance: (1) Seller, at Seller's election and upon written notice to Buyer, may declare this Contract null and void and of no further legal effect; or (2) Buyer, upon written notice to Seller, which shall include written evidence from the lender of Buyer's inability to obtain financing as provided in Paragraph 9 of this Contract, may declare this Contract null and void and of no further legal effect. In either case, the deposit shall be disbursed in accordance with the Deposit paragraph of this Contract. If Buyer has complied with all of Buyer's obligations under this Contract, including those with respect to applying for financing and seeking to obtain financing, then the Release of Deposit agreement shall provide that the deposit shall be returned to Buyer.

11. ALTERNATE FINANCING: Provided Buyer timely and diligently pursues the financing described in Paragraph 9 **"Financing"**; Paragraph 10 **"Financing Application and Commitment"**; and the provisions of Paragraph 28 **"Buyer Responsibility"**, Buyer, at Buyer's election, may also apply for alternate financing. If Buyer, at Buyers sole option, obtains a written commitment for financing in which the loan amount, term of note, amortization period, interest rate, down payment or loan program differ from the financing as described in Paragraph 9, or any addendum to this Contract, the provision of Paragraph 10 or any addendum to this Contract shall be deemed to have been fully satisfied. Such alternate financing may not increase costs to Seller or exceed the time allowed to secure the financing commitment as provided in Paragraph 10, or any addendum to this Contract.

12. HOME AND/OR ENVIRONMENTAL INSPECTION: Buyer acknowledges, subject to Seller acceptance, that Buyer is afforded the opportunity, at Buyer's sole cost and expense, to condition Buyer's purchase of the Property upon a Home Inspection and/or Environmental Inspection in order to ascertain the physical condition of the Property or the existence of environmental hazards.   If Buyer desires a Home Inspection and/or Environmental Inspection contingency, such contingency must be included in an addendum to this Contract. Buyer and Seller acknowledge that Brokers, agents or subagents are not responsible for the existence or discovery of property defects.

Inspection(s) Addenda Attached _____   Inspection(s) Declined _____   _____
                          Buyer   Buyer   **Buyer   Buyer**

13. INCLUSIONS/EXCLUSIONS: Included in the purchase price are all permanently attached fixtures, including all smoke detectors. Certain other **now existing items** which may be considered personal property, whether installed or stored upon the property, are included if box below is checked.

INCLUDED	INCLUDED	INCLUDED	INCLUDED
☐ Alarm System	☐ Exhaust Fan(s) # ___	☐ Pool, Equip. & Cover	☐ Trash Compactor
☐ Built-in Microwave	☐ Exist. W/W Carpet	☐ Refrigerator(s) # ____	☐ Wall Oven(s) # _____
☐ Ceiling Fan(s) # ___	☐ Fireplace Screen/Doors	☐ w/ice maker	☐ Water Filter
☐ Central Vacuum	☐ Freezer	☐ Satellite Dish	☐ Water Softener
☐ Clothes Dryer	☐ Furnace Humidifier	☐ Screens	☐ Window A/C Unit(s)
☐ Clothes Washer	☐ Garage Opener(s) # ___	☐ Shades/Blinds	# _____
☐ Cooktop	w/remote(s) # ____	☐ Storage Shed(s) # ____	☐ Window Fan(s)
☐ Dishwasher	☐ Garbage Disposer	☐ Storm Doors	# _____
☐ Drapery/Curtain Rods	☐ Hot Tub, Equip. & Cover	☐ Storm Windows	☐ Wood Stove
☐ Draperies/Curtains	☐ Intercom	☐ Stove or Range	
☐ Electronic Air Filter	☐ Playground Equipment	☐ T.V. Antenna	

ADDITIONAL INCLUSIONS (SPECIFY):_____

ADDITIONAL EXCLUSIONS (SPECIFY):_____

14. AGRICULTURALLY ASSESSED PROPERTY: The Property, or any portion thereof, may be subject to an Agricultural Land Transfer Tax as imposed by Section 13-301 et seq. of the Tax-Property Article, Annotated Code of Maryland, by reason of the Property's having been assessed on the basis of agricultural use. Agricultural taxes assessed as a result of this transfer shall be paid by _____.

15. FOREST CONSERVATION AND MANAGEMENT PROGRAM: Buyer is hereby notified that this transfer may be subject to the Forest Conservation and Management Program imposed by Section 8-211 of the Tax-Property Article, Annotated Code of Maryland. Forest Conservation and Management program taxes assessed as a result of this transfer shall be paid by the_____.

Maryland Association of REALTORS® Residential Sales Contract

16. LEAD-BASED PAINT:

A. FEDERAL LEAD-BASED PAINT LAW: Title X, Section 1018, the Residential Lead-Based Paint Hazard Reduction Act of 1992 (the Act), requires the disclosure of certain information regarding lead-based paint and lead-based paint hazards in connection with the sale of residential real property. Unless otherwise exempt, the Act applies only to housing constructed prior to 1978. A Seller of pre-1978 housing is required to disclose to Buyer, based upon Seller's actual knowledge, all known lead-based paint hazards in the Property and provide Buyer with any available reports in the Seller's possession relating to lead-based paint or lead-based paint hazards applicable to the Property. Seller, however, is not required to conduct or pay for any lead-based paint risk assessment or inspection. At the time that the offer to purchase is entered into by Buyer, Seller is required to provide Buyer with the EPA pamphlet entitled "Protect Your Family From Lead In Your Home" and a "Disclosure of Information on Lead- Based Paint and Lead-Based Paint Hazards" form. **Seller is required under the Act to provide Buyer with a ten (10) day time period (or other mutually agreeable time period) for Buyer, at Buyer's expense, to conduct a risk assessment or inspection for the presence of lead-based paint and/or lead-based paint hazards unless Buyer waives such assessment or inspection by indicating such waiver on the Lead-Based Paint Disclosure form. Notwithstanding the right of the Buyer under the Act to conduct a risk assessment inspection for presence of lead-based paint and/or lead-based paint hazards, Seller is not required by the Act to permit Buyer, and Buyer shall have no right, to rescind this Contract based upon the results of such inspection, even if the inspection reveals the presence of lead-based paint and/or lead-based paint hazards within the Property, unless otherwise provided in a written addendum to this Contract. (If applicable, see Lead-Based Paint Hazard Inspection Addendum.) Seller and any agent involved in the transaction are required to retain a copy of the completed Lead-Based Paint Disclosure form for a period of three (3) years following the date of settlement. A SELLER WHO FAILS TO GIVE THE REQUIRED LEAD-BASED PAINT DISCLOSURE FORM AND EPA PAMPHLET MAY BE LIABLE UNDER THE ACT FOR THREE TIMES THE AMOUNT OF DAMAGES AND MAY BE SUBJECT TO BOTH CIVIL AND CRIMINAL PENALTIES.**

Seller represents and warrants to Buyer, Broker(s), Broker(s)' agents and subagents, intending that they rely upon such warranty and representation, that the property:

(**Seller to initial applicable line**): _____ was constructed prior to 1978
                                    OR _____ was not constructed prior to 1978
                                    OR _____ the date of construction is uncertain.

If the Property was constructed prior to 1978 or if the date of construction is uncertain, as indicated by Seller's initial above, Buyer and Seller mutually agree that the requirements of the Act shall apply to the sale of the Property. Buyer and Seller acknowledge that the real estate brokers and salespersons involved in the sale of the Property have no duty to ascertain or verify the date of construction and assume no such duty or responsibility. Buyer and Seller agree, represent and warrant, each unto the other, that no binding and enforceable contract shall be deemed to exist or to have been formed unless the requirements of the Act have been complied with prior to the execution of this Contract by Buyer and Seller. Buyer and Seller represent and warrant that each intended, as a material term of the offer and acceptance, that the requirements of the Act be complied with as an express condition of the formation of a binding and enforceable contract by and between the parties.

Buyer and Seller acknowledge by their respective initials below that they have read and understand the provisions of this paragraph.

_____(BUYER) _____(BUYER)   _____(SELLER) _____(SELLER)

B. MARYLAND LEAD POISONING PREVENTION PROGRAM: Under the Maryland Lead Poisoning Prevention Program (the "Maryland Program"), any residential dwelling constructed prior to 1950 which is leased for residential purposes is required to be registered with the Maryland Department of the Environment (MDE). Any residential dwelling constructed between 1950 and 1978, which is leased for residential purposes, may be registered with the MDE at the election of the owner.

Seller hereby discloses that the property:

1. *(Seller to initial applicable line)* _____ is currently registered in the Maryland Program
                                    _____ is NOT currently registered in the Maryland Program

If the Property was constructed prior to 1950 and Buyer intends to lease the Property effective immediately following settlement or in the future, Buyer shall be required to register the Property with the Maryland Department of the Environment within thirty (30) days following the date of settlement or within thirty (30) days following the conversion of the Property to rental property as required by the Maryland Program. Buyer shall be responsible for full compliance under the Maryland Program, including but not limited to, registration; inspections; lead-paint risk reduction and abatement procedures; payment of all fees, costs and expenses; and the notice requirements to tenants as well as the requirements of qualified offers.

F I G U R E   9.1 (CONTINUED)

Maryland Association of REALTORS® Residential Sales Contract

Buyer acknowledges by Buyer's initials below that Buyer has read and understands the provisions of this paragraph.
_____(BUYER)   _____(BUYER)

2. If the Property is already registered under the Maryland Program as indicated in Paragraph 16.B.1., Seller further discloses to Buyer that an event as defined under the Maryland Program (including, but not limited to, notice of the existence of lead-based paint hazards or notice of elevated blood lead levels from a tenant or state, local or municipal health agency) *(Seller to initial applicable line)* _____ has; or _____ has not occurred which obligates Seller to perform either the modified or full risk reduction treatment of the Property as required under the Maryland Program. If an event has occurred which obligates Seller to perform either the modified or full risk reduction treatment of the Property, Seller hereby discloses the scope of such treatment as follows:_____
_____
_____
If such event has occurred, Seller *(Seller to initial applicable line)* _____ will, or _____ will not perform the required treatment prior to transfer of title of the Property to Buyer.
Buyer acknowledges by Buyer's initials below that Buyer has read and understands the provisions of this paragraph.
_____(BUYER)   _____(BUYER)

17. ADDENDA: The Addenda checked below, which are hereby attached, are made a part of this Contract:
☐ Affiliated Business Disclosure Notice
☐ Cash/Conventional Financing Appraisal Contingency
☐ Condominium Resale Notice
☐ Conservation Easement
☐ Disclosure of Licensee Status
☐ First-Time Maryland Home Buyer Transfer & Recordation Tax
☐ Homeowners Association Notice
☐ Kickout
☐ Lead-Based Paint Hazard Inspection
☐ Lead-Based Paint and Lead-Based Hazards Disclosure of Information
☐ Local City/County Certifications/Registrations
☐ Local City/County Notices/Disclosure

☐ Maryland Non-Resident Seller Transfer Withholding Tax
☐ Notice to Buyer and Seller – Maryland Residential Real Property Disclosure/Disclaimer Act
☐ On-Site Sewage Disposal System Inspection
☐ Property Subject to Ground Rent
☐ Property Inspection s
☐ Purchase Price Escalation
☐ Sale, Financing, Settlement or Lease of Other Real Estate
☐ Seller's Purchase of Another Property
☐ Third Party Approval
☐ Water Quality

☐ Other Addenda/Special Conditions: _____
_____

18. TERMITE INSPECTION: Buyer, at Buyer's expense, (if VA, then at Seller's expense) is authorized to obtain a written report from a Maryland licensed pest control company that, based on a careful visual inspection, there is no evidence of termite or other wood-destroying insect infestation in the residence or within three (3) feet of the residence; and damage due to previous infestation has been repaired. The provisions of this paragraph also shall apply to: (1) the garage or within three (3) feet of the garage (whether attached or detached); (2) any outbuildings located within three feet of the residence or garage; and (3) a maximum of ten (10) linear feet of the nearest portion of a fence on Seller's Property within three feet of the residence or garage. If there is evidence of present infestation as described above, or if damage caused by present or prior infestation is discovered, Seller, at Seller's expense, shall repair any damage caused by present or prior infestation and have the present infestation treated by a licensed pest control company. If the cost of treatment and repair of such damage exceeds 2% of the purchase price, Seller may, at Seller's option, cancel this Contract, unless Buyer, at Buyer's option should choose to pay for the cost of treatment and repairs exceeding 2% of the purchase price, then this Contract shall remain in full force and effect. If such report reveals damage for which the cost of treatment and repair exceeds 2% of the purchase price, Seller's decision regarding treatment and repair of damage shall be communicated in writing to Buyer within five (5) days from receipt of the report, after which Buyer shall respond to Seller in writing with Buyer's decision within three (3) days from receipt of Seller's notification of Seller's decision. If Seller does not notify Buyer in writing of Seller's decision within five (5) days from receipt of report, Buyer may, at Buyer's option, pay

F I G U R E   9.1 (CONTINUED)

Maryland Association of REALTORS® Residential Sales Contract

for the cost of treatment and repairs exceeding 2% of the purchase price. If Buyer does not want to pay for the cost of treatment and repairs exceeding 2% of the purchase price, Buyer may terminate this Contract upon written notice delivered to Seller. In the event this Contract is terminated under the terms of this paragraph, the Deposit(s) shall be disbursed in accordance with the Deposit paragraph of this Contract.

19. DEPOSIT: If the Deposit is held by a Broker as specified in Paragraph 7(c) of this Contract, Buyer hereby authorizes and directs Broker to hold the Deposit instrument without negotiation or deposit until the parties have executed and accepted this Contract. Upon acceptance, the initial Deposit and additional Deposits (the "Deposit"), if any, shall be placed in escrow as provided in Paragraph 7(e) of this Contract and in accordance with the requirements of Section 17-502(b)(1) of the Business Occupations and Professions Article, Annotated Code of Maryland. If Seller does not execute and accept this Contract, the initial Deposit instrument shall be promptly returned to Buyer. The Deposit shall be disbursed at settlement. In the event this Contract shall be terminated or settlement does not occur, Buyer and Seller agree that the Deposit shall be disbursed by Broker only in accordance with a Release of Deposit agreement executed by Buyer and Seller. In the event Buyer and/or Seller fail to complete the real estate transaction in accordance with the terms and conditions of this Contract, and either Buyer or Seller shall be unable or unwilling to execute a Release of Deposit agreement, Buyer and Seller hereby acknowledge and agree that Broker may distribute the Deposit in accordance with the provisions of Section 17-505(b) of the Business Occupations and Professions Article, Annotated Code of Maryland.

20. DEED AND TITLE: Upon payment of the purchase price, a deed for the Property containing covenants of special warranty and further assurances (except in the case of transfer by personal representative of an estate), shall be executed by Seller and shall convey the Property to Buyer. Title to the Property, including all chattels included in the purchase, shall be good and merchantable, free of liens and encumbrances except as specified herein; except for use and occupancy restrictions of public record which are generally applicable to properties in the immediate neighborhood or the subdivision in which the Property is located and publicly recorded easements for public utilities and any other easements which may be observed by an inspection of the Property. Buyer expressly assumes the risk that restrictive covenants, zoning laws or other recorded documents may restrict or prohibit the use of the Property for the purpose(s) intended by Buyer. In the event Seller is unable to give good and merchantable title or such as can be insured by a Maryland licensed title insurer, with Buyer paying not more than the standard rate as filed with the Maryland Insurance Commissioner, Seller, at Seller's expense, shall have the option of curing any defect so as to enable Seller to give good and merchantable title or, if Buyer is willing to accept title without said defect being cured, paying any special premium on behalf of Buyer to obtain title insurance on the Property to the benefit of Buyer. In the event Seller elects to cure any defects in title, this Contract shall continue to remain in full force and effect; and the date of settlement shall be extended for a period not to exceed fourteen (14) additional days. If Seller is unable to cure such title defect(s) and is unable to obtain a policy of title insurance on the Property to the benefit of Buyer from a Maryland licensed title insurer, Buyer shall have the option of taking such title as Seller can give, or terminating this Contract and being reimbursed by Seller for cost of searching title as may have been incurred not to exceed 1/2 of 1% of the purchase price. In the latter event, there shall be no further liability or obligation on either of the parties hereto; and this Contract shall become null and void; and all Deposit(s) shall be disbursed in accordance with the Deposit paragraph of this Contract. In no event shall Broker(s) or their agent(s) have any liability for any defect in Seller's title.

21. CONDITION OF PROPERTY AND POSSESSION: At settlement, Seller shall deliver possession of the Property and shall deliver the Property vacant, clear of trash and debris, broom clean and in substantially the same condition as existed on the Date of Contract Acceptance. All electrical, heating, air conditioning, plumbing (including well and septic), and any other mechanical systems and related equipment, appliances and smoke detector(s) included in this Contract shall be in working condition. Buyer reserves the right to inspect the Property within five (5) days prior to settlement. **EXCEPT AS OTHERWISE SPECIFIED IN THIS CONTRACT, INCLUDING THIS PARAGRAPH, THE PROPERTY IS SOLD "AS IS"'.** The obligations of Seller as provided in this paragraph shall be in addition to any Disclosure and Disclaimer Statement as required by Section 10-702, Real Property Article, Annotated Code of Maryland and any provision of any inspection contingency addendum made a part of this Contract.

22. ADJUSTMENTS: Ground rent, homeowner's association fees, rent and water rent shall be adjusted and apportioned as of date of settlement; and all taxes, general or special, and all other public or governmental charges or assessments against the Property which are or may be payable on a periodic basis, including Metropolitan District Sanitary Commission, Washington Suburban Sanitary Commission, or other benefit charges, assessments, liens or encumbrances for sewer, water, drainage, paving, or other public improvements completed or commenced on or prior to the date hereof, or subsequent thereto, are to be adjusted and apportioned as of the date of settlement and are to be assumed and paid thereafter by Buyer, whether assessments have been levied or not as of date of settlement if applicable by local law. Any heating or cooking fuels remaining in supply tank(s) at time of settlement shall become the property of Buyer.

F I G U R E   9.1 (CONTINUED)

Maryland Association of REALTORS® Residential Sales Contract

23. SETTLEMENT COSTS: Buyer agrees to pay all settlement costs and charges including, but not limited to, all Lender's fees in connection herewith, including title examination and title insurance fees, loan insurance premiums, all document preparation and recording fees, notary fees, survey fees where required, and all recording charges, except those incident to clearing existing encumbrances or title defects, except if Buyer is a Veteran obtaining VA financing, those prohibited to be paid by a Veteran obtaining VA financing, which prohibited charges shall be paid by Seller.

24. TRANSFER CHARGES:

A. IN GENERAL. Section 14-104 of the Real Property Article, Annotated Code of Maryland provides that, unless otherwise negotiated in the contract or provided by State or local law, the cost of any recordation tax or any State or local Transfer Tax shall be shared equally between the Buyer and Seller.

B. FIRST-TIME BUYER. Under Section 14-104(c) of the Real Property Article, the entire amount of recordation and local transfer tax shall be paid by the Seller of property that is sold to a first-time Maryland homebuyer, unless there is an express agreement that the recordation tax or any state or local transfer tax will not be paid entirely by the Seller.

RECORDATION AND LOCAL TRANSFER TAX. If the Buyer is a first-time Maryland homebuyer, Buyer and Seller expressly agree, in accordance with Section 14-104(c) of the Real Property Article, Annotated Code of Maryland, that payment of recordation tax and local transfer tax shall be shared equally between the Buyer and Seller unless a "First-time Maryland Homebuyer Transfer and Recordation Tax Addendum" is attached, which contains a different express agreement.

STATE TRANSFER TAX: Under Section 13-203(b) of the Tax-Property Article, Annotated Code of Maryland, the amount of state transfer tax due on the sale of property to a first-time Maryland homebuyer is reduced from 0.50% to 0.25% and shall be paid entirely by the Seller. Buyer is hereby notified that to ensure receipt of the above reduction, Buyer should so indicate on Page 10 of this Contract and complete the required affidavit at settlement indicating that the Buyer is a first-time Maryland homebuyer.

25. BROKER LIABILITY: Brokers, their agents, subagents and employees do not assume any responsibility for the condition of the Property or for the performance of this Contract by any or all parties hereto. By signing this Contract, Buyer and Seller acknowledge that they have not relied on any representations made by Brokers, or any agents, subagents or employees of Brokers, except those representations expressly set forth in this Contract.

26. BROKER'S FEE: All parties irrevocably instruct the settlement officer to collect the fee or compensation and disburse same according to the terms and conditions provided in the listing agreement and/or agency representation agreement. Settlement shall not be a condition precedent to payment of compensation.

27. SELLER RESPONSIBILITY: Seller agrees to keep existing mortgages free of default until settlement. All violation notices or requirements noted or issued by any governmental authority, or actions in any court on account thereof, against or affecting the Property at the date of settlement of this Contract, shall be complied with by Seller and the Property conveyed free thereof. The Property is to be held at the risk of Seller until legal title has passed or possession has been given to Buyer. If, prior to the time legal title has passed or possession has been given to Buyer, whichever shall occur first, all or a substantial part of the Property is destroyed or damaged, without fault of Buyer, then this Contract, at the option of Buyer, upon written notice to Seller, shall be null and void and of no further effect, and the deposits shall be disbursed in accordance with the Deposit paragraph of this Contract.

28. BUYER RESPONSIBILITY: If Buyer has misrepresented Buyer's financial ability to consummate the purchase of the Property, or if this Contract is contingent upon Buyer securing a written commitment for financing and Buyer fails to apply for such financing within the time period herein specified, or fails to pursue financing diligently and in good faith, or if Buyer makes any misrepresentations in any document relating to financing, or takes (or fails to take) any action which causes Buyer's disqualification for financing, then Buyer shall be in default; and Seller may elect by written notice to Buyer, to terminate this Contract and/or pursue the remedies set forth under the Default paragraph of this Contract.

29. HOMEOWNER'S ASSOCIATION: The Property is not part of a development subject to the imposition of mandatory fees as defined by the Maryland Homeowner's Association Act, unless acknowledged by attached addendum.

30. GROUND RENT: If the Property is subject to ground rent and the ground rent is not timely paid, the ground lease holder (i.e., the person to whom the ground rent is payable) may bring an action under Section 8-402.3 of the Real Property Article, Annotated Code of Maryland. As a result of this action, a lien may be placed upon the property. If the Property is subject to ground rent, Sections 14-116 and 14-116.1 of the Real Property Article provide the purchaser, upon obtaining ownership of the Property, with certain rights and responsibilities relative to the ground rent. (If the Property is subject to ground rent: See Property Subject to Ground Rent Addendum.)

F I G U R E   9.1 (CONTINUED)

Maryland Association of REALTORS® Residential Sales Contract

31. SALE/SETTLEMENT OR LEASE OF OTHER REAL ESTATE: Neither this Contract nor the granting of Buyer's loan referred to herein is to be conditioned or contingent in any manner upon the sale, settlement and/or lease of any other real estate unless a contingency for the sale, settlement and/or lease of other real estate is contained in an addendum to this Contract. Unless this Contract is expressly contingent upon the sale, settlement and/or lease of any other real estate, Buyer shall neither apply for nor accept a financing loan commitment which is contingent upon or requires as a pre-condition to funding that any other real estate be sold, settled and/or leased.

32. LEASES: Seller may neither negotiate new leases nor renew existing leases for the Property which extend beyond settlement or possession date without Buyer's written consent.

33. DEFAULT: Buyer and Seller are required and agree to make full settlement in accordance with the terms of this Contract and acknowledge that failure to do so constitutes a breach hereof. If Buyer fails to make full settlement or is in default due to Buyer's failure to comply with the terms, covenants and conditions of this Contract, the initial Deposit and additional Deposits (the "Deposit") may be retained by Seller as long as a Release of Deposit Agreement is signed and executed by all parties, expressing that said Deposit may be retained by Seller. In the event the parties do not agree to execute a Release of Deposit Agreement, Buyer and Seller shall have all legal and equitable remedies. If Seller fails to make full settlement or is in default due to Seller's failure to comply with the terms, covenants and conditions of this Contract, Buyer shall be entitled to pursue such rights and remedies as may be available, at law or in equity, including, without limitation, an action for specific performance of this Contract and/or monetary damages. In the event of any litigation or dispute between Buyer and Seller concerning the release of the Deposit, Broker's sole responsibility may be met, at Broker's option, by paying the Deposit into the court in which such litigation is pending, or by paying the Deposit into the court of proper jurisdiction by an action of interpleader. Buyer and Seller agree that, upon Broker's payment of the Deposit into the court, neither Buyer nor Seller shall have any further right, claim, demand or action against Broker regarding the release of the Deposit; and Buyer and Seller, jointly and severally, shall indemnify and hold Broker harmless from any and all such rights, claims, demands or actions. In the event of such dispute and election by Broker to file an action of interpleader as herein provided, Buyer and Seller further agree and hereby expressly and irrevocably authorize Broker to deduct from the Deposit all costs incurred by Broker in the filing and maintenance of such action of interpleader including but not limited to filing fees, court costs, service of process fees and attorneys' fees, provided that the amount deducted shall not exceed the lesser of $500 or the amount of the Deposit held by Broker. All such fees and costs authorized herein to be deducted may be deducted by Broker from the Deposit prior to paying the balance of the Deposit to the court. Buyer and Seller further agree and expressly declare that all such fees and costs so deducted shall be the exclusive property of Broker. If the amount deducted by Broker is less than the total of all of the costs incurred by Broker in filing and maintaining the interpleader action, then Buyer and Seller jointly, and severally, agree to reimburse Broker for all such excess costs upon the conclusion of the interpleader action.

34. MEDIATION OF DISPUTES: Mediation is a process by which the parties attempt to resolve a dispute or claim with the assistance of a neutral mediator who is authorized to facilitate the resolution of the dispute. The mediator has no authority to make an award, to impose a resolution of the dispute or claim upon the parties or to require the parties to continue mediation if the parties do not desire to do so. Buyer and Seller agree that any dispute or claim arising out of or from this Contract or the transaction which is the subject of this Contract shall be mediated through the Maryland Association of REALTORS®, Inc. or its member local boards/associations in accordance with the established Mediation Rules and Guidelines of the Association *or* through such other mediator or mediation service as mutually agreed upon by Buyer and Seller, in writing. Unless otherwise agreed in writing by the parties, mediation fees, costs and expenses shall be divided and paid equally by the parties to the mediation. If either party elects to have an attorney present that party shall pay his or her own attorney's fees.

Buyer and Seller further agree that the obligation of Buyer and Seller to mediate as herein provided shall apply to all disputes or claims arising whether prior to, during or within one (1) year following the actual contract settlement date or when settlement should have occurred. Buyer and Seller agree that neither party shall commence any action in any court regarding a dispute or claim arising out of or from this Contract or the transaction which is the subject of this Contract, without first mediating the dispute or claim, unless the right to pursue such action or the ability to protect an interest or pursue a remedy as provided in this Contract, would be precluded by the delay of the mediation. In the event the right to pursue such action, or the ability to protect an interest or pursue a remedy would be precluded by the delay, Buyer or Seller may commence the action only if the initial pleading or document commencing such action is accompanied by a request to stay the proceeding pending the conclusion of the mediation. If a party initiates or commences an action in violation of this provision, the party agrees to pay all costs and expenses, including reasonable attorneys' fees, incurred by the other party to enforce the obligation as provided herein. The provisions of this paragraph shall survive closing and shall not be deemed to have been extinguished by merger with the deed.

FIGURE   9.1 (CONTINUED)

Maryland Association of REALTORS® Residential Sales Contract

35. ATTORNEY'S FEES: In any action or proceeding between Buyer and Seller based, in whole or in part, upon the performance or non-performance of the terms and conditions of this Contract, including, but not limited to, breach of contract, negligence, misrepresentation or fraud, the prevailing party in such action or proceeding shall be entitled to receive reasonable attorney's fees from the other party as determined by the court or arbitrator.   In any action or proceeding between Buyer and Seller and/or between Buyer and Broker(s) and/or Seller and Broker(s) resulting in Broker(s) being made a party to such action or proceeding, including, but not limited to, any litigation, arbitration, or complaint and claim before the Maryland Real Estate Commission, whether as defendant, cross-defendant, third-party defendant or respondent, Buyer and Seller jointly and severally, agree to indemnify and hold Broker(s) harmless from and against any and all liability, loss, cost, damages or expenses (including filing fees, court costs, service of process fees, transcript fees and attorneys' fees) incurred by Broker(s) in such action or proceeding, providing that such action or proceeding does not result in a judgment against Broker(s).

As used in this Contract, the term "Broker(s)" shall mean: (a) the two (2) Brokers as identified on Page 11 of this Contract; (b) the two (2) named Sales Associates identified on Page 11 of the Contract; and (c) any agent, subagent, salesperson, independent contractor and/or employees of Broker(s). The term "Broker(s)" shall also mean, in the singular, any or either of the named Broker(s) and/or Sales Associate(s) as identified or, in the plural, both of the named Brokers and/or Sales Associates as identified.

This Paragraph shall apply to any and all such action(s) or proceeding(s) against Broker(s) including those action(s) or proceeding(s) based, in whole or in part, upon any alleged act(s) or omission(s) by Broker(s), including, but not limited to, any alleged act of misrepresentation, fraud, non-disclosure, negligence, violation of any statutory or common law duty, or breach of fiduciary duty by Broker(s). The provision of this Paragraph shall survive closing and shall not be deemed to have been extinguished by merger with the deed.

36. NOTICE OF BUYER'S RIGHT TO SELECT SETTLEMENT SERVICE PROVIDERS: Buyer has the right to select Buyer's own title insurance company, title lawyer, settlement company, escrow company, mortgage lender or financial institution as defined in the Financial Institutions Article, Annotated Code of Maryland.   Buyer acknowledges that Seller may not be prohibited from offering owner financing as a condition of settlement.

37. LIMITED WARRANTY: NOTICE TO BUYER: IF A WARRANTY PLAN IS BEING OFFERED WITH THE PURCHASE OF THE PROPERTY, IT MAY BE A LIMITED WARRANTY. SINCE SUCH WARRANTY PLANS DO NOT COVER STRUCTURAL DEFECTS AND MAY NOT COVER PRE-EXISTING DEFECTS, BUYER SHOULD REQUEST THE REAL ESTATE AGENT TO PROVIDE BUYER WITH ANY BROCHURE WHICH DESCRIBES THE PLAN IN ORDER TO DETERMINE THE EXTENT OF COVERAGE PROVIDED BY THE WARRANTY.

38. PROPERTY INSURANCE BROCHURE: An informational brochure published by the Maryland Association of REALTORS®, Inc. titled "The New Reality of Property Insurance – What You Should Know" is available to explain current issues relative to obtaining insurance coverage for the Property to be purchased.

39. GUARANTY FUND: NOTICE TO BUYER: BUYER IS PROTECTED BY THE REAL ESTATE GUARANTY FUND OF THE MARYLAND REAL ESTATE COMMISSION, UNDER SECTION 17-404 OF THE BUSINESS OCCUPATIONS AND PROFESSIONS ARTICLE OF THE ANNOTATED CODE OF MARYLAND, FOR LOSSES IN AN AMOUNT NOT EXCEEDING $25,000 FOR ANY CLAIM.

40. SINGLE FAMILY RESIDENTIAL REAL PROPERTY DISCLOSURE NOTICE: Buyer is advised of the right to receive a "Disclosure and Disclaimer Statement" from Seller (Section 10-702 Real Property Article, Annotated Code of Maryland).

41. MARYLAND NON-RESIDENT SELLER: If the Property is not the Seller's principal residence and the Seller is a non-resident individual of the State of Maryland or is a non-resident entity which is not formed under the laws of the State of Maryland or qualified to do business in the State of Maryland, a withholding tax from the proceeds of sale may be withheld at the time of settlement except as otherwise provided by Maryland law. (See Maryland Non-Resident Seller Transfer Withholding Tax Addendum.)

42. INTERNAL REVENUE SERVICE FILING: Buyer and Seller each agree to cooperate with the settlement officer by providing all necessary information so that a report can be filed with the Internal Revenue Service, as required by Section 6045 of the IRS Code. To the extent permitted by law, any fees incurred as a result of such filing will be paid by the Seller.

43. NOTICE TO BUYER CONCERNING THE CHESAPEAKE AND ATLANTIC COASTAL BAYS CRITICAL AREA: Buyer is advised that all or a portion of the property may be located in the "Critical Area" of the Chesapeake and Atlantic Coastal Bays, and that additional zoning, land use, and resource protection regulations apply in this

F I G U R E   9.1 (CONTINUED)

Maryland Association of REALTORS® Residential Sales Contract

area. The "Critical Area" generally consists of all land and water areas within 1,000 feet beyond the landward boundaries of state or private wetlands, the Chesapeake Bay, the Atlantic Coastal Bays, and all of their tidal tributaries. The "Critical Area" also includes the waters of and lands under the Chesapeake Bay, the Atlantic Coastal Bays and all of their tidal tributaries to the head of tide. For information as to whether the property is located within the Critical Area, Buyer may contact the local Department of Planning and Zoning, which maintains maps showing the extent of the Critical Area in the jurisdiction. Allegany, Carroll, Frederick, Garrett, Howard, Montgomery and Washington Counties do not include land located in the Critical Area.

44. WETLANDS NOTICE: Buyer is advised that if all or a portion of the Property being purchased is wetlands, the approval of the U.S. Army Corps of Engineers will be necessary before a building permit can be issued for the Property. Additionally, the future use of existing dwellings may be restricted due to wetlands. The Corps has adopted a broad definition of wetlands which encompasses a large portion of the Chesapeake Bay Region. Other portions of the State may also be considered wetlands. For information as to whether the Property includes wetlands, Buyer may contact the Baltimore District of the U.S. Army Corps of Engineers. Buyer may also elect, at Buyer's expense, to engage the services of a qualified specialist to inspect the Property for the presence of wetlands prior to submitting a written offer to purchase the Property; or Buyer may include in Buyer's written offer a clause making Buyer's purchase of the Property contingent upon a satisfactory wetlands inspection.

45. FOREST CONSERVATION ACT NOTICE: If the Property is a tract of land 40,000 square feet or more in size, Buyer is notified that, unless exempted by applicable law, as a prerequisite to any subdivision plan or grading or sediment control permit for the Property, Buyer will be required to comply with the provisions of the Maryland Forest Conservation Act imposed by Section 5-1601, et seq. of the Natural Resources Article, Annotated Code of Maryland, including, among other things, the submission and acceptance of a Forest Stand Delineation and a Forest Conservation Plan for the Property in accordance with applicable laws and regulations. Unless otherwise expressly set forth in an addendum to this Contract, Seller represents and warrants that the Property is not currently subject to a Forest Conservation Plan, Management Agreement or any other pending obligation binding the owner of the Property under said Act; further, Seller represents and warrants that no activities have been undertaken on the Property by Seller in violation of the Forest Conservation Act.

46. NOTICE CONCERNING CONSERVATION EASEMENTS: If the Property is encumbered by a Conservation Easement as defined in Section 10-705 of the Real Property Article, Annotated Code of Maryland, the contract must contain a notice concerning the easement, which is contained in an attached addendum. This Paragraph does not apply to the sale of property in an action to foreclose a mortgage or deed of trust. (If the Property is encumbered by a Conservation Easement: See Conservation Easement Addendum.)

47. FOREIGN INVESTMENT TAXES-FIRPTA: Section 1445 of the United States Internal Revenue Code of 1986 provides that a Buyer of residential real property located in the United States must withhold federal income taxes from the payment of the purchase price if (a) the purchase price exceeds Three Hundred Thousand Dollars ($300,000.00) and (b) the seller is a foreign person. Unless otherwise stated in an addendum attached hereto, if the purchase price is in excess of Three Hundred Thousand Dollars ($300,000.00), Seller represents that Seller is not a non-resident alien, foreign corporation, foreign partnership, foreign trust or foreign estate (as those terms are defined by the Internal Revenue Code and applicable regulations) and agrees to execute an affidavit to this effect at the time of settlement.

48. CRIMINAL ACTIVITY AND SEXUAL OFFENDERS. Buyer may contact the state, county or municipal police departments in which the Property is located or check the "Sex Offender Registry" at the Maryland Department of Public Safety and Correctional Services website in order to ascertain criminal activity in the vicinity of the Property or the presence of registered sexual offenders who live or work within the vicinity of the Property. Buyer acknowledges that Buyer is solely responsible to inquire of such matters before signing this Contract. Buyer shall have no right to cancel this Contract based upon criminal activity or the presence of registered sexual offenders in the vicinity of the Property. Buyer further acknowledges that no real estate licensee involved in the sale or purchase of the Property, whether acting as the agent for Seller or Buyer, has any duty nor assumes any duty or responsibility to ascertain criminal activity or the presence of registered sexual offenders in the vicinity of the Property.

49. MILITARY INSTALLATIONS: This Section does not apply in Allegany, Carroll, Frederick, Garrett, Howard, Montgomery, and Washington Counties. Buyer is advised that the Property may be located near a military installation that conducts flight operations, munitions testing, or military operations that may result in high noise levels.

50. NOTICE TO THE PARTIES: Brokers, their agents, subagents and employees, make no representations with respect to the following:
(a) Water quantity, quality, color, or taste or operating conditions of public and/or private water systems.

F I G U R E   9.1 (CONTINUED)

Maryland Association of REALTORS® Residential Sales Contract

(b) Location, size or operating condition of on-site sewage disposal systems.

(c) The extensions of public utilities by local municipal authorities, existence or availability of public utilities, and any assessments, fees or costs for public utilities which might be imposed by local municipal authorities, should public utilities be extended or available to the subject Property. (Buyer should consult the Department of Public Works to determine the availability of proposed future extensions of utilities.)

(d) Lot size and exact location. If the subject Property is part of a recorded subdivision, Buyer can review the plat upon request at the Record Office. If the subject Property is not part of a recorded subdivision, Buyer may verify exact size and location through a survey by a licensed engineer or land surveyor, at Buyer's expense.

(e) Existing zoning or permitted uses of the Property: Buyer should contact the Zoning Office and/or a licensed engineer to verify zoning and permitted uses.

(f)   Brokers/agents are not advising the parties as to certain other issues, including without limitation: soil conditions; flood hazard areas; possible restrictions of the use of property due to restrictive covenants, subdivision, environmental laws, easements or other documents; airport or aircraft noise; planned land use, roads or highways; and construction materials and/or hazardous materials, including without limitation flame retardant treated plywood (FRT), radon, radium, mold spores, urea formaldehyde foam insulation (UFFI), synthetic stucco (EIFS), asbestos, polybutylene piping and lead-based paint. Information relating to these issues may be available from appropriate governmental authorities. This disclosure is not intended to provide an inspection contingency.

(g) Buyer and Seller each assume full responsibility for selecting and compensating their respective vendors.

51. NON-ASSIGNABILITY: This Contract may not be assigned without the written consent of Buyer and Seller. If Buyer and Seller agree in writing to an assignment of this Contract, the original parties to this Contract remain obligated hereunder until settlement.

52. PARAGRAPH HEADINGS: The Paragraph headings of this Contract are for convenience and reference only, and in no way define or limit the intent, rights or obligations of the parties.

53. COMPUTATION OF DAYS: As used in this Contract, and in any addendum or addenda to this Contract, the term "days" shall mean consecutive calendar days, including Saturdays, Sundays, and holidays, whether federal, state, local or religious. A day shall be measured from 12:00:01 a.m. to and including 11:59:59 p.m. E.S.T. For the purposes of calculating days, the count of "days" shall begin on the day following the day upon which any act or notice as provided in this Contract, or any addendum or addenda to this Contract, was required to be performed or made.

54. ENTIRE AGREEMENT: This Contract and any addenda thereto contain the final and entire agreement between the parties, and neither they nor their agents shall be bound by any terms, conditions, statements, warranties or representations, oral or written, not herein contained. The parties to this Contract mutually agree that it is binding upon them, their heirs, executors, administrators, personal representatives, successors and, if permitted as herein provided, assigns. Once signed, the terms of this Contract can only be changed by a document executed by all parties. This Contract shall be interpreted and construed in accordance with the laws of the State of Maryland. It is further agreed that this Contract may be executed in counterparts, each of which when considered together shall constitute the original Contract.

55. ELECTRONIC DELIVERY: The parties agree that this Contract offer shall be deemed validly executed and delivered by a party if a party executes this Contract and delivers a copy of the executed Contract to the other party by telefax or telecopier transmittal, or delivers a digital image of the executed document by email transmittal.

Buyer's Signature _____ Date _____   Seller's Signature _____ Date _____

Buyer's Signature _____ Date _____   Seller's Signature _____ Date _____

DATE OF CONTRACT ACCEPTANCE: _____

Contact Information: ☐ **Check if First-Time Maryland Homebuyer**
BUYER / NAME(S):_____
MAILING ADDRESS:_____

SELLER / NAME(S):_____
MAILING ADDRESS:_____

F I G U R E   9.1 (CONTINUED)

Maryland Association of REALTORS® Residential Sales Contract

Information provided for reference only:

LISTING BROKER: _____ BRANCH OFFICE: _____

OFFICE PHONE: _____ FAX: _____ BROKER/AGENT MLS ID: _____

OFFICE ADDRESS: _____

SALES ASSOCIATE: _____ E-Mail: _____ PHONE: _____

ACTING AS: ☐ LISTING BROKER AND SELLER AGENT; OR
            ☐ INTRA - COMPANY AGENT WITH BROKER AS DUAL AGENT

SELLING BROKER: _____ BRANCH OFFICE: _____

OFFICE PHONE: _____ FAX: _____ BROKER/AGENT MLS ID: _____

OFFICE ADDRESS: _____

SALES ASSOCIATE: _____ E-Mail: _____ PHONE: _____

ACTING AS: ☐ SELLER AGENT (WHETHER "COOPERATING AGENT" OR "SELLING AGENT"); OR
            ☐ BUYER AGENT; OR
            ☐ INTRA - COMPANY AGENT WITH BROKER AS DUAL AGENT

by the seller. In such a transaction, the seller must also pay the entire amount of recordation and local transfer tax, unless there is an express agreement between the parties to the contrary. Other details on this matter appeared in Chapter 8 of this book.

Notice of HOA Fees

If the property is subject to a homeowners' association (HOA) and to the imposition of *mandatory HOA fees*, this fact must be disclosed to purchasers in the purchase agreement, usually by reference to the public record. Similar reference should be included about a residential property within a condominium regime.

Limit on Buyer Protection from Guaranty Fund

Contracts for the sale of real estate must contain a *notice of purchaser protection* by the Real Estate Guaranty Fund for actual losses in an amount not to exceed $25,000 for any one transaction.

Handling of Earnest (Deposit) Monies

A real estate broker must promptly place all earnest (deposit) monies in a special non-interest-bearing account, unless directed to do otherwise by both buyer and seller. Contracts in which a licensee holds an earnest deposit should also authorize that broker to disperse the deposit according to the rules now contained in Section 505 of the Brokers Act (Title 17). Details of these rules are found in Chapter 3, under "Disposition of Trust Money."

Choice of Settlement and Similar Service Providers

The Brokers Act mandates that contracts reveal that buyers of single-family dwellings may not be required to employ specific title insurance, settlement, or escrow companies or title attorneys but may choose their own. (See Chapter 1.)

Agricultural Land Transfer Tax

Every seller is also required to notify the purchaser when land being transferred may be subject to agricultural land transfer tax. The statewide MAR Residential Contract of Sale provides that sellers who fail to notify buyers in accordance with this requirement are liable to those buyers for the agricultural land transfer tax that the buyers will have to pay. This provision can, of course, be removed from the contract language by negotiation before it is signed.

Conservation Easements Disclosure

The purchaser has a *right to rescind* a contract for the sale of property encumbered by a "conservation easement" if

1. the seller fails to give, on or before entering into the contract of sale, or within 20 days afterward, a copy of all conservation easements encumbering the property; and
2. the contract of sale fails to contain a statement with specified information about the conservation easement and the purchaser's rights and responsibilities, in conspicuous type to the effect that

    this property is encumbered by one or more conservation easements or other restrictions limiting or affecting uses of the property and owned by the Maryland Environmental Trust, the Maryland Historical Trust, the Maryland Agricultural Land Preservation Foundation, the Maryland Department of Natural Resources, or a land trust (the "Conservation Easements"). Maryland law requires that the seller deliver to the buyer copies of all Conservation Easements,

    and notice of the requirement that, within 30 calendar days after the property is sold, the *purchaser* must give notice of the transfer, including specified information, to the owner of the conservation easement.

"Critical Areas"

All contracts for sale of property suitable for one or two single-family units entered into after October 1, 2004, have been required to contain the following language:

Notice to Buyer Concerning the Chesapeake and
Atlantic Coastal Bays Critical Area

Buyer is advised that all or a portion of the property may be located in the "Critical Area" of the Chesapeake and Atlantic Coastal Bays, and that additional zoning, land use, and resource protection regulations apply in this area. The "Critical Area" generally consists of all land and water areas within 1,000 feet beyond the landward boundaries of state or private wetlands, the Chesapeake Bay, the Atlantic Coastal Bays, and all of their tidal tributaries. The "Critical Area" also includes the waters of and lands under the Chesapeake Bay, the Atlantic Coastal Bays, and all of their tidal tributaries to the head of tide. For information as to whether the property is located within the Critical Area, buyer may contact the local Department of Planning and Zoning, which maintains maps showing the extent of the Critical Area in the jurisdiction. Allegany, Carroll, Frederick, Garrett, Howard, Montgomery, and Washington Counties do not include land located in the Critical Area.

Notice of Possible High Noise Levels Due to Military Installations

A notice in the wording below must appear in residential sales transactions in all areas of the State except Allegany, Carroll, Frederick, Garrett, Howard, Montgomery, and Washington Counties. However, all local laws requiring a statement or notice substantially similar to this statement shall prevail over this requirement.

Buyer is advised that the property may be located near a military installation that conducts flight operations, munitions testing, or military operations that may result in high noise levels.

Other Required Clauses

The *Real Property* Article requires that contracts of sale must also include the following notices and disclosures, where applicable:

- Notice pertaining to sale of real property in Prince George's County creating subdivision
- Notice pertaining to resale of condominium unit
- Notice pertaining to initial sale of lot in development containing more than 12 lots
- Notice pertaining to resale of any lot or initial sale of lot in development containing 12 or fewer lots
- Notice pertaining to initial sale of lot not intended to be occupied or rented for residential purposes
- Notice pertaining to initial sale of cooperative interests
- Notice of liability for agricultural land transfer tax
- Notice to purchaser pertaining to sale of certain land in Prince George's County that the land being sold is subject to a development impact fee and the unpaid amount of that fee
- Notice pertaining to sale of certain agriculturally assessed land in St. Mary's and Charles Counties

Baltimore City and most counties have various additional contract requirements unique to their jurisdictions. Information about these requirements is available from local boards or associations for use by their members. For example, contracts for the sale of multiple-dwelling property in Baltimore City must contain a clause whereby the seller guarantees that the property being purchased complies with the Baltimore City Multiple-Dwelling Code and that the license will be delivered to the buyer at the time of settlement.

Property in Maryland not served by public sewerage and water systems is subject to the State Department of Health and Mental Hygiene laws and regulations pertaining to individual sewerage disposal systems and wells. The licensee must provide the buyer of unimproved land with a notice that if the property being purchased is to be used for residential purposes, the buyer, before signing the contract, should ascertain the status of sewerage and water facilities and, if required, whether the property will be approved for installation of a well and/or private sewerage system.

The Department of Veterans Affairs (VA), the Federal Housing Administration (FHA), and many private lenders require an evaluation by the local health department of the sewerage system and the water supply on residential property prior to settlement. When this is required, a bacteriologic sample must be collected from the well and analyzed by the health department. Consequently, licensees involved in such a transaction must allow sufficient time for these procedures when estimating a settlement date. Assistance and information are available from the Department of Health and Mental Hygiene, O'Connor Building, 201 W. Preston Street, Baltimore, MD 21201 or from local health boards.

Contingency and Other Clauses

To express the exact agreement of the parties to a contract and to protect the best interests of their clients, licensees often employ contingency and other addenda. Licensees should avoid drafting the language of such clauses themselves but rather make use of forms with wording drafted by competent legal counsel. Such forms are typically available from realty boards and associations of which licensees are members. Additional disclosure clauses and contingency language often address such matters as the following:

- Details of financing
- Impact of appraisal
- Buyer's prompt loan application and receipt of lender's commitment
- Lenders' fees and charges and who will receive the benefit of any favorable changes due to market conditions
- Home inspections and their impact
- Sale of purchasers' home and any release (kickout) clause
- Existence and extent of any leasehold interests
- Disposition of any agricultural crops
- Party to pay fees for IRS filing
- Requirements for mediation
- Limitations on participating brokers' (and their affiliates') liability for any untoward happening
- Agreement to following English Rule for payment of attorneys after a dispute is decided
- Placing the risk of casualty loss upon the seller until such time as the purchaser occupies or settlement is held
- Assurance that the seller will deliver the property free from municipal (or similar) code violations of which the seller has been notified

- Seller's commitment to deliver possession upon settlement or other specified date
- Details of any presettlement occupancy agreement
- Various inspection contingencies
- Presence of any financial contingencies

Survival

A statement in a contract asserting that the entire contract (or specific portions) shall "survive and not be merged into the deed" allows enforcement of incomplete portions of that contract after settlement for either 3 or 12 years from the date of the contract. If no "survival" language appears in a contract, its terms are "merged into the deed" at settlement (i.e., they are no longer subject to suits for enforcement after delivery of deed at settlement). To be "merged" could better be thought of as "submerged"—as in "drowned."

Release from Contract of Sale

When one party is unable or unwilling to consummate a contract of sale and the other party agrees to release that party, the broker should provide a competently drafted release form for signatures of both parties. If, on the other hand, the parties do not agree, upon release, as to how any deposits are to be distributed, the broker is free to follow the statutory procedure described in Chapter 3.

■ OPTION AGREEMENTS

In Maryland, a **lease purchase option agreement** is a lease agreement containing a clause that gives the tenant some power to purchase the landlord's interest in real property. No lease option purchase of improved residential property is valid in Maryland unless it contains the statement in capital letters "THIS IS NOT A CONTRACT TO BUY" and a clear statement of the option agreement's purpose and effect with respect to the purchase of the property that is the subject of the option.

Even though details of times, prices, dates, financing, prorations, settlement expenses, and so forth—everything needed for a contract of sale—are clearly set forth in the option, it still "IS NOT A CONTRACT TO BUY." It is, rather, a unilateral contract that would become bilateral and binding on both parties only if option rights are exercised by the optionee.

Similarly a **lease with option to renew** is not a contract to renew but still should contain all details of the situation created should the optionee decide to exercise the option and renew, e.g., recitation of any changes in rent or other significant matter and reiteration, by reference to the original agreement, of other details that would not change.

In *every* option, an **option price** (consideration for the option itself) must be recited, in addition to the price or rental to be paid were the option to be exercised.

■ CONSTRUCTION CONTRACTS

Prior to the signing of a contract for the construction of a single-family dwelling using alternating current (AC) electrical service and a public water system, a builder must, under certain conditions, offer prospective buyers the option of having a sprinkler system installed. Some jurisdictions in the state already require that such systems be installed in new homes in addition to smoke detectors.

■ NEW HOME WARRANTIES AND DEPOSITS

Before entering into contracts for sale or construction of new homes, builders must disclose to purchasers on a State-mandated form whether they participate in a **new home warranty** security plan and the extent of that plan. If builders do not participate in a new home warranty plan, they must disclose, among other things, that without a new home warranty, the purchaser may be afforded only certain limited (statutory) warranties.

The disclosure must also state that builders of new homes, although *registered*, are not required to be *licensed* by the State and are not required to be licensed by most local jurisdictions. Purchasers who acknowledge by their signature that they have been so informed then have five working days to rescind their contract and recover all money paid for their purchases. Contracts for purchase or construction of new homes that do not contain this notice are voidable by the buyers. Builders are, however, required to register with the Home Builder and Home Builder Sales Representative Registration Unit in the Consumer Protection Division of the Office of the Maryland Attorney General, thus bringing some oversight of that industry under State government influence. If builders' registrations are revoked, they are no longer allowed to sell homes they have built. Since October 1, 2008, salespersons selling a builder's new homes also need to be similarly registered, but no longer need to hold real estate sales licenses. The fee for their registration for a two-year period is $200. Builders pay a $600 fee.

Any person knowingly misrepresenting the existence of a new home warranty is subject to a fine not exceeding $50,000, imprisonment for not more than two years, or both, in addition to other penalties provided by the *Real Property* Article.

In connection with the sale and purchase of new, single-family residential units, including condominiums that are not completed at the time of contracting the sale, if the vendor or builder obligates purchasers to pay any sum of money before units have been completed and the realty has been granted to the purchaser, the builder or vendor is required to

- ■ deposit or hold the sums in an escrow account to ensure their return to purchasers who are entitled to them, or
- ■ obtain and maintain a corporate surety bond to provide return of deposits to purchasers who are entitled to them.

The *Maryland Custom Home Protection Act*, found in the *Real Property* Article, provides certain protections for buyers of newly constructed homes. This law sets standards for contract payments, surety bonds, contract requirements, mortgage loans, and sales by licensed real estate brokers. Detailed provisions govern brokers' handling of deposit monies.

■ INSTALLMENT CONTRACTS

Maryland statutes provide protections for purchasers of residential property under **installment contracts,** which are stronger than the protections provided by common law. Some Maryland requirements for sale of residential property by installment contract are presented in Chapter 12. The principles text presents general information on installment contracts in its chapters on contracts and finance.

■ DISCLOSURE REQUIREMENTS OF INITIAL SALES OF CONDOMINIUMS

A contract for the initial sale or resale of a condominium unit requires the disclosure of certain information to the purchaser before the execution of the contract. The buyer of a condominium unit has 15 days (for initial sale) or 7 days (for resale) from the signing of such a contract within which to rescind the agreement for any reason at all. Looking at the law's requirements from another perspective, the developer must deliver all required papers to condominium purchasers 15 days prior to settlement. Purchasers cannot waive this requirement in a sales contract. However, they are permitted to proceed to settlement without having received the required papers. If they do so, they still retain the right to rescind the transaction for up to one year. A contract for the initial sale of a residential condominium unit to a member of the public must also contain notice of the developer's warranties.

■ RESIDENTIAL PROPERTY DISCLOSURE AND DISCLAIMER STATEMENT

The required use of the Residential Property Disclosure and Disclaimer Statement is presented in Chapter 4. Failure to present the Statement to purchasers in a timely fashion may enable them to rescind the contract as late as the day when settlement is to take place—or at least until they apply for the loan required for the purchase.

Use of the Disclosure and Disclaimer Statement is *not* required in

- the initial sale of a single-family residential real property that has never been occupied or for which a certificate of occupancy has been issued within one year before the seller and buyer enter into a contract;
- the transfer of properties exempt from transfer tax under the *Tax-Property Article* (land installment contracts and certain options to purchase require the use of the statement);
- sale by a lender, an affiliate, or a subsidiary of a lender of property acquired by foreclosure or by deed in lieu of foreclosure;
- a sheriff's sale, tax sale, or sale by foreclosure, partition, or court-appointed trustee;
- a transfer by a fiduciary in the course of the administration of a decedent's estate, guardianship, conservatorship, or trust;
- the transfer of a single-family residential real property to be converted by the buyer into use other than residential use or to be demolished; or
- the sale of unimproved real property.

AGENCY DISCLOSURE FORM

A properly completed agency disclosure form, "Understanding Whom Agents Represent," should be attached to or otherwise accompany the original sales agreement from signing to settlement. The properly completed and maintained form can prove useful in defending against either party's charge of "undisclosed dual agency."

POWERS OF ATTORNEY

Attorneys-in-fact (now called "Agents") in powers of attorney are *persons* granted authority in *documents* called **powers of attorney** to perform, in place of their grantor, certain actions such as selling or conveying property on behalf of the owner who granted the power. When a deed or other instrument is signed by an attorney-in-fact ("Agent") who is acting under such a document—properly signed and acknowledged—that document must be recorded *either before or on* the same day the deed or mortgage is placed in the public record. It may even be recorded after the deed has been recorded if

- the power of attorney was both dated and acknowledged on or before the effective date of the deed;
- the power of attorney had not been revoked up to the time of the recording of the deed; and
- the deed recorded contained or was accompanied by an affidavit from the attorney-in-fact (agent) stating he or she had no actual knowledge that the person who granted the power of attorney had either revoked it, had become legally disabled, or had been incompetent at the time of the agent's signing the deed.

It is prudent, in all cases involving powers of attorney, for licensees preparing for settlement to check with closing and title officers well before the scheduled closing to make sure such powers of attorney are in a form acceptable to the settlement officers and to the lending institutions involved.

DUTIES AND OBLIGATIONS OF LICENSEES

The Regulations of the Commission set forth a number of duties and obligations that real estate licensees have to clients, the public, and fellow licensees with respect to contracts. These include

- prompt presentation of all written offers and counteroffers,
- reduction of all agreements to a written form that clearly sets forth all the obligations of the parties,
- obtaining proper signatures on all forms, and
- giving and retaining copies of all signed agreements.

■ EQUITABLE TITLE AND RISK OF LOSS

When a contract of sale has been signed by all parties, the buyers receive **equitable title.** This is called the *doctrine of equitable conversion.* Under Maryland common law, possession of equitable title places the risk of loss due to accidental damage to the premises *on the buyers* who hold an **executory contract**—one that exists between contract signing and closing. This is true unless the sellers cause the damage or the buyers have taken presettlement, physical possession of the premises. To offset this possibility, most contracts in Maryland include a provision that the sellers will bear any casualty losses until settlement or occupancy—whichever occurs first. Licensees should see that this issue is addressed in any contract they negotiate.

■ RESIDENTIAL SALES CONTRACT PROVIDED FOR MARYLAND Realtors®

The residential sales contract form that appears as Figure 9.1 is provided to members of the Maryland Association of Realtors® for their exclusive use. The Association also provides an array of addenda for specific situations and to meet certain legal requirements. Examples are the "Lead-Based Paint Hazard Inspection Addendum," required by federal law in residential sales of structures built before 1978, and the "First-Time Maryland Home Buyer Transfer and Recordation Tax Addendum."

QUESTIONS

1. In Maryland, contracts for the sale of real estate must be
    1. in writing to be enforceable.
    2. on a standard printed form.
    3. signed by the seller only.
    4. signed by the buyer only.

2. Oral contracts for the sale of real estate are
    1. valid.
    2. called parol agreements.
    3. enforceable in a court of law.
    4. illegal.

3. Licensees buying or selling real property *MUST*
    1. advise the other party of the fact that they are real estate licensees.
    2. advise lending institutions of their licensure.
    3. write to the Real Estate Commission.
    4. advise the Attorney General.

4. Which of the following is *NOT* required to be disclosed in a Maryland real estate sales contract?
    1. That a leasehold interest is involved in the sale
    2. That the owner/seller is a real estate licensee
    3. The existence of possible tax charges for agricultural land development
    4. The title insurance company name

5. Use of the "Critical Areas" notice is required
    1. in all counties with major waterways.
    2. only in counties bordering on Atlantic or Chesapeake waterways.
    3. in all counties, regardless of whether they are affected by such regulation.
    4. throughout the State, except in Allegany, Carroll, Frederick, Garrett, Howard, Montgomery, and Washington counties.

CHAPTER 10

Transfer of Title

■ KEY TERMS

adverse possession	donor	legatees
attested	elective share	nominate
beneficiaries	grantor	notorious
constructive notice	heirs	nuncupative wills
custodian	holographic wills	pretermitted
deed	hostile	residue
devise	intestate	surviving issue
devisees	issue	transfer tax
documentary stamp tax	legacy	

■ OVERVIEW

Title to land in Maryland, as elsewhere, can pass by descent, devise, adverse possession, gift, grant, escheat, eminent domain, erosion, accretion, reliction, foreclosure, and tax and sheriff's sales. This chapter deals with transfers of title by descent, action of law, will, and deed.

■ TRANSFER OF TITLE BY DESCENT

Surviving spouses are provided for by the Maryland Law of Descent and Distribution, which abolished dower and curtesy. This statute also names other classes of heirs who inherit property owned by decedents who die **intestate** (without a valid will). An example of situations involving intestacy that the law addresses is that of a surviving spouse

- and a minor child: each gets half;
- and no minor children but with **surviving issue** (adult children and perhaps their children): spouse gets $15,000 and half of the **residue** (rest);
- and no **issue** (children) but surviving parents: spouse gets $15,000 and half of the remainder;
- and no surviving issue or parents: spouse takes all.

When the decedent is not intestate but leaves a will that gives the spouse less than the portions provided in each situation above—perhaps as little as nothing—the spouse may renounce the will and elect (choose) to claim a larger amount that may be authorized by statute. This is called the survivor's **elective share.**

Title to real property of decedents passes immediately to their *personal representatives* (formerly called *administrators*) in situations without a valid will. These individuals pay decedents' debts and estate taxes and then distribute the remainder of the estate according to statute under supervision of the court.

Persons who receive property *by descent* are called **heirs.** Persons who receive property *through a will* are called **beneficiaries.** Beneficiaries are of two types: **devisees,** who receive real property (a **devise**), and **legatees,** who receive personal property (a **legacy**).

If the decedent was both intestate and entirely without heirs, the estate is converted to cash, and that cash paid to the Maryland Medical Assistance Program if the decedent received long-term care benefits from that program. If that is not the case, the cash is paid to the board of education in the county in which the personal representative was granted authority to administer the estate.

TRANSFER OF TITLE BY ACTION OF LAW

To obtain title to real estate through **adverse possession,** an adverse user must be in actual possession of the property, and that possession, alone or combined with that of a sequence of previous adverse owners, must have been continuous for at least 20 years. The possession also must be or have been open, **notorious** (known to others), exclusive, **hostile** (without permission), and—because Maryland law does not recognize "squatters' rights"—under claim of right or color of title. Each of those terms has a very specific legal meaning. Situations involving adverse possession can be very technical and should always be handled with guidance from competent legal counsel.

TRANSFER OF TITLE BY WILL

There are statutory requirements for a valid will. Persons age 18 or over, who are of sound mind and are legally competent, may make a will. Wills should be prepared carefully by testators' attorneys, signed by the maker, and witnessed by two persons as required by law. While surviving spouses can contest wills that grant them less than what would have been their intestate share, other heirs, such as testators' children, may not do so.

Omitted Children

Children born after a testator's will is signed and before the testator's death are said to be **pretermitted** (omitted). This category also includes children of the decedent who had not yet been born at the time of the decedent's death. Under common law, pretermitted children do not have a share in the decedent's estate. However, Maryland statute has set aside this aspect of common law and treats pretermitted children as if they were born before the will was signed.

Nuncupative (oral) **wills** are not recognized in Maryland. **Holographic wills** (those in the handwriting of the testator) are recognized if they are properly **attested** (witnessed).

■ TRANSFER OF TITLE BY DEED

Maryland statutes also set forth requirements for a valid deed. A **deed** must be prepared in writing by an attorney or by one of the parties, be executed by a competent grantor at least 18 years of age, state the actual consideration or be accompanied by an affidavit that states it, and give a legally sufficient property description.

Deeds must be typewritten and in English to be recorded, although an accompanying official consular translation into English satisfies this requirement for a deed written in another language.

A deed signed only by the **grantor** (the one granting the property) is effective if delivered and accepted by the grantee. It is called a *deed poll*. In contrast, transfers of property belonging to a minor and of properties involving corporate sellers or purchasers are situations in which both grantees and the grantors are required to sign the deed.

Recordation of Deeds and Mortgages

Maryland law specifies that the transfer of any fee or freehold estate, any declaration or limitation of use, and any estate extending beyond seven years (such as a deed or a long-term lease) shall be effective only if the deed is executed and recorded. Chapter 13 of this book also points out that leases for more than seven years must be recorded. Title to property passes, *as between the parties*, upon delivery and acceptance of a valid deed. Consequently, unrecorded deeds are valid between grantors and grantees and also against third parties, but only those third parties with actual notice. Grantees under unrecorded deeds are subject to having their equitable title interests extinguished if their grantor subsequently grants the property to others who are unaware of the earlier transfer. The law requires that deeds be recorded to alert potential purchasers of land to the possible interests of others. Recording deeds can also protect grantees against third persons who do not have actual notice. The recording of a deed constitutes **constructive notice** as of date of recording. Deeds are recorded in the county where the land lies. For land lying in more than one county, the deed must be recorded in each of the counties.

Recordation requires acknowledgment before a notary or other authorized public officer and payment of all required transfer taxes, ad valorem taxes, and special assessments. The deed is considered made (done) *on the date it is signed, sealed, and delivered*, even though acknowledged at a later date and recorded still later.

Mortgages or deeds of trust (but not deeds) are exempt from the recordation tax if they secure home loans made for the initial purchase or for renovation of the mortgagor's (borrower's) principal residence.

■ TAXES ON CONVEYANCES

The **documentary stamp tax** (so-called because, historically, its payment was indicated by attaching actual revenue stamps to the deed) is a Maryland State tax levied at the rate of $0.55 per $500 or fraction thereof on the full sales price of the property. Several cities and counties have added their own stamp tax.

Another State tax is the Maryland **transfer tax.** It is 0.5 percent of the full consideration except for transfers to a first-time Maryland homebuyer, as explained in Chapter 8. Cities and counties collect additional transfer taxes.

"Subject to" Transfers Between Relatives and Transfers by Assumption Not Taxed

Transfers between many classes of relatives—among others—including step-siblings, in-laws, and former spouses, are exempt from recordation and transfer taxes only on the amount of mortgage indebtedness assumed by the transferee.

■ AGRICULTURAL TRANSFER TAX

The agricultural transfer tax is calculated by the Assessments Office and is payable at the time of property transfer. It is imposed when land subject to agricultural ad valorem tax assessment is sold with nonagricultural use in view. The student is referred to the full discussion and resources given in Chapter 8.

■ MARYLAND UNIFORM TRANSFERS (GIFTS) TO MINORS ACT

This law authorizes a **donor** (one who gives a gift) to **nominate** (name) a **custodian** to act on behalf of the minor beneficiary (the one receiving the gift). The designation, powers, and responsibilities of a custodian and procedures for transfers of custodial property and claims against such property are set forth in the statute. Use of legal counsel is important in such a transfer.

QUESTIONS

1. One requirement for obtaining title to the property of another by adverse possession is that the claimant *MUST*

    1. post a sign on the subject property.
    2. notify the original owner in writing.
    3. have been in possession of the property at least 20 years.
    4. own the adjoining land.

2. The Maryland Law of Descent and Distribution

    1. can affect estates of those not leaving a valid will.
    2. ensures that surviving spouses receive part of any estate.
    3. can affect the estates of both those leaving a valid will and those dying intestate.
    4. does all of the above.

3. To be valid between the parties, a deed to Maryland real property must meet all the following requirements, *EXCEPT* that it be

    1. voluntarily delivered during the lifetime of the grantor.
    2. in writing and signed.
    3. signed by a grantor who is competent.
    4. recorded.

4. To be eligible for recordation, a deed conveying Maryland real estate *MUST*

    1. only show a nominal consideration.
    2. be in the handwriting of the grantee.
    3. have been prepared by an attorney or by one of the parties.
    4. be witnessed by two persons not mentioned in the deed.

5. In Maryland, a valid will *MUST*

    1. be delivered during the lifetime of the testator/testatrix.
    2. be signed by at least one of the beneficiaries.
    3. be acknowledged before an officer of the court (notary public).
    4. have a minimum of two witnesses.

CHAPTER 11

Title Records

■ KEY TERMS

judicial injunction   report of title

■ OVERVIEW

According to Maryland State law, deeds, mortgages, ground leases, and other instruments creating an estate in real estate for longer than seven years must be recorded. This practice benefits owners, prospective purchasers, and lenders. Recording benefits buyers, who need to know who claims to own the property they are considering. It protects grantees by giving constructive notice to the world of their claim of interest in a property. It also enables lenders to know if a mortgage loan applicant is the "owner of record" of the property being mortgaged and if there are any financial encumbrances against the property of which they have not been told.

■ DETAILS OF RECORDATION

Deeds and Mortgages   To be eligible for recordation, a deed must state the full consideration actually paid for the property. If that information is not shown the deed, it must be stated in an affidavit attached to the deed for the deed to be recorded. Only deeds acknowledged before a notary public or similar official may be recorded.

Deeds and mortgages on real estate are recorded by the clerk of circuit court in each county and Baltimore City. Recording must take place in the county or city *where the land is located*. If property is located in two counties, it must be recorded in *both*, with each county receiving a recording fee proportional to the amount of land located in the county, as shown by the tax assessment. Occasionally, recordings are made in a county other than that in which the property is located.

It should be noted that Maryland has only one system of recording and uses only grantor and grantee indices (indexes). The Torrens system, described in the main text, is not used in Maryland.

Real estate records are sorted into two indices: one by the names of grantors and one by names of grantees. Because Maryland law regards mortgages as conveying legal title to the lender/mortgagee (or to the trustees in the cases of deeds of trust), mortgagors (borrowers) are in the grantor index, and mortgagees and trustees are in the grantee index. Purchasers who finance a property by giving a mortgage (or deed of trust) to a financial institution are already grantees named in the deed they received. They are then regarded as grantors in the deed of trust (or mortgagors when a mortgage is used) they give to a financial institution. They have to become grantees for a property before they can be grantors—transferring the property to their lender or their lender's trustee. In the first instance, their names will be recorded in the grantee index; in the second, in the grantor index.

No deed conveying real estate may be recorded in any county of Maryland until all taxes and other public assessments or charges on the property have been paid and the record of ownership has been transferred on the tax assessment books to the grantee who is named in the deed to be recorded. If the deed transfers all of the real estate owned by the grantor in the county, then, in many counties, all of the grantor's personal property tax (if any) must also be paid prior to recording.

In Baltimore City, a deed conveying real estate may not be recorded if there is an outstanding unpaid water bill of more than $50. In Harford County, no deed conveying real estate may be recorded if *any* water bill is unpaid. Licensees preparing for settlement should check requirements in the county or municipality where the property that is the subject of the transaction is located.

In addition to transfer taxes, fees are charged for recording deeds and other documents. These fees are set by the counties. In many counties, recording costs $3 per page, or portion thereof, plus $1 for each name to be recorded in the grantor-grantee index. One who records a document takes it to the office of the clerk of court, pays the proper amount of documentary stamps and transfer tax stamps, pays the recording fee, and leaves the document with the clerk. The clerk's staff then reproduces the document in the public record, stamps the original to indicate where the information has been recorded, and returns it to the person designated to receive it.

Leases

Recording of leases that are for periods longer than seven years serves to protect lessees if mortgage lenders foreclose on their landlord. It also provides protection against certain persons to whom the landlord is indebted and judgment already rendered. *Lease* recordation costs are often as great as the costs for recording *deeds*. However, most leases of seven years or less are not subject to the recordation tax.

Plats of Subdivision

The law requires that subdividers have plats of subdivision approved by State and local authorities before recording those plats. Documents such as listings, sales contracts, and deeds typically refer to recorded plats by *liber and folio* (book and page). Such reference to the properly recorded plat in a later document can satisfy the need for exact property description. No lot within a subdivision can be offered for sale until the plat of subdivision has been recorded.

Recordation and development of individual lots in a subdivision are regulated on a local level by the county in which the property is located. Licensees should always be sure that the deeds to the individual lots for sale in a subdivision have been properly recorded and that all local laws regarding recordation have been met before advertising the lots for sale. Failure to do so could result in a **judicial injunction,** which would halt the marketing of the property. In addition, depending on the situation, the licensees may also be in violation of the State license law and, thus, subject to suspension or revocation of their real estate licenses.

■ TITLE EVIDENCE

In Maryland, it is customary for buyers in a real estate transaction to authorize the ordering of title evidence at their expense, although this, like so many other things, is negotiable. Generally, buyers will choose a title (settlement) company whose legal staff will (among other things)

- order an abstract of title to be prepared and, based on that abstract, prepare a **report** (opinion) **of title** as to whether the present condition of the title, as contained in the public record, is marketable; or
- acting as licensed representatives of a title insurance company, issue a preliminary title insurance policy (a title insurance *binder*) based on favorable abstract data.

The person performing settlement is required by statute to explain owner's title insurance at the closing meeting and make it available (offer to sell it) to residential purchasers. A policy of title insurance is the most frequently used form of title evidence in Maryland.

Note that Maryland law requires that the following notice be given to buyers, printed in bold type in the body of each sales contract presented by licensees: **YOU ARE ENTITLED TO SELECT YOUR OWN TITLE INSURANCE COMPANY, SETTLEMENT COMPANY, ESCROW COMPANY, OR TITLE ATTORNEY.**

■ PREREQUISITES TO RECORDING

No fee simple deed, mortgage, or deed of trust may be recorded, unless it bears a certification that the instrument has been prepared by attorneys admitted to practice before the Maryland Court of Appeals, under the supervision of such attorneys, or by one of the parties to the instrument. Various localities impose other requirements.

■ UNIFORM COMMERCIAL CODE

The Uniform Commercial Code (UCC) is in effect in Maryland. Two provisions of this code may affect real estate practices:

1. The use of chattel mortgages on fixtures or contents has been replaced by use of security agreements and financing statements.
2. The bulk sales provision applies when a person sells all of the stock in trade when selling a business.

The principles text contains more information about the UCC.

QUESTIONS

1. Buyers who purchase a parcel of real estate that is located in two counties should record in
   1. the county with the larger portion.
   2. the county with the smaller portion.
   3. the State capital.
   4. both counties.

2. When a parcel of Maryland real estate is sold, title search is customarily ordered on behalf of the
   1. seller.
   2. buyer.
   3. broker.
   4. seller and broker together.

3. Deeds and mortgages may be recorded in each county with the
   1. clerk of circuit court.
   2. Torrens system office.
   3. personal property tax office.
   4. municipal office of planning and zoning.

4. Deeds and mortgages conveying real estate in Maryland are NOT
   1. indexed under the name of the grantor.
   2. indexed under the name of the grantee.
   3. indexed under the name of the selling broker.
   4. referenced to previously recorded conveyances.

5. Which of the following is NOT true concerning requirements for recording a deed?
   1. It may be drafted (prepared) by one of the parties.
   2. It may be witnessed rather than notarized.
   3. It may be drafted (prepared) by an attorney.
   4. It must be notarized.

12

Real Estate Financing

■ KEY TERMS

balloon clause	maturity date	tax and insurance
deed in trust	mortgagee	expense account
deed of release	mortgagor	title theory
deed of trust	notice of sale	trustee sale
deed of trust financing	power-of-sale clause	trustee's deed
judicial mortgage	satisfaction of mortgage	vendees
foreclosure	secondary mortgage	
junior lenders	surplus money action	

■ OVERVIEW

Most real estate is purchased using borrowed funds. Both the traditional mortgage and the deed of trust are common in Maryland and are used in both third-party and owner financing. The State allows, but stringently regulates, another form of owner financing—the installment land contract.

■ NOTE TO STUDENT

The **deed of trust**—also called a *trust deed*—is different from a **deed in trust**, which is used to place property into a trust. Both are different from a **trustee's deed**, by which property is transferred out of a trust by the trustee. The student should review the discussion of these terms in the principles text.

■ MORTGAGE AND DEED OF TRUST LOANS

Maryland is considered a **title theory** state, as defined in the main text. A lender who records a properly signed and delivered mortgage or deed of trust holds legal title to the real estate pledged. Maryland's mortgage and deed of trust foreclosure and sale laws, however, are similar to those of a lien theory state, except that lenders, rather than delinquent landlords, *are allowed to collect rents* on investment properties during the foreclosure process.

Deeds of trust are used throughout the state as financing instruments for real estate. **Deed of trust financing** is a three-party arrangement involving borrower (the trustor), trustee, and lender (beneficiary). This arrangement is so popular in Maryland that it is sometimes called a *Potomac Mortgage*.

The deed of trust forms used in Maryland have a **power-of-sale clause,** which gives the trustee authority to sell pledged property in the event of borrower's default. In such a case, there is no court action. After giving adequate public notice, the trustee has the property sold at a **trustee sale** (a public auction). Some mortgages contain language granting the mortgagees the power-of-sale clause.

The money the trustee obtains from the sale is then applied to the principal of the mortgage debt plus the accrued interest and legal costs caused by the sale. Any money left, over and above what is due any lienholder, is returned to the defaulted borrower.

In Maryland, only a natural person and not a corporation or partnership may serve as trustee under a deed of trust and sell the property in case of default under the provisions of the document's power-of-sale clause. In some other jurisdictions, any person, including corporations and partnerships, may serve.

■ DEFAULT, FORECLOSURE, AND DEFICIENCY

The parties to a mortgage are the **mortgagor** (borrower) and the **mortgagee** (lender). If the borrower defaults, the lender who wishes to foreclose seeks a court order to sell the mortgaged property at public auction, unless there is a power-of-sale clause in the mortgage. When the funds from a **judicial** (court-ordered) **mortgage foreclosure** sale are insufficient to satisfy the debt, a judgment may be issued against the borrower for the deficiency. However, when a deficiency occurs after a nonjudicial foreclosure, either by a trustee or by the mortgagee under a power-of-sale clause, no such judgment is entered. Deficiency actions are not allowed in Federal Housing Administration (FHA) loans, and the Department of Veterans Affairs (VA) is reluctant to allow them.

■ AVOIDING FREQUENT FUTURE FORECLOSURES

Emergency legislation in 2008 was designed to reduce the likelihood of future waves of foreclosure like the one in the first decade of the 21st century. Based on the premise that borrowers had been lured into debt beyond their means and lenders had turned a blind eye to applicants' poor credit history, the legislation sought to require understandable explanations so that the terms of every mortgage agreement would be understandable to borrowers. People who sign off on application information at every level must be identified, and stiff penalties are specified for failing to follow the new guidelines. Additionally, lenders will be penalized for pressuring appraisers to inflate appraisals to fit unrealistic offers, and so on.

■ REDUCING RESIDENTIAL MORTGAGE DEFAULTS AND FORECLOSURES

Preventive Legislation

In 2008, the *Protection of Homeowners in Foreclosure Act* was passed forbidding *mortgage fraud*, defined as

■ knowingly making any deliberate misstatement, misrepresentation, or omission (or using such misrepresentations by others) during the mortgage lending process with the intent that they be relied on by a mortgage lender, borrower, or any other party to the mortgage lending process;

■ receiving any proceeds or any other funds related to the closing of a mortgage loan involving such misstatements and misrepresentations;

■ conspiring to do either of the above; or

■ recording any document related to a mortgage loan that the filer knows to contain such misstatements.

Violation of this law can bring felony convictions and maximum penalties of $5,000 and imprisonment for not more than 1 year, $15,000 and 15 years if the victim is a vulnerable adult, and $100,000 and 20 years for a pattern of violation of mortgage fraud.

Other Preventive Legislation

Identifying lenders and originators when mortgages first recorded. Subject to issuance of new rules by the Commissioner of Financial Regulation, to be accepted for recordation, a mortgage must contain the names of, and other information about, both the mortgage originator and the mortgage lender. Rules for these latter disclosures and penalties for failure to make them are to be determined and published by the Commissioner. Actions to foreclose filed prior to April 3, 2008, did not have to meet these requirements.

Remedial legislation: slowing the foreclosure process. Changes in law in 2008 require that, with certain exceptions, an action to foreclose a mortgage on residential property may not be filed until either 90 days after default or 45 days after notice of intent to foreclose is sent to the delinquent borrower and the owner of the property—whichever is later. This replaces the previous 15-day minimum waiting period.

Curbing misleading practices of faux "consultants." Legislation passed in 2007, and strengthened in 2008, imposes heavy penalties on unauthorized persons who offer or attempt to perform foreclosure "rescue." During the wave of mortgage difficulties in the present decade, predatory "rescuing" behavior by parties who actually intend to be foreclosure purchasers rather than "rescuers" has included representations that the foreclosure purchasers

- will "save" a homeowner's house (or similar language),
- are acting as "advisors" to the delinquent homeowner, and/or
- hold certifications or licenses they do not actually hold.

Such representations and many other promises often persuaded unwary homeowners to agree to actions resulting in loss of their home, being stripped of any equity they had in it, and forfeiture of their good credit.

The 2008 Maryland *Mortgage Fraud Protection Act* requires foreclosure consultants, except attorneys and certain others, to be licensed as real estate brokers and to provide homeowners with their research on values related to a defaulting property. It also requires that contracts and agreements with—and notices and disclosures to—defaulting borrowers during foreclosure consulting be in the language of the defaulting borrowers—that language used in the interviews with them. It makes a violation of the Act an unfair or deceptive trade practice under the Maryland Consumer Protection Act, punishable by fines of as much as $10,000 and three years imprisonment.

■ MORTGAGE INTEREST RATE LIMITS AND PREPAYMENT

In Maryland, there is no limit on the rate of interest lenders may charge in first mortgage loans. The state interest ceiling on second mortgage loans and land installment contracts is 24 percent. The written agreement between mortgagor and mortgagee must specify the rate of interest.

If the agreement between mortgagor and mortgagee does *not* expressly limit prepayment and/or impose a penalty for it, a mortgage debt can be prepaid at any time without penalty. But when such a penalty *has* been agreed to, it may not exceed two month's advance interest on the total of all amounts prepaid within a 12-month period that are more than one-third of the original loan.

For example:

> Original loan: $90,000 for 10 years at 8%
> Partial prepayments made in Year 3: $25,000 + $15,000 = $40,000
> This $40,000 is $10,000 more than 1/3 of the original loan.
> Therefore, two months' interest on $10,000 at 8% = $133.33 prepayment charge.

Legislation in 2008 established that if a bank pays various expenses of a borrower (closing expenses) and the borrower later prepays the loan, the bank may then recover from the borrower—at any time before the end of the loan's term—all the costs it had incurred on the borrower's behalf and the amount will not be regarded as prepaid interest, or a "prepayment penalty." The procedure merely makes the borrower repay the closing costs that the lender had previously advanced on the borrower's behalf.

Banks' ability to recover such costs has been the subject of sharp controversy, pitting Maryland courts against federal regulators, who hold that federal powers preempt powers of states in regulating nationally related banks and their subsidiaries. In short, Maryland's restrictions were stricter than federal ones on banks' recovering borrowers' settlement costs that the banks had paid. The new law may put this conflict to rest.

A lender who violates the usury ceiling for second mortgages, except for a bona fide error of computation, may collect only the principal amount of the loan and may not collect *any* interest, costs, or other charges with respect to the loan. In addition, a lender who *knowingly* violates any provision of this portion of the law shall forfeit to the borrower three times the amount of interest and charges already collected in excess of that authorized by law, or $500, whichever is greater.

■ MORTGAGE EXPENSE ACCOUNTS

Under Maryland law, lending institutions (banks, savings banks, and savings associations) that require a **tax and insurance expense account** for first mortgage loans must pay interest on these funds at passbook rate but not less than 3 percent. The interest is computed on the average monthly balance in the escrow account and paid annually by crediting the borrower's account with the amount of interest due. This payment is reported to the IRS on a Form 1099. The requirement to pay interest continues even when loans are sold into the secondary market, if the original lending institution continues to service them.

■ DISCRIMINATION

Under Maryland law, a lender may not refuse loans to any person based solely on geographic area, neighborhood, race, religion, color, age, sex, disability, marital status, familial status, or national origin. However, a lender may refuse to make a loan based on higher than normal risks connected with the loan.

■ GROUND RENT: FHA/DVA LOANS

The Department of Veterans Affairs will guarantee loans only on properties subject to ground rent that are located in Anne Arundel County, Baltimore City, Baltimore County, and the Joppatowne subdivision in Harford County. If a veteran purchases leasehold property located in another part of the State using such financing—formerly called a *GI loan*—the ground rent must be redeemed on or prior to the date of closing.

For Federal Housing Administration (FHA) loans on Maryland property held subject to a ground rent, the residential mortgage limit must be reduced by the capitalization value of the annual ground rent. Ground rents are discussed in Chapter 13 of this book.

■ RELEASE OF MORTGAGE LIEN

When a mortgage note has been fully repaid by the borrower, the lender must prepare and provide to the borrower a release of lien document. This may be either a **satisfaction of mortgage** or a **deed of release.** Although the lender will often record this instrument, it is the borrower's responsibility to ensure that the document actually does get recorded.

In some instances, a mortgagee simply enters the statement of release directly in the margin of the recorded mortgage instrument; then that document is rerecorded so that the public record will indicate the release. Recording the release provides public notice that the original mortgage lien has been canceled.

■ MORTGAGE PRESUMED PAID

A mortgage or deed of trust will be presumed to have been paid and the lien created by that document removed if a period of 12 years has elapsed since the last payment date called for in the instrument (its **maturity date**). Alternatively, if the maturity date cannot be ascertained and 40 years have elapsed since the date of the document's recording, the mortgage will be presumed paid and the lien extinguished.

■ FORECLOSURES AND TRUSTEE SALES

The mortgage or deed of trust—but not the note—must be recorded before a lender may start foreclosure proceedings in case of borrower default. State law requires that to record a residential mortgage or deed of trust, a lender must execute and attach an affidavit to each mortgage stating

■ that the mortgage document accurately sets forth the amount of the loan, and
■ that the entire amount was disbursed when the mortgage was executed or delivered to the lender by the borrower.

When a mortgage does not contain a provision giving the mortgagee the power of sale, a foreclosure sale ordered and supervised by the court is the lender's final remedy for default by the borrower.

Because there is no statutory right of redemption in Maryland, a defaulted borrower has to make redemption by paying the necessary funds to the mortgagee *before* the sale has been completed—that is, before the court officer delivers the sale deed to the foreclosure purchaser.

Mortgagees or trustees are permitted to purchase properties in default at their sale rather than selling them to satisfy debts, provided they have diligently attempted to obtain the best possible price for each property on the market.

Holders of subordinate interests in real property may record a request for a **notice of sale,** requiring holders of superior interests in property to give notice of an impending foreclosure sale. They must file a **surplus money action** to receive any of the proceeds of a scheduled foreclosure sale that are not used to satisfy superior liens. If holders of such junior liens fail to do these things, their liens will be extinguished, no matter how large the proceeds from the sale.

Note that a foreclosure sale under a deed of trust or mortgage in default may terminate any leaseholds on the property that began after the deed of trust was executed and recorded. Leaseholds entered into before the date of the mortgage may survive, if they meet requirements for recordation of leases longer than seven years. Tenants whose leases contain subordination agreements or who have later granted such agreements will not be protected. Strict foreclosure, as described in the principles text, is not recognized in Maryland.

■ LAND INSTALLMENT CONTRACTS

The State law regarding land installment contract sales of real estate is found in the Annotated Code of Maryland in Title 10 of the *Real Property* Article. Note that this law applies only to the sale of improved properties, occupied or to be occupied by the purchaser for a dwelling, or of an unimproved, subdivided lot or lots intended to be improved for residential purposes. In other cases, common-law rules apply with fewer protections for **vendees** (purchasers).

Land installment contracts should be prepared and processed by attorneys. The purchaser may rescind the contract and demand that all sums paid be returned if the vendor does not record the contract within 15 days of its being signed by all parties. Land installment contract financing also requires cumbersome ongoing reporting by the vendor for protection of the purchaser.

■ JUNIOR FINANCING

The maximum interest rate a lender may charge in Maryland for a **secondary mortgage** (what Maryland statutes call a mortgage other than a first mortgage) is 24 percent; the maximum loan origination fee that may be charged is $250 or 10 percent of the proceeds of the loan, whichever is less. Only an actual cost, such as a recording fee or title insurance, may be charged in addition to the origination fee. A lender may refinance a junior loan not more than once in any 12-month period and not more than twice during any 5-year period. The *Commercial Law* Article of the Maryland Annotated Code sets forth the details.

Maryland law permits all fees, discounts, and points allowed or required under federally related second mortgage purchase programs. However, the points and the contract interest rate combined may not exceed an annual percentage rate (APR) of 24 percent.

Prohibited Practices   Junior (secondary loan) **lenders** in Maryland are prohibited from certain practices, including the following:

- ■ Attempting to have debtors waive their legal rights
- ■ Requiring accelerated payments for any reason other than default

■ Having debtors execute assignments of wages for payment of loans
■ Charging a fee to execute a release after a loan is paid

Balloon Payments   Maryland Secondary Mortgage Law requires that lenders, including private sellers, who take back a second mortgage containing a **balloon clause** (a clause that makes the final payment significantly larger than previous payments) grant—upon the borrower's request—an automatic, one-time, six-month extension beyond the maturity date. This provision applies to second mortgage loans made for buying residential property for owner occupancy.

■ RESIDENTIAL PROPERTY LOAN NOTICES

Lenders who make loans on residential property are required to provide prospective borrowers with a written notice informing them of their right to choose an attorney or a title insurance company. This notice must be provided within three days of their application for the loan. Lenders are also required to notify applicants that by completing their loan applications, they are terminating any right they might have had to rescind the contract for lack of a Property Disclosure and Disclaimer statement. The Secondary Mortgage Loan Law is Title 12 of the *Commercial Law* Article.

QUESTIONS

1. Mortgages on Maryland real property
   1. must be recorded to be valid between lender and borrower.
   2. may not be refused to any persons because of their religion.
   3. by law must be for a minimum ten-year term.
   4. may be foreclosed by strict foreclosure if in default.

2. Hugh James purchased his home with the aid of a balloon second mortgage that has reached the end of its term. Now that the balloon payment is coming due, he
   1. must pay the final (balloon) payment immediately or risk foreclosure.
   2. is entitled to automatic refinancing of the remaining balance.
   3. automatically receives a six-month extension.
   4. must be granted a six-month extension if he now requests it from the lender.

3. When Thomas Lowell obtained a loan to purchase a new home from BNN Savings Bank, BNN failed to record the mortgage document. The mortgage does not give BNN the power of sale in case of default. Which of the following is TRUE?
   1. As things stand, BNN Savings Bank will be able to enforce the mortgage in a court of law if Lowell defaults on his loan.
   2. If Lowell defaults on the loan, BNN cannot foreclose on the mortgage until the instrument is recorded.
   3. As mortgagor, it is Lowell's obligation to record the mortgage for his own protection.
   4. If Lowell defaults on the loan, BNN could sell the property without foreclosure action.

4. Bonita Harrison needs $365,000 to purchase a new home from a builder. She borrows it from First Maryland Savings Bank. Which of the following security arrangements may First Maryland Savings Bank use?
   1. Mortgage or deed of trust
   2. Real estate trust
   3. Installment contract
   4. Deed of release

5. Alpha Spurlin obtains a 30-year loan from Liberty Savings Association to purchase a Baltimore condominium unit. Along with monthly payments of principal and interest, the lender requires that she pay amounts for deposit into an escrow account for the later payment of taxes and property insurance. Which of the following is TRUE?
   1. Liberty Savings must pay Spurlin interest on these escrow deposits when the loan is paid off.
   2. Spurlin may require the lender to maintain her escrow account in an interest-bearing depository.
   3. Liberty Savings must credit Spurlin's account with passbook-rate interest—but not less than 3 percent—on her escrow deposits annually.
   4. Spurlin must pay the lender a minimum of 3 percent interest for maintaining such an account for her.

CHAPTER

13

Leases

■ KEY TERMS

cognovit clause
common-law estates
confess judgment clause
constructive eviction
constructive notice
damages
dispossess
dispossession
  proceedings

distraint
exculpatory clause
holding over
inception of a lease
leased fee
leasehold
lease with option to
  purchase
memorandum of lease

periodic tenancies
possession
recorded
security deposits
tenant rights
warranty of habitability

■ OVERVIEW

Leaseholds in Maryland are the four familiar **common-law estates:** (1) leases for a specified time period ("for years"), (2) leases from period to period ("from year to year"), (3) tenancies at will, and (4) tenancies at sufferance. Long-term ground leases, an example of the first type, are common in certain areas.

■ MARYLAND GROUND RENTS

Ground leases exist in many areas in the State. Some of them may be redeemed (freed from ground rent) after specified periods, while others are irredeemable. The ground lease tenant typically owns the improvements located on the rented ground. One reason developers might establish a ground rent would be to keep the selling price of houses they have built within the financial reach of more purchasers. The purchaser of a house under ground rent does not have to purchase the lot, just rent it. If the purchaser/tenant does not pay the rent, however, the owner of the ground can record, and then foreclose, a lien on the property and thus take title to it in fee, together with the improvements (buildings) on it. This would leave the original purchaser with nothing—neither the house nor the land.

Ground rental is money paid to the landowner (landlord) by a tenant who possesses the landlord's land by virtue of a lease. Such leases usually give tenants possession of land for a specific term not to exceed 99 years. Possession of the land reverts (goes back) to the fee simple landowner when the lease finally expires, if it is terminated by the tenant's default, or if it is not renewed. Some ground leases have options for renewal for additional terms, either at predetermined, graduated rentals, or at rentals to be based on reappraisal of the land and improvements at the time of renewal.

It is apparently the intention of the Maryland legislature to end as many ground leases on residential property in Maryland as possible. "Residential" is defined as property with four or fewer residential units.

Legislation passed in 2007 made all previously irredeemable residential ground leaseholds subject to redemption on September 30, 2010, unless the ground landlords (the "holders" of ground leases) record their intention to preserve irredeemability. In that event, the leases are extended for ten years. At the end of the extension, the owners again may record such intentions, and so on, every ten years. If notice of intention to preserve irredeemability is not filed before 2010 or before any ten-year renewal term expires, the land becomes subject to redemption by the tenant by capitalizing the annual ground rent at 6 percent.

As amended in 2007, the law now states that any residential ground lease—that is not an irredeemable ground lease—for a term of 15 years or longer may be redeemed *at any time* (no more waiting periods of 3 or 5 years) at the option of the tenant upon 30 days notice to the landlord. If the lease were created on any date between April 6, 1888, and July 1, 1982, it may be redeemed at 6 percent; if created since July 2, 1982, at 12 percent. (Redemption at 12 percent costs half as much as redemption at 6 percent.) Properties may be redeemed for lesser sums if stipulated in the leases, or they may be redeemed for any sum to which the parties agree at the time of redemption.

A transferee who becomes holder of a ground lease is now required to notify the leasehold tenants, within 30 days of becoming owner, of their right to redeem the property and invite them to contact the new holder for details of such procedure.

Settlement agents must inform purchasers who borrow money to purchase a residential property that is under redeemable ground rent that it is redeemable for a specified cost and that the cost can be rolled into the amount of the (purchase) loan being made.

Creation of a Ground Rent

Since 2007, owners of a fee simple or leasehold estates in residential property that is suitable for—or being used for—four or fewer dwelling units *may not subject them to ground leases or ground subleases.* Some properties may still be subjected to ground leases: commercial property, mobile home sites, condos, co-ops, and other residential uses involving more than four dwellings.

Ground Rent Disclosure

When property subject to ground rent is sold, the contract of sale must inform the buyer that nonpayment of the ground rental may result in

■ loss of the entire property, in fee, to the ground landlord; and
■ termination of the buyer's leasehold.

Owners, or licensees representing them, when posting signs on ground rent property for sale, are required to show on the sign *the amount of annual ground rental and cost of capitalization* in numbers as large and clear as the numbers showing the price of the property.

Land subject to ground rent is not held in fee simple. The holder (ground landlord) has a **leased fee,** and the tenant/occupant has a **leasehold.** Therefore, if a contract of sale for property subject to ground rent does not disclose existence of the ground rent, yet the agreement calls for delivery of fee simple title to the purchaser, the seller must redeem the property before settlement. If the property is irredeemable, the seller cannot deliver fee simple title and will be in breach of contract.

■ MARYLAND RESIDENTIAL LEASES

In the *Real Property* Article, the Maryland Statute of Frauds provides that to be enforceable, leases that end in less than one year need not be in writing. However, those whose term is more than one year must be written. The time periods are measured from the **inception of a lease**—the date the lease agreement is made, not the date of permitted occupancy—until the end of its term.

Leases longer than seven years must be **recorded.** Recordation of a document requires acknowledgment before a notary public or similar official. Note, however, that even when such leases have not been properly recorded, they are still valid and binding between the original parties, against their creditors, and against their successors and assignees who have actual notice of the lease or who acquire the property when a tenant is in actual occupancy. **Possession** (occupancy) of property by a tenant under a lease for seven years or less gives **constructive notice** of the tenant's rights. However, occupancy at any time under an unrecorded lease that is for longer than seven years does not give such notice. It is clear that recording the longer lease serves to protect the tenant, while mere occupancy under a shorter (seven years or less) lease would be enough to protect the tenant. Although the law requires that any lease for a term longer than seven years be recorded, a recorded **memorandum of lease** satisfies this requirement.

Postsettlement Occupancy Excepted

No portions of the Landlord and Tenant statute dealing with residential leases apply when, after the sale of an owner-occupied residence, the sellers and purchasers agree that sellers may remain in possession for 60 days or less. This is called a *postsettlement occupancy agreement.*

Disclosure of Representation

Licensees must provide written disclosure of agency representation to both lessors and lessees when negotiating any residential lease for *longer than 125 days*. This disclosure must be made no later than the first scheduled face-to-face meeting between the licensees and any prospective tenant or landlord. Please review the discussion on disclosure of representation in Chapter 2.

Residential Security Deposits

Landlords may not require **security deposits** of more than two months' rental, and they must give tenants receipts for these deposits. Failure to do so makes them liable to tenants for the sum of $25. More importantly, landlords are liable to tenants for up to three times any security deposit taken in excess of this limit, plus reasonable attorney fees.

Within 30 days of their receipt, deposit monies must be placed and maintained by landlords or their agents in accounts opened for this sole purpose in a branch of a federally insured bank or a savings institution licensed to do business in Maryland.

In lieu of such accounts, a landlord may hold security deposits in insured certificates of deposit issued by banks, described above, or in securities issued by the federal government or the State of Maryland. The total of all these deposit accounts, certificates, and securities must be sufficient in amount to equal all the security deposits for which a landlord or landlord's broker is liable. Broker licensees' records of these funds must be available for inspection by members of the Commission or its agents during normal business hours.

A further statutory protection of residential tenants is that their security deposits held by landlords are protected against attachment by creditors of either the landlords or the tenants.

Residential tenants, when their landlords agree, may now purchase a surety bond to protect their landlords for losses usually covered by the usual rental security deposit. If the landlords agree, tenants may meet security deposit requirements of their landlords by making an all-cash deposit, paying part in cash and providing the other part with a surety bond, or covering it all with a surety bond. The use of such bonds needs the agreement of both landlords and tenants. Tenants may not be required to protect the landlord in an aggregate amount greater than the sum of two months' rental, no matter what the composition of the coverage is. Landlords may not *require* the use of a surety bond at all.

Tenants pay a premium for the bond that protects the landlord for an amount up to two months' rental. The premium for this protection is not returnable, and, unlike a cash security deposit, earns the tenants no interest. Landlords have no interest to pay when there is no cash payment to them as security deposits but only surety bonding.

The law imposes—for the protection of tenants—many protective requirements for landlords' use of such bonds. Tenants have similar protections from the bonding company, if those companies violate detailed requirements imposed on them. The usual penalty against a landlord or a bonding company involves loss of the right to keep any of the security deposit or to claim any payment under the bond or an award to the tenants of three times the amount of money improperly withheld from them plus "reasonable attorney fees." If tenants purchase bonds and landlords then refuse use of bonds, the insurer must return the premiums paid and any other charges associated with applications.

At the time leases are written, landlords must give tenants written notice of various **tenant rights.** One example is the right to demand from landlords, at the beginning of leases, written reports of property condition inspections made in the presence of the new tenants. They must request these property-condition inspections by certified mail within 15 days of taking occupancy. Landlords who fail to provide these reports to tenants who make the proper request become liable to the tenants for as much as three times the amount of any security deposit taken. This amount could be offset (reduced) by amounts due in unpaid rent and tenant damages to the premises.

Tenants also have the right to request by certified mail—sent at least 15 days before their intended move-out—to be present at the final inspection. Landlords must set dates between five days before and five days after intended move-outs and notify the tenants in writing of these dates.

When leases are terminated, landlords must return tenants' security deposits within 45 days, together with simple interest at the statutory rate—presently 3 percent per annum. Interest accrues at six-month intervals from the day the tenant gives the security deposit and does not compound.

Security deposits may be withheld by landlords at the end of leases to cover

- unpaid rent;
- losses due to breach or violation of lease terms (the landlord is entitled only to the actual financial loss—**damages**—caused by the breach); and
- cost of repairs to leased premises because of damage to the leased premises by the tenants or their families, guests, agents, invitees, or employees in excess of ordinary wear and tear.

Landlords who wish to withhold deposits to compensate them for damages must present to their tenants, within 45 days of the termination of the tenancy, written statements of amounts actually expended in the repair of damages. Estimates without paid receipts do not satisfy this requirement. Once again, failure to comply with this requirement makes landlords liable to tenants for three times the amount of security deposits wrongfully withheld, plus reasonable attorney fees. In addition, landlords may lose their right to recover from the security deposit any unpaid rent or rental income lost due to breach of lease. A legal action concerning security deposits may be brought by tenants any time during tenancy or within two years after its termination. Tenants may not waive any of the protections provided in this section of the law. Any provision purporting to do so in a lease agreement would be of no force and effect. Regrettably, there is no prohibition against having such a "waiver" in a lease, even when its purpose appears to be intimidation of the tenants.

State law requires that landlords maintain systems of orderly records showing dates of payment and amounts of rent paid by tenants. Landlords must also retain copies of receipts given to tenants for cash rental payments.

■ MISCELLANEOUS REQUIREMENTS

Note that Baltimore County and City landlords must give tenants of multifamily dwellings notice when they are located in *floodplain areas*.

Owners of residential rental units in Baltimore City must file an *annual registration statement* with the Baltimore City Commissioner of Housing and Community Development, whether the units are occupied or not, and pay a registration fee. Other jurisdictions also may have registration requirements and conduct periodic inspections.

Owners of multifamily residential rental property (property having five or more residential units) are required by State law to post in a conspicuous place a sign listing the name, address, and telephone number of the property owner or managing agent. The information may instead be included in the lease or shown on rental receipts.

■ SALE OF LEASED PREMISES

Unless specified to the contrary in the lease, the purchaser of a property occupied by a tenant under a lease is bound by the conditions and terms of that lease, just as the original landlord was. A purchaser of rented property not wishing to become a landlord should include a clause in the property purchase contract requiring that the premises be delivered unoccupied and vacant at the time of settlement. Baltimore City and several other jurisdictions require that a landlord give residential tenants the *right of first refusal* before leased premises can be sold to someone else.

■ TERMINATION OF PERIODIC TENANCIES

The requirements to terminate **periodic tenancies** differ throughout the State. In all counties except Montgomery County and Baltimore City, the landlord must give the tenant *written* notice to terminate, as follows:

■ One week for a week-to-week tenancy
■ One month for a month-to-month tenancy
■ Three months for a year-to-year tenancy

By contrast, a tenant's *parol* (oral) *notice* is sufficient to terminate such tenancies. If landlords can prove that the tenants gave such notice, they do not need to give their own notice to those tenants.

In Montgomery County, the parties may agree in writing to longer or shorter notice periods. However, the local laws of Baltimore City generally require that a landlord give the following written notices to terminate:

■ 60 days for a tenancy of less than one year, or at sufferance
■ 90 days for a periodic tenancy
■ 30 days in all other cases

A tenant may terminate any of these tenancies by giving the landlord 30 days' notice.

Holding Over

When a landlord consents to a tenant's **holding over** (remaining on the premises after the end of the lease term), the tenant becomes a week-to-week tenant if the lease status was week-to-week prior to the holding over. In all other cases, the tenant becomes a month-to-month tenant, unless the lease provides otherwise and this lease provision (stating otherwise) is initialed by the tenant.

A tenant under a lease who *unlawfully* holds over beyond the termination of the lease is liable to the landlord for actual damages that may be caused by the holding over.

Landlords' Rights to Summary Dispossession

Landlords who give the required notice or have court orders for termination of tenancy may **dispossess** tenants and repossess property by simple court suit before a district court judge. The length of notice landlords must give tenants before beginning **dispossession proceedings** is generally one month in renewable monthly tenancies or in tenancies with a fixed term and no provision for renewal. For automatically renewable yearly tenancies, this notice (with certain exceptions) is three months; for renewable monthly or weekly tenancies, it is one month or one week.

Tenant Refusal to Comply

If the tenant or person in possession refuses to comply with the written request to remove from the property, the landlord may make a complaint in writing to the district court of the county where the property is located. The court issues a summons, served by the sheriff to the tenant, to appear before the court, and an attested copy is affixed to the property in a conspicuous place. This is considered sufficient notice.

Back Rent on Renewal of Lease

Tenants or assignees who apply to their landlords for renewal under a covenant in their leases giving them the right to renew must produce vouchers or evidence showing payment of rent accrued for three years preceding this demand and application. If tenants do not provide such proof, landlords, before executing the renewal of the lease, are entitled to demand and recover not more than three years' back rent, in addition to any renewal fine that may be provided for in the lease. This commonly occurs in situations involving ground rent.

Failure to Demand Rent

If there is no demand or payment of rent for more than 20 consecutive years, landlords lose not only the unpaid rental but also the reversion of the property. Therefore, a landlord's failure to demand rent for 20 years could result in the tenant's receiving fee simple title. Landlords under any legal disability when the 20-year period expires have 2 years after the removal of the disability to assert their rights.

Receipts for Tenants' Rental

In Anne Arundel County, unless the tenant makes payment by check or rents the property for commercial or business purposes, the landlord is required to give the tenant a receipt showing the amount of payment and the time it covers. If convicted of violating this section of the law, any person or agent forfeits the rent for the period in question.

In other counties, when the tenant makes payment other than by check, the landlord or the landlord's agent must simply give the tenant a receipt.

Surrender of Premises   When a lease contains a covenant or promise by the tenant to leave, restore, surrender, or yield the leased premises in good repair, this does not bind the tenant to erect any similar building or pay for any building destroyed by fire or otherwise, if the damage was not due to the negligence or fault of the tenant.

Landlords may ask the district court to seize and sell tenants' personal property for unpaid rent by filing a petition. Landlords may do this only if tenancy has continued for longer than three months (by written lease or periodic tenancy) or was *at will*. **Distraint** is the term used for a landlord's right both to seize and sell such property and for the court's action in awarding this right.

A rental agreement must clearly state information such as when tenancy expires, when rent accrues, or whether rent is to be paid in advance or in arrears. If it does not, a court may find the agreement's terms too vague and deny the landlord's request for distraint.

■ PROHIBITED RESIDENTIAL LEASE PROVISIONS

In Maryland, the following provisions are prohibited in residential leases:

- A provision (**cognovit clause**) that authorizes an attorney for the landlord to plead the tenant guilty (**confess judgment clause**) on a claim arising from the lease, especially failure to pay rental
- A provision under which the tenant agrees to waive or forgo any rights or remedies against the landlord as provided by law
- A provision allowing the landlord to charge a penalty for late payment of rent that is more than 5 percent of the amount of rent due for the period in which the rent is delinquent. (In weekly rentals, this late charge may not exceed $3 per week or $12 per month.)
- Any provision under which the tenant waives the right to a jury trial
- Any provision under which the tenant agrees to a period for the landlord's notice to quit (in the event that the tenant breaches the lease terms) that is less than the period prescribed by law (Both parties, however, are free to agree to a period that is *longer* than that prescribed by law.)
- Any provision authorizing the landlord to take possession of the leased premises or any of the tenant's personal property, unless the lease has been terminated by operation of law and such personal property has been abandoned by the tenant
- Any **exculpatory clause**—that is, language in the lease intended to exempt or hold the landlord harmless from liability to the tenant or any other person for any injury, loss, damage, or liability arising from the landlord's omission, fault, negligence, or other misconduct on or about the leased premises in areas that are not under the tenant's control (e.g., stairways, elevators, hallways, and so forth)
- A provision (not specifically signed or initialed by the tenant) allowing the automatic renewal of the lease term for a period longer than one month

■ A requirement that the tenant give the landlord a longer period of notice to terminate the tenancy than the period granted the landlord to similarly notify the tenant

All of the preceding provisions, if included in a Maryland lease, are considered *unenforceable*. Landlords who threaten or attempt to enforce one or more of these provisions may be liable to a tenant for actual damages and attorney's fees incurred as a result. Unfortunately for tenants, there is no penalty for a landlord's merely including these clauses in a lease.

■ WITHHOLDING RENT

Maryland law requires that a landlord provide and maintain premises for residential tenants that are free of defects and do not present substantial and serious threats of danger to the life, health, and safety of the tenants. Where hazardous conditions exist on leased property, a tenant may give the landlord written notice by certified mail of the conditions and then wait as long as 30 days. If the hazardous conditions are not corrected within that period, a tenant may withhold rent from the landlord or pay it into an escrow account for necessary repairs. Such conditions include fire or health hazards or other defects that may threaten the safety or occupancy of renters, such as

■ lack of adequate sewage disposal facilities;
■ infestation of rodents in two or more dwelling units; or
■ failure to meet the standards set in the *Environment* Article at §6-815 or §6-819 for dealing with lead-based paint hazards. (See Table 13.1 and Chapter 14 in this book.)

Such a situation is *not* **constructive eviction**, because in constructive eviction, tenants finds any continued occupancy impossible and so move out.

The Baltimore City Code holds that there is an implied **warranty of habitability** by a landlord that the premises are fit for human habitation. It also provides for remedies for tenants if the premises are unsafe and dirty to the extent that the tenants' health is threatened. The warranty of habitability differs from *rent escrow laws* in that tenants already have the use of their rent money to make those repairs the landlord has failed to complete. Under the rent escrow law, rent must be paid into an account, where it is held until the repairs are made.

The district court can order tenants to pay rents into a *rent escrow account* of the court or administrative agency of the county. If the tenant fails to pay rent accrued or as it becomes due, the court, on certification of the account, can give judgment in favor of the landlord and issue a warrant for possession. On final disposition of the action, the rent escrow account is distributed in accordance with a judgment or hearing.

Note that minor, not dangerous, defects or housing code violations that go uncorrected are not considered just cause for nonpayment of rent.

Tenants' Rights to End Leases and Receive Relocation Expenses

If owners of affected properties fail to comply with applicable risk reduction standards to make their properties lead-safe, tenants may make formal, documented written requests to be released from their leases and receive up to $2,400 relocation expense awards for moving to properties that meet risk-reduction standards. Landlords have three days to produce valid risk-reduction satisfaction certificates, lead-free certificates, or certification that required work has been completed. If owners fail to provide such information in accordance with this request within three business days, tenants may bring actions in District Court for the relief requested: termination of lease, relocation expenses, and reasonable attorney fees.

■ LEASE AGREEMENT FORMS

A number of lease forms are available from local realty boards or associations, property owner associations, and tenant organizations. Any landlord who offers more than four dwelling units for rent on one parcel of property or at one location and who rents by means of written leases substantially increases the requirements concerning the form of written leases.

■ RETALIATORY EVICTIONS

A landlord may not evict tenants, increase rent, or decrease any services to which they are entitled for tenants' doing any of the following:

■ Filing written complaints with the landlord or with a public agency against the landlord
■ Filing a lawsuit against the landlord
■ Joining a tenants organization

■ PEACEABLE AND QUIET ENTRY

Landlords are required by law to ensure that tenants may peaceably and quietly enter the leased premises at the beginning of the lease. Failure to do so allows the tenant, on written notice to the landlord before possession is delivered, to rescission of the lease, abatement of rent, or actual damages.

■ SAFETY REQUIREMENTS

Tenant safety is an ongoing concern of landlords and their agents and property managers.

Compliance with Risk Reduction Laws

Licensees helping to rent older properties must be prepared to protect their clients and their customers meet the lead-based paint hazards disclosure requirements outlined in Table 13.1.

TABLE   13.1

Lead-Based Paint Disclosure and Registration Requirements

Dates	Federal Compliance Requirements
Built before 1/1/1978 "Targeted Property"	Both of the following must be given to all lessees at the beginning of every tenancy and again every two years. Tenants' receipt of these is to be verified by their signature. 1. EPA Booklet, *Protect Your Family From Lead in Your Home*, to be given to all lessees at the beginning and renewal of every lease 2. "Lead Based Paint (Rental) Disclosure Form," to be given and signed, and copies kept.

	Maryland Compliance Requirements
Built before 1/1/1950 "Affected Property"	1. The property must be registered with the Maryland Department of the Environment and then reregistered annually. 2. Before a property is rented, it must be inspected by state-approved inspectors and any necessary abatement performed. 3. Maryland Department of the Environment Pamphlet *Notice of Tenants' Rights* and the EPA Booklet, *Protect Your Family From Lead in Your Home* are to be given to tenants at the beginning of every tenancy, every two years thereafter, and whenever the rental changes.

See Chapter 14 for more details on lead-based paint hazards.

Sprinkler Systems

Sprinkler systems must be installed in every newly constructed dormitory, hotel, lodging or rooming house, town house, and multifamily residential dwelling. Sprinkler systems are not required, however, if a dwelling unit is not serviced by a public water supply system.

Smoke Detectors

Smoke detectors must be installed in all multifamily buildings and hotels constructed before 1975 and having four to nine units and in *all* buildings—*regardless of when they were built*—having more than nine units. The landlord is responsible for the installation, repair, or replacement of the detectors. The *occupant* of a one-family, two-family, or three-family residential dwelling constructed before July 1975 is required to equip the apartment with at least one approved smoke detector and to maintain the smoke detector. A smoke detector operated both by battery and by alternating current (AC) must be installed in every newly constructed residential dwelling unit. At least one smoke detector must be installed on each level, including basements but not attics.

Carbon Monoxide Alarms

All residential housing—including apartments and condos as well as commercial properties that contain sleeping quarters—that uses fossil-based fuel for any heating, cooling, cooking, or lighting purpose must be equipped with hard-wired carbon monoxide alarms within specified distances of sleeping areas and connected to a central system. Systems must conform to various national and State building technical specifications. This requirement applies to structures with building permits issued after January 1, 2009.

■ LEASE OPTION AGREEMENTS

A **lease with option to purchase** includes any lease that contains a clause giving the tenant the right to purchase the landlord's interest in the property until some specified date. No lease option on improved residential property in Maryland, with or without a ground rent interest, is valid unless it contains the statement "THIS IS NOT A CONTRACT TO BUY" in capital letters. It must also contain a clear statement of the option's purpose and effect with respect to the ultimate purchase of the property. The purchase price of the property as well as a consideration for the option privilege itself—even if only a nominal (token) amount—must both be recited.

■ MOBILE HOME PARKS

Title 8A of the *Real Property* Article sets forth the rights and responsibilities of mobile home park tenants and owners. It addresses such matters as park rules, maintenance, and tenancy.

■ SOURCES OF ASSISTANCE

Baltimore Neighborhoods Inc., a private nonprofit civil rights agency working in behalf of fair housing and tenants' rights in the Baltimore area, publishes guides to laws covering tenant-landlord relations in Baltimore City, the counties, and the State. These guides, revised annually to incorporate new laws, may be purchased from the organization at 2217 St. Paul St., Baltimore, MD 21218. The organization's Web address is *www.bni-maryland.org*.

Students can also find the text of the Landlord and Tenant Law, in the Real Property Article, at *www.michie.com*. Once there, choose "Michie's Code of Maryland," then "Real Property," then "Title 8."

QUESTIONS

1. Sampson sold a house he owned that was occupied by Rawlins under a one-year lease having six months to run. Therefore,
   1. Rawlins must vacate at the closing of the sale.
   2. Rawlins's lease continues until its expiration.
   3. the lease terminates at closing.
   4. the lease is not binding on the new owner.

2. A landlord holding a tenant's security deposit of $2,400 is required to
   1. credit the tenant with $72 interest after one year.
   2. allow the tenant 5 percent simple interest per year.
   3. return the deposit within 30 days after termination of the lease.
   4. give the tenant a receipt or be liable to the tenant for a sum of $1,200.

3. In Maryland, which of the following leases does NOT need to be acknowledged, recorded, and in writing?
   1. Seven-year apartment lease
   2. Eight-year residential lease
   3. Nine-year commercial lease
   4. Ten-year residential lease

4. Jane Builder has just completed a new house, which she is offering for sale at $240,000 with fee simple title. If, to satisfy an immediate buyer, she creates a ground lease requiring $720 a year ground rent at a 6 percent redemption rate, then
   1. the property may not be redeemed for at least 50 years.
   2. she can reduce the price to $228,000.
   3. she can reduce the price to $225,600.
   4. the in-fee price would be $235,680.

5. Arthur Buyer is interested in purchasing a residence for $325,000 with a ground rent of $1,250. Arthur will receive
   1. a deed conveying to him a fee simple interest.
   2. a leasehold estate subject to an annual ground rent of $1,250.
   3. no deed until such time as he redeems the ground rent.
   4. a fee simple deed after paying ground rent for five years.

6. A woman who bought and occupied her home but has to pay a semiannual ground rent owns a real estate interest called a(n)
   1. fee simple estate.
   2. leasehold estate.
   3. estate at will.
   4. estate at sufferance.

7. Ground rents are sometimes originated to
   1. reduce the amount of cash required to purchase a property.
   2. force the tenant to keep the property in good repair.
   3. provide further assurances to the mortgagee.
   4. prevent the lender from foreclosing.

8. The ground rent on a residence is $600 a year, and the lease has been in effect for more than five years. A redemption at
   1. 5 percent will require $6,000.
   2. 6 percent will require $10,000.
   3. 10 percent will require $7,500.
   4. 12 percent will require $15,000.

9. The right of a residential landlord to have a court seize and sell a tenant's personal property for unpaid rent is called
   1. ejectment.
   2. abandonment.
   3. dispossession.
   4. distraint.

10. Which of the following provisions, if included in residential leases in Maryland, is enforceable?
    1. Tenants agree to pay the landlord a 5 percent penalty for late rent payments.
    2. Tenants agree to let landlords use their pass-keys to take possession of tenants' property if tenants fall more than one month behind in rent payments.
    3. Tenants agree to waive or forgo any rights or remedies against landlords provided by law.
    4. Tenants waive their rights to jury trial.

14

Environmental Issues and Real Estate Transactions

■ KEY TERMS

affected properties
asbestos
carcinogenic

jointly and severally
methyl tertiary-butyl ether
(MTBE)

mold
storage tanks

■ OVERVIEW

Maryland, like most states, faces complex environmental challenges. Almost all of them call for balancing economic vitality with environmental concerns, human safety, and quality of life. These tensions can pit the rights of property owners against the wishes of others for preservation or restoration of natural resources. Nationwide, literally hundreds of statutes, ordinances, and regulations are written each year to address these matters.

Various resources dealing with Maryland environmental concerns and programs are available at the Web site of the Maryland Department of the Environment (MDE): *www.mde.state.md.us*.

■ MULTIPLE CHALLENGES

Environmental concerns include the loss of woodlands, farmlands, tidal and non-tidal wetlands. These concerns overlap other ecological issues, such as endangered species, clean air, clean water, fisheries, and other wildlife. Recreation and camping needs are also part of the puzzle.

Hazards to human health include auto emissions and other air and/or water pollution from ozone, asbestos, radon, radium, lead-based paint, wastewater sewage, industrial waste, leakage from underground storage tanks, and acid rain.

■ MEETING THE CHALLENGES

The Maryland Smart Growth Initiative is designed to motivate local jurisdictions in the State to plan more effectively for growth without "suburban sprawl"—the wasteful use of space accompanying construction of housing further and further from urban centers. In the words of the *Maryland Manual Online*, "Maryland is committed to limiting sprawl development by revitalizing older neighborhoods and redirecting growth to already developed areas, thereby saving the State's farmland, open spaces, and natural resources." For a better understanding of smart growth in this State, consult the Maryland Office of Smart Growth at *www.smartgrowth.state.md .us/sginmd.htm*.

■ MULTILEVEL APPROACHES

The State reaches upward, outward, and inward in its efforts: upward toward federal agencies, outward toward neighboring states, and inward to subdivisions and municipalities. To this last group, the State typically grants enabling powers to authorize their participation through zoning and other environmentally related activities. Various subdivisions are authorized to set standards even more rigorous than those set by the State. If they are less strict than the State's, the more rigorous State laws prevail.

Cooperative Approaches

It is rare that an environmental issue can be handled effectively by the Maryland State government acting alone. Its activities and interests overlap and interact with those of the federal government, neighboring states, State subdivisions and municipalities, and private and corporate citizens.

■ ENFORCEMENT

Enforcement of standards set forth in statutes, regulations, and ordinances is carried out by the MDE except in cases where county enforcement capabilities and resources are comparable to those of that department. The Secretary of MDE may delegate enforcement powers to such counties for a two-year period.

■ THE CHESAPEAKE BAY

The Chesapeake Bay, nearly 200 miles long and fed by 48 major rivers, 100 smaller rivers, and thousands of other tributaries, is the largest and most productive estuary in the United States. It covers 64,000 square miles and provides habitat for myriad species of plants and animals. Its 15-million-person population is expected to swell to 18 million by 2020.

Chesapeake Bay Critical Area Act

This law identifies the *Critical Area* as all land within 1,000 feet of the average high-water line of tidal waters or the landward edge of tidal wetlands and all waters of and lands under the Chesapeake Bay and its tributaries.

The 2008 General Assembly strengthened this and supporting laws by

- giving the Critical Area Commission authority to update and enforce the law,
- allowing the State to revoke the licenses of builders who knowingly violate the law,
- increasing the no-build buffer zone for new subdivisions in rural areas from 100 feet to 200 feet, and
- tightening the rules about where new housing can be located.

The Buffer

The original act had designated as the *Buffer* a 100-foot, natural vegetation, forested zone from the mean high-water line, landward from tidal waters and from the edge of tidal wetlands. That buffer is now 200 feet. The buffer's trees filter runoff water returning to streams and reduce sediments, fertilizers, and toxic substances. Human activities in the area are sharply reduced because of their adverse impact on the nearby waterways and wildlife. No disturbance of the buffer may be permitted by local jurisdictions unless an applicant can meet strict provisions for a variance.

A wealth of interesting and useful information on this matter is found at the Web site of the Critical Area Commission for the Chesapeake and Atlantic Coastal Bays: *www.dnr.state.md.us/criticalarea*.

■ FILLING OF WETLANDS RESISTED

Filling wetlands, for whatever purpose, is regarded as one of the most environmentally pernicious of actions. It may be permitted only when no alternative course of action is available or when the person seeking a permit will create new areas of wetland to compensate for those being filled. The replacement area ratios (new-to-lost) range from 1:1 to 4.5:1.

■ IMPACT ON RESIDENTIAL REAL ESTATE

Many of these environmental issues directly and indirectly affect availability of residential housing. Preserving agricultural space and wetlands reduces the amount of land available for development. Indeed, the present policy of Maryland is not just to maintain but to *increase* the total area of all State wetlands.

In seeking to achieve environmental and public safety goals, the State and its subdivisions impose regulatory and impact fees and increasingly require costly safety measures and techniques that protect both people and the environment. By slowing development and imposing fees on developers—fees that are then passed along to consumers—governments make it more costly for people to buy homes in less developed areas. This is intended to guide renewal of older, developed areas and more intense use of that land, rather than "sprawling" into rural and semirural areas.

One statutory requirement that affects every licensee is that *all* contracts for sale of property suitable for one or two single-family units contain the "Notice to Buyer Concerning the Chesapeake and Atlantic Coastal Bays Critical Area," quoted in full in Chapter 9.

■ MARYLAND DEPARTMENT OF THE ENVIRONMENT

Targeting Asbestos

Within the MDE, the Air and Radiation Management Administration, among its other duties, sets and enforces standards for **asbestos** removal and encapsulation projects and licenses people who work in that field. Much attention of the Department is directed toward asbestos identification and its containment in or removal from public buildings such as public schools, colleges, and universities.

However, asbestos is found in varying amounts in single-family homes, with older homes often having greater amounts. Until the 1970s, asbestos, because of its insulating properties, was a popular component of siding, kitchen floor tiles, and heating and cooling insulation. Licensees should not attempt to answer questions about asbestos and should neither minimize nor exaggerate its effects. Refer questions to companies that are licensed to deal with asbestos.

Waste Management Administration

Also within the MDE is the Waste Management Administration, which deals with environmental restoration and land redevelopment, oil control, lead poisoning, solid waste, scrap tires, sewage sludge, and hazardous materials. It oversees aboveground **storage tanks** for oil and gas and underground tanks for the storage of regulated substances. It seeks to identify, prioritize, and abate contaminated sites.

Owners of certain underground storage tanks containing petroleum products must remove or pay for the removal of tanks that leak. MDE regulations set standards for evidence of the financial responsibility of property owners for costs of cleanup, corrective action, and liability.

Of ongoing concern is the presence of **methyl tertiary-butyl ether (MTBE)** in the air and in groundwater. This substance has been increasingly used to replace tetraethyl lead in gasoline as an agent to reduce knocking in gasoline motors. As federal requirements for clean air get stricter, more MTBE is used. The increased use of such reformulated gasoline (RFG) produces less carbon monoxide (CO) from automobile operation, but, inevitably, some of the MTBE additive gets into the ground and the air—some from spills, some from leaking underground storage tanks (LUSTs), and some from simple evaporation.

MTBE is suspected of being **carcinogenic** (cancer causing), although this characteristic has not yet been proven. Yet, even before MTBE reaches suspected unsafe levels, drinking water infiltrated by it has an unpleasant taste and odor. This problem is especially bothersome in areas where there is no public water supply and citizens use individual wells. Moreover, once MTBE is released into the environment, it breaks down into tertiary butyl alcohol (TBA), which cannot be detected by taste and odor at similar levels of concentration. Enforcement of remediation is most active in areas that do not have public water and where levels from 20 to 40 parts per billion have been detected. Where wells have been affected, property transfers by sale have often been halted. Proper filtration can abate the problem but imposes considerable cost on the party responsible for its installation.

Legislation passed in 2005 now requires the MDE to provide notice to the local health department upon a finding by the Department of specified oil contaminants, including MTBE, in groundwater samples. The local health department then provides owners of property located within one-half mile of a site found to be contaminated with a notice of that fact. The person responsible for an oil discharge is liable for the costs of providing the notice.

Water Management Administration

Among the most important functions within the MDE are those given to the Water Management Administration, which seeks to protect *drinking water*. With its team of inspectors, it also oversees tidal and nontidal wetlands, floodplains, water appropriations, waterway and floodplain construction, sediment control, stormwater management, coal mining, and oil and gas exploration.

Mold

There are a great many varieties of **mold,** some toxic, some irritating, some mildly annoying, and some (such as penicillin) very useful. Mold identification and removal—and the training of technicians to do those things—has become an industry in itself. It is a complex subject about which there is considerable interest, modest knowledge, and quite a bit of fear. There are 50 Web sites offering legal help for people who have found mold in their houses for every 1 Web site giving information about the problem. The presence of mold has inspired dramatic litigation, with some celebrity homeowners suing builders and others for millions of dollars in damages and medical costs.

It is physically difficult to remove toxic mold from a home once it is identified. However, even greater human and financial costs threaten persons who have physical reactions to the presence of mold. Licensees are urged not to disturb mold by, for example, pulling out bathroom drywall or wallpaper. Even dead mold triggers severe allergic reactions in some persons. Licensees are never to assure buyers or tenants that a home is mold-free or even mold-safe. Give no reassurances but do not generate unnecessary fears. Refer all questions to attorneys and certified, licensed experts.

Mold formation can be reduced by proper ventilation of areas where water may condense or drip. Household relative humidity greater than 40 percent encourages mold growth. It thrives on moisture, wood, paper, and darkness. A house with improperly installed roof "flashing" or poorly maintained soffits, drains, and downspouts allows water to find its way into wall spaces, where it joins all the other factors that foster mold growth. Engineering inspections of houses will often reveal situations that can produce mold, even if they do not find the mold itself. Much of Maryland has favorable conditions for mold growth year-round, so proper home construction and maintenance are the leading methods of reducing mold infestation, related respiratory diseases, and possible consequent litigation.

■ REDUCTION OF LEAD RISK IN HOUSING ACT

Maryland's *Reduction of Lead Risk in Housing Act* seeks "to reduce the incidence of childhood lead poisoning, while maintaining the stock of available affordable rental housing." This act, the environmental law that affects more existing Maryland residential properties than any other law, undergirds Maryland's Lead Paint Poisoning Prevention Program.

To see the full text of the *Reduction of Lead Risk in Housing Act*, go to *www.michie.com* and choose "Maryland Code," then "Environment," then "Title 6," then "6-801."

There is broad-based scientific agreement that exposure to lead-based paint can produce devastating results in young children, newborns, and fetuses. This law is an earnest attempt to reduce the exposure of children under age six and of pregnant women to the effects of lead-based paint in residential rental properties built before 1978.

Lead Paint Poisoning Abatement

State and federal legislation concerning lead levels in certain rental properties impose substantial responsibilities and burdens on investor-owners of many income properties and on their agents. At the same time, these laws allow investors to limit their liability for lead poisoning by following certain procedures.

Legislation in 2005 redefined the elevated blood lead level that triggers notification by local health departments as 15 (rather than 20) micrograms per deciliter. It expanded coverage in the original law to include exterior structures, such as playground equipment and benches. It requires that an inspection report state that all interior and exterior surfaces are lead-free or that the interior is lead-free and the exterior surfaces that were chipping, peeling, or flaking have been restored with non-lead-based paint.

Children and Mothers Targeted for Protection

Maryland's Lead Paint Poisoning Prevention Plan makes children under age six and pregnant women with elevated blood lead (EBL) levels eligible for specific financial relief for medical treatment ($7,500) and for relocation to lead-safe housing ($9,500). These amounts come from either landlords or their insurance companies. Investors wishing to limit their liability to their tenants for lead poisoning must bring their property into compliance with lead-safe standards and keep it that way.

Plan Encourages Modest Settlements

The plan doesn't actually limit, or cap, the liability of landlords. Rather, it makes them eligible to present "qualified offers" of amounts up to $7,500 for medical expenses and up to $9,500 for relocation and rent supplement expenses to their tenants found to have EBL levels. If tenants with EBL levels accept the "qualified offer," they give up the right to sue the landlord for larger sums. In exchange, they get their money when they need it and don't have to face the prolonged uncertainty of initiating a lawsuit that may be particularly difficult to win.

Companies insuring residential properties that are or have been made lead-free or lead-safe are required to provide liability coverage for lead paint poisoning up to $17,000 (the total of $7,500 and $9,500).

Active Enforcement

The law is vigorously enforced. Moreover, its requirements increase periodically. Note: **Affected properties** (see Chapter 13) are those constructed before 1950 that contain at least one rental dwelling unit; the term also refers to an individual unit within such a multiunit building, as well as residential rental properties built between 1950 and 1977, for which the owner has opted to comply with this law.

Properties to Be Registered

One statute, in effect since October 1994, divides residential rental properties into two significant groups, based on dates of construction:

1. Before 1950
2. From 1950 through 1977

Based on those classifications, tens of thousands of rental dwelling properties are registered with the MDE. Owners must register every residential rental built before 1950 for a $15 fee and then pay annual renewal fees, also $15, for each. For example, an owner with a home built before 1950, divided into four apartments, must register each unit for $15 and then pay $60/year renewal fees as long as the properties remain in rental use. The annual renewal amount is also $15 per rental unit for post-1950 units whose owners may opt to join the program. The "opt-in" program makes such owners eligible to make qualified offers in the event children are found to be poisoned by lead in properties.

Licensees' Responsibilities

Licensees acting as management agents for landlords who have affected residential rental properties share their clients' legal responsibilities. Consequently, they must become familiar with aspects of inspection, lead reduction procedures, property registration, periodic renewal of registration, insurance, and limitation of liability with respect to lead-paint issues. The State—through its leadership and agencies—is manifesting its determination to pursue the goal of a lead-safe rental environment for the children of Maryland.

■ FEDERAL LAW ALSO APPLIES

The requirements of Maryland law are in addition to and do not take the place of the requirements set forth in federal law concerning lead in residential properties built prior to 1978. The federal law requires distribution of information in the form of the booklet *Protect Your Family From Lead in Your Home* both to potential tenants and to purchasers of properties built before 1978. This 17-page booklet can be seen at and downloaded from *www.epa.gov/lead/pubs/leadpdfe.pdf*.

Additional HUD/EPA requirements require giving *purchasers* a form, "Disclosure of Lead-Based Paint and Lead-Based Paint Hazards." The form becomes a part of the contract to purchase. It allows purchasers to demand as much as a ten-day interval to secure a lead assessment inspection of the property and to rescind the contract if sellers will not correct any deficiencies that are found. But the inspection or risk assessment period can be lengthened, shortened, or waived by mutual written consent between the purchaser and the seller.

The form also contains the sellers' disclosure of all known lead-paint hazards in the property and a lead warning statement. It requires the purchasers' signatures

FIGURE 14.1

Lead-Based Paint Disclosure Form

Disclosure of Information on Lead-Based Paint and/or Lead-Based Paint Hazards

Lead Warning Statement

Every purchaser of any interest in residential real property on which a residential dwelling was built prior to 1978 is notified that such property may present exposure to lead from lead-based paint that may place young children at risk of developing lead poisoning. Lead poisoning in young children may produce permanent neurological damage, including learning disabilities, reduced intelligence quotient, behavioral problems, and impaired memory. Lead poisoning also poses a particular risk to pregnant women. The seller of any interest in residential real property is required to provide the buyer with any information on lead-based paint hazards from risk assessments or inspections in the seller's possession and notify the buyer of any known lead-based paint hazards. A risk assessment or inspection for possible lead-based paint hazards is recommended prior to purchase.

Seller's Disclosure

(a) Presence of lead-based paint and/or lead-based paint hazards (check (i) or (ii) below):

   (i) _____ Known lead-based paint and/or lead-based paint hazards are present in the housing (explain).

   _____

   (ii) _____ Seller has no knowledge of lead-based paint and/or lead-based paint hazards in the housing.

(b) Records and reports available to the seller (check (i) or (ii) below):

   (i) _____ Seller has provided the purchaser with all available records and reports pertaining to lead-based paint and/or lead-based paint hazards in the housing (list documents below).

   _____

   (ii) _____ Seller has no reports or records pertaining to lead-based paint and/or lead-based paint hazards in the housing.

Purchaser's Acknowledgment (initial)

(c) _____ Purchaser has received copies of all information listed above.

(d) _____ Purchaser has received the pamphlet *Protect Your Family from Lead in Your Home.*

(e) Purchaser has (check (i) or (ii) below):

   (i) _____ received a 10-day opportunity (or mutually agreed upon period) to conduct a risk assessment or inspection for the presence of lead-based paint and/or lead-based paint hazards; or

   (ii) _____ waived the opportunity to conduct a risk assessment or inspection for the presence of lead-based paint and/or lead-based paint hazards.

Agent's Acknowledgment (initial)

(f) _____ Agent has informed the seller of the seller's obligations under 42 U.S.C. 4852d and is aware of his/her responsibility to ensure compliance.

Certification of Accuracy

The following parties have reviewed the information above and certify, to the best of their knowledge, that the information they have provided is true and accurate.

Seller	Date	Seller	Date
Purchaser	Date	Purchaser	Date
Agent	Date	Agent	Date

Note: This is the form given by sellers to purchasers. The landlord-to-tenant form is different.

regarding receipt of this information, receipt of the EPA/HUD pamphlet, and their decision as to whether they will make use of the maximum ten-day contingency period.

Even owners who sell or rent their own property without the aid of real estate licensees are required to provide the form and the pamphlet. The rental form makes *no* provision for an inspection period but otherwise contains essentially the same information as the form for sales. It refers, of course, to *lessors* and *lessees* rather than to *purchasers* and *sellers*. Figure 14.1 presents a typical form for *sales*. The student should remember that a different form is used for *rental* transactions, which does not contain a ten-day period for lead inspection and subsequent cancellation.

The form contains many blanks that require a response—either an initial or a check mark. Licensees should make certain that there is such a response in *every* blank. When one or more blanks are not responded to, this is treated as *failure* to meet the federal requirement. Using the form intended for rental situations for a sale—and vice versa—also fails to satisfy the law.

When a licensed agent makes any of these mistakes, both the licensee *and* the principal—whether homeseller or landlord—are held responsible. Fines of up to $10,000 may be imposed, and an assessment of treble damages can be levied for deliberate failure. Fines are assessed **jointly and severally** (that is, not proportionately). Therefore, the licensee should scrutinize every form for appropriateness and completeness before delivering it to its recipient.

There is actually no "official federal form" for either a rent or a sale situation. But any form used is required to have "substantially the same language" as the wording prescribed in HUD regulations. Many associations of brokers, therefore, provide HUD's language in both forms, word for word.

Unlike the federal law, Maryland statutes require inspection and, if necessary, remediation by owners of "affected residential rental property" (as defined in 6-801[b] of the *Environment* Article) in addition to delivery of the MDE *Notice*

T A B L E   14.1

Federal and Maryland Requirements for Residential Structure Lead-Paint Poisoning Disclosure Literature

Built Dates Are Inclusive	Lease	Sale	Federal Requirements	MD Requirements
1/1/1979 and forward (Fed) and 1/1/1978 and forward (MD)	Y	Y	n/a	n/a
1950–1978 (Fed) 1950–1977 (MD)	Y	Y	EPA Booklet & Rental Disclosure Form	n/a
Before 1/1/1950	Y		EPA Booklet & **Rental** Disclosure Form	MDE Notice
Before 1/1/1950		Y	EPA Booklet & **Sale** Disclosure Form	n/a

to Tenants every time such properties have change of occupancy *or* an increase in rent. The six-page MDE booklet, *Notice of Tenants' Rights*, is available for download at *www.mde.state.md.us/assets/document/LeadCoordination/tenants_rights.pdf*.

The requirements for distribution of lead-based paint literature by both the Federal government and Maryland are presented in Table 14.1.

QUESTIONS

1. All the following are direct sources of Maryland air pollution *EXCEPT*
   1. radon.
   2. leakage from underground storage tanks.
   3. asbestos.
   4. automobile emissions.

2. Preservation of open space and ecological challenges
   1. are concerns that must be addressed separately.
   2. are not appropriate issues for State government to address.
   3. overlap in many ways.
   4. can best be dealt with by individual municipalities.

3. The Maryland Smart Growth Initiative, in addition to other things,
   1. is a disguised "no-growth" plan.
   2. seeks to develop new areas in a systematic and orderly fashion.
   3. seeks to revitalize older neighborhoods.
   4. encourages reduction in density of housing.

4. Environmental regulations imposed by local jurisdictions within the State
   1. must not be stricter than those imposed by the State itself.
   2. may be stricter than those imposed by the State.
   3. are authorized by federal mandate.
   4. do not require State enabling acts.

5. Most environmental issues
   1. can usually be handled by the State alone.
   2. require cooperation between the State and local municipalities.
   3. require cooperation among local municipalities, the State, and other states.
   4. involve local, State, regional (interstate), and federal cooperation.

6. The Chesapeake Bay Critical Area Act
   1. does not clearly define what a *Critical Area* is.
   2. establishes buffer zone size at 1,000 feet.
   3. keeps local governments from approving virtually any disturbance of the land in a buffer zone.
   4. defines *Critical Area* as all land within 200 feet of high-water line of tidal bodies and within 200 feet of the dry edge of tidal wetlands.

7. A buffer zone
   1. preserves and protects trees and other natural vegetation, mainly to help purify the air.
   2. extends 200 feet further inland than does a Critical Area.
   3. is meant to provide wildlife a safe habitat.
   4. provides a pleasant area for fishing and hunting.

8. Filling of wetlands is
   1. regarded as mildly hurtful to the environment.
   2. allowed only as a last resort.
   3. subject to multiple levels of regulation.
   4. no longer allowed under any circumstance.

9. Environmental actions by state and local governments seek to produce all of the following effects *EXCEPT* an
   1. increase in the amount of land available for real estate development.
   2. increase in the size of the State's wetland areas.
   3. increase in the cost of housing in less-developed areas.
   4. increase in the intensity of land use in older, developed areas.

10. Inclusion of the "Notice to Buyer Concerning the Chesapeake and Atlantic Coastal Bays Critical Area"

    1. is required in all contracts for the sale of real property in the State.
    2. is required in all contracts for the sale of Maryland residential property.
    3. is not required in certain Maryland counties.
    4. informs purchasers whether the property they are purchasing is located in the Critical Area of the Chesapeake and Atlantic Coastal Bays.

CHAPTER 15

Fair Housing

■ KEY TERMS

complainant   natural person   respondent

conciliation agreement

■ OVERVIEW

Competent real estate licensees realize that fair housing compliance is very demanding. Licensees must have knowledge of applicable federal, State, and local laws, each of which often has its own list of protected groups and of prohibited and required activities. In this chapter, you may notice some similarities and some differences among State, federal, and local laws regarding fair housing.

In this chapter, the term *Commission* refers to the State of Maryland Commission on Human Relations.

■ COMMISSION ON HUMAN RELATIONS

Nine members, appointed by the Governor for staggered six-year terms, comprise the Human Relations Commission. The members choose their own chairperson and are served by an Executive Director and a Deputy Director. The Executive selects an attorney to serve as the Commission's General Counsel. The body meets monthly with additional special meetings after five days' notice to the members.

In addition to its work with fair housing, the Commission works to reduce discrimination in employment and in public accommodations. It not only follows up on complaints from the public but may also take the initiative and generate complaints when at least three of its members agree to do so. The Commission is also subject to the very law from which it receives its authority in that it must not show partiality or favoritism in its own staffing and personnel policies. All State agencies, departments, boards, and their employees are similarly subject to Article 49b, the Human Relations Commission law.

Processing Complaints

Complaints *to the Commission* must be made within one year of the alleged discriminatory action or the end of such action, whichever is later. Complaints must be in writing and under oath. When a complaint is received, the Executive Director considers it and refers it to staff for investigation. Copies of the written staff report submitted to the Executive Director are then sent both to the **complainant** (the aggrieved party making the complaint) and to the **respondent** (the party accused of discriminatory behavior). If the respondent is also a real estate licensee, a copy of the report is sent to the state Real Estate Commission.

If the report concludes that a discriminatory act probably has been committed, staff members seek to deal with the matter by conference, conciliation, and persuasion. If no agreement is reached between complainant and respondent, a report of that fact is sent to all parties.

If the initial conclusion of staff is that there is no probable cause, the report is considered a "final order," which can then be appealed by the complainant to a circuit court in the county where the alleged violation occurred.

When there is found to be probable cause and no agreement is reached, all findings are certified by staff. A written notice is then sent in the name of the Commission to the respondent requiring an answer to the charges at a public hearing before a hearing examiner to be held in the county of the alleged violation.

If conciliation is productive, a written **conciliation agreement** is signed by the parties. Its terms are made public, unless the parties request they not be *and* the Commission determines such disclosure would not serve the purposes of the statute.

Up to this point, all proceedings are nonpublic and held in strict confidence. Indeed, a Commission member or one of its staff members who violates this confidentiality can be punished by a fine of not more than $1,000 and a term of not more than one year in prison.

At a public hearing, the General Counsel makes the case in support of the complaint. The respondent may give written answer, be heard in person, call and examine witnesses, and be represented by counsel.

When hearing examiners find (conclude) that respondents have engaged in a discriminatory practice, they may order them to

- cease and desist,
- take positive action to remedy the situation,

■ reinstate or rehire (in an employment dispute), or

■ provide any other appropriate equitable relief.

If the finding is that there was no discriminatory practice, the examiner shall issue and file an order of dismissal. False and/or malicious complaints are punishable by a fine of not more than $500 and/or one year in prison.

If a respondent fails to do what is ordered, the Commission may sue to enforce compliance with any order within its authority.

Alternative Complaint Procedure

Whereas complaints to the Human Relations Commission must be made within one year, the complainant may apply *to a court* for relief at any time up to two years from the time of the alleged discriminatory event or breach of a conciliation agreement.

A civil action (suit) may be initiated against the respondent in a circuit court in the appropriate county before or even during the early stages of the processing of a complaint by the Commission. However, when this happens, the administrative hearing process on the same alleged discriminatory practice must stop immediately. The complainant is required to notify all parties of initiating civil action.

■ FAIR HOUSING LAWS

Persons who believe they are being discriminated against in a Maryland property transaction—whether it involves real property or personal property—because of their race may, by virtue of the 1866 federal Civil Rights Act, petition a federal court to order an end to the discrimination. Alternatively, they may choose to file a complaint with the Maryland Human Relations Commission if they experience discrimination in a residential real estate–related transaction. Aspects of a real estate–related transaction that would be covered include not only selling and brokerage but also appraisal, insuring, and lending, either for rental, purchase, or improvement and repair of a home.

Because Maryland has laws and enforcement mechanisms that have been adjudged "substantially equivalent" to the federal *Fair Housing Act of 1968*, as amended, residential discrimination complaints are handled by State agencies and by State courts. Complaints made to HUD are referred by HUD to the Commission.

The federal Fair Housing Act of 1968 as amended in 1988 may be found at *www .usdoj.gov/crt/housing/title8.htm.*

Those seeking help under the Maryland law—Article 49b, *Human Relations Commission,* §19 and following—will find that the protected categories are similar to, but go beyond, those in the federal law. In addition to the federal categories of race, color, religion, sex, familial status, national origin, and disability, Maryland includes *marital status* and *sexual orientation.* The Act defines *sexual orientation* as "identification of an individual as to male or female homosexuality, heterosexuality, or bisexuality."

Note that Maryland statutes call for the use of the phrase "individual with a disability" to replace "handicapped person."

Exceptions

The Maryland law has exceptions to its antidiscrimination requirements that parallel those in the 1968/1988 federal Fair Housing Act.

In both, an individual is permitted to discriminate in the sale or rental of a single-family dwelling if the property is sold or rented without the help of any broker, of any person in the business of selling or renting dwellings, or of any agent of either of these. The seller must use no discriminatory advertising in marketing the property. Unlike the federal law, Maryland's Article 49B makes no requirement about the number of properties such seller may own or how many may be sold within a specified time period.

The law allows an owner-occupant of a single-family principal residence to reject tenant applicants *for rooms* based on sex, marital status, and/or sexual orientation.

Also, the owner of a building of *five* or fewer rental units *who occupies one of those units* may also reject applicants in the three categories above. This contrasts with the federal law's standard of a total of *four* or fewer units.

TABLE 15.1

Protected Groups for Housing in Certain Maryland Counties

	PROTECTED CATEGORIES								
	Federal Categories: race, color, religion, sex, national origin, disability, familial status	State Categories: race, color, religion, sex, national original, disability, familial status, sexual orientation, marital status	Age	Occupation/ Source of Income	Political Opinion	Personal Appearance	Marital Status	Ancestry	Creed
JURISDICTION									
Howard County	X	X	X	X	X	X	X		
Frederick County	X	X	X				X		
Prince George's County	X	X	X	X	X	X	X		
Calvert County	X	X	X				X		
Montgomery County	X	X	X	X				X	
City of Rockville	X	X	X	X					X

Maryland's other exceptions closely follow those in the federal Fair Housing Act by permitting exclusion of certain protected groups under specific circumstances:

- Religious organizations may limit rental accommodations to one sex and to members of the organization's religious denomination.
- Private clubs may refuse nonmembers who seek accommodations.
- Owners may refuse to rent or sell to persons convicted of manufacture or distribution of illegal drugs.
- Operators of housing for the elderly may reject occupancy (not owner-ship) by families with young children. *Either* of two situations permit such exclusion:

  1. All residents of the community are required to be age 62 and above.
  2. At least one person age 55 or more resides in 80 percent of the units.

- Owners need not rent to families larger in number than the limits set for occupancy by local government units. Such "reasonable occupancy stan-dards" are typically based on adequacy of number of rooms and square foot-age of units for safe occupancy.

Counties, municipalities, and other local governments are also empowered to enact ordinances and extend protection to additional groups. These may not be less strict than the statewide requirements.

All jurisdictions recognize the federal "core" of protected categories: race, color, religion, national origin, sex, handicap (*disability*, in Maryland), and familial sta-tus. The State and some counties and cities have added others. *Marital status* and *sexual orientation* are added by the State of Maryland and most of its jurisdictions; *occupation* and *personal appearance*, by Howard and Prince George's Counties; *ancestry* and *source of income*, by Montgomery County; and *ancestry* by the City of Rockville.

Sources of law relating to enforcement include the *Civil Rights Act of 1866*; *The Civil Rights Act of 1964*; *The Fair Housing Act of 1968*, as amended; Article 49B of the Maryland Code; §17-526 of the Business Occupations and Professions Article of the Maryland Code; Chapter 27 of the Montgomery County Code; Title 12, Subtitle 2 of the Howard County Code; Division 12, Subdivision I of the Prince George's County Code; and Chapter 13 of the Laws of Rockville. Although not comprehensive, this list is suggestive of the number of laws governing and protect-ing the people of Maryland in the area of fair housing.

DISCRIMINATION IN HOUSING

Examples listed in the Maryland statute of unlawful discriminatory housing prac-tices against protected groups include

- refusing to sell, rent, or negotiate after a bona fide offer;
- making unavailable or denying a dwelling or representing that a property is not available for inspection, sale, or rent when it is in fact available;
- discriminating in terms, conditions, or privileges of sale or rental of a dwelling;
- discriminating in the provision of related services or facilities;

■ making or ordering to be made any publication, notice, or statement concerning properties for sale or rent indicating any preference, limitation, or discrimination; and

■ seeking, *for profit,* to induce any person to sell or rent a dwelling by making representations regarding the entry of a protected group into an area.

Special Provisions for Individuals with Disabilities

In addition to the protections in the previous list, the following prohibited acts are added on behalf of persons with disabilities:

■ Discrimination against an applicant with a disability or a nondisabled applicant who will have a person with a disability residing in the dwelling after it is sold, rented, or made available

■ Discrimination in sale, rental, or availability of a property

■ Discrimination in terms, conditions, or privileges of sale or rental or in connection with the dwelling after sale or rental

■ Refusal to permit reasonable modifications of existing premises occupied or to be occupied by individuals with disabilities, as needed to give the disabled person full enjoyment of the dwelling and made at the tenants' expense and with the tenants' agreement to restore the premises to their condition before the modification (This right also applies to unit owners and residents in condominiums.)

■ Refusal to make reasonable accommodations in rules, policies, practices, or services when such accommodations are necessary to give persons with disabilities equal opportunity to use and enjoy a dwelling

■ Failure to design or construct a multifamily dwelling for first occupancy so that the public use and common areas are readily accessible to and usable by persons with disabilities. All doors for passage into and within all premises within the dwelling must be wide enough to accommodate wheelchairs, and all premises must have suitable adaptive design features (for example, an accessible route into and through the dwelling; light switches, electrical outlets, thermostats, and other environmental controls in accessible locations; reinforcements in bathroom walls to allow later installation of grab bars; and kitchens and bathrooms designed so that individuals in wheelchairs can maneuver about the space).

Discrimination in Real Estate Services

The law forbids any person or business entity that engages in real estate–related transactions

■ to discriminate against any person in making available a transaction or in the terms or conditions of a transaction because of membership in a protected group; or

■ to deny access to, or membership in, or participation in a multiple listing service, brokers' organization, or other service, organization, or facility relating to the business of selling or renting dwellings or to discriminate in the terms or conditions of membership or of participation based on protected group status.

Maryland statute makes it unlawful to coerce, intimidate, threaten, interfere with, or retaliate against persons who seek to exercise the rights granted by this law or against persons who encourage others to exercise their rights. Persons guilty of such actions may be fined not more than $1,000, suffer imprisonment for not more than one year, or both. If the violation results in bodily injury, penalties may range up to $10,000 and ten years in prison; if it results in death, imprisonment may be for any term of years or for life.

Enforcement of Agreements

The Commission may sue to enforce an agreement that a respondent in a case has breached.

At the time a complaint is first received, the Commission itself may also initiate a civil action in the circuit court of the county where the property is located for relief of the complaining party. Having done this, the Commission may still proceed with its administrative proceedings. But if an aggrieved party initiates a civil action under federal or State law seeking relief for a discriminatory housing practice, the Commission may review the complaint and refer the matter to the State Attorney General but then may not continue to hear the same charges.

Anyone who deliberately submits false information to the Commission as it investigates; who fails to make full disclosure; or who changes previous records, reports, or accounts shall be fined not more than $100,000 or imprisoned for not more than one year, or both.

Aggrieved persons may begin civil actions in an appropriate State court not later than two years after the discriminatory action. But they may file no civil action based on the same discrimination after the Commission or a State or local agency has succeeded in producing a conciliation agreement except to enforce that agreement.

Relief granted in a civil action may not set aside any lease or sales contract to other bona fide purchasers or tenants who did not have actual notice of the filing of a complaint with the Commission or of the civil action.

Pattern of Discrimination

When the Commission believes there is a pattern of discrimination or resistance to the rights granted by this law, it may commence a civil action in circuit court. The court may award preventive relief or grant temporary or permanent injunctions and restraining orders against those responsible for violations. The court may also award—in addition to attorney fees—monetary damages to aggrieved persons in amounts not to exceed $50,000 for a first violation and $100,000 for subsequent violations.

■ COMMERCIAL PROPERTY

Neither the owners or the operators of commercial property, their agents and employees, nor any persons licensed or regulated by the State may discriminate against an individual in the terms, conditions, or privileges of property leased for commercial usage or in the provision of services or facilities in connection with the property, because of the individual's race, color, religion, sex, age, physical disability, marital status, or national origin.

■ THE REAL ESTATE BROKERS ACT

The Brokers Act also addresses discrimination against protected groups.

Whether or not acting for monetary gain, a person may not knowingly induce or attempt to induce another person to sell or rent a dwelling or otherwise transfer real estate or knowingly discourage or attempt to discourage another person from purchasing real estate

■ by making representations regarding the entry or prospective entry into a neighborhood of individuals of a particular race, color, sex, religion, or national origin;

■ by making representations regarding the existing or potential proximity of real property owned or used by individuals of a particular race, color, sex, religion, or national origin; or

■ by representing that the existing or potential proximity of real property owned or used by individuals of a particular race, color, sex, religion, or national origin will or may result in the lowering of property values; a change in the racial, religious, or ethnic character of the block, neighborhood, or area; an increase in criminal or antisocial behavior in the area; or a decline in the quality of schools serving the area.

This contrasts with both Human Relations Commission Law and the federal Fair Housing Act, which require *the profit motive* for such blockbusting.

A person may not provide *financial assistance* by loan, gift, or otherwise to another person if the person has actual knowledge that the financial assistance will be used in a transaction that results from a violation of these prohibitions.

Solicitation of Residential Listings

If one of the purposes of the solicitation or attempted solicitation is to change the racial composition of a neighborhood, a person may not solicit or attempt to solicit the listing of residential properties for sale or lease by in-person, door-to-door solicitation, telephone solicitation, or mass distribution of circulars.

Baltimore County law generally forbids canvassing by any person—licensee or not—to generate listings or simply to confer with owners or tenants about real estate. By *canvassing*, the law means door-to-door solicitation or solicitation by use of circulars, visitations, or telephone. However, solicitations when the solicitor, or the employer of the solicitor, has been invited or requested by the owner or tenant are permitted.

Baltimore County law provides several methods of canvassing that are *not* considered solicitation. These include advertisements in bona fide newspapers of general circulation or on radio or television, literature distributed through the U.S. mail, legitimate personal referrals, contacts with property owners resulting from the owners' having personally advertised the property for sale, and solicitation for the purpose of obtaining information for appraisals or similar collection of general sales or market data.

Violation of either the Baltimore City or Baltimore County law is punishable as a misdemeanor, with possible penalties upon conviction of a fine, imprisonment, or both.

Laws concerning solicitation vary from jurisdiction to jurisdiction. It is the responsibility of licensees to be familiar with the local laws where they perform acts of real estate brokerage.

Conservation Areas

The Brokers Act empowers the Real Estate Commission to identify and designate certain localities as *conservation areas.* In these areas and for limited time periods, all advertising of properties for sale and the use of For Sale signs is suspended. Brokerage firms may not solicit listings from owners of such properties but may list them when approached by their owners. This is done for the purpose of preserving racial stability in the affected locality in the event of a threatening volume of real estate transactions. Requirements for establishing such areas are presently so cumbersome that not one such area has been designated for almost a quarter century.

■ ENFORCEMENT

A person aggrieved by a fair housing violation may have to decide the avenue through which to seek redress—whether through a local, county, State, or federal agency.

Federal Laws

In the area of race, aggrieved persons may go directly to federal district court for injunctive relief. For race *and* other matters, they may sue in local courts for damages. If complaint of an alleged Maryland violation is reported to HUD, HUD will refer the matter to the Maryland Human Relations Commission, because Maryland laws are "substantially equivalent" to the federal fair housing laws.

State Enforcement

Complaints made or referred to the Maryland Human Relations Commission are investigated, mediated, and resolved by agreements enforceable in the courts.

Financial Penalties

If the Maryland Human Relations Commission, after proper investigation and hearing, concludes that a respondent—the person against whom the charge was brought—has engaged in any of the unlawful practices listed above, it may seek an order assessing a civil penalty against the respondent not exceeding $500 for a first offense. If it is the second offense within five years, the penalty can be in an amount not more than $1,000. If there were two prior offenses within the last seven years, the maximum penalty would be $2,500.

If the respondent is a **natural person**—an individual rather than a firm or organization—the penalty may be imposed without regard to the time periods between previous violations.

Fair housing provisions of the Brokers Act may be enforced administratively by the State Real Estate Commission or judicially by the Office of the Attorney General. Courts and other government agencies finding licensees guilty of discrimination are required to report their findings to the Real Estate Commission.

Local Laws and Their Enforcement

Chartered counties are empowered to enforce fair housing law violations with fines or penalties not to exceed those provided in the federal Fair Housing Act Amendments of 1988 and 1993. Many counties use their own Human Rights or Human Relations Commissions instead of, or in addition to, possible court enforcement.

■ DISCRIMINATION IN FINANCING

It is unlawful for any bank, savings association, credit union, insurance company, or other creditor to deny a housing loan or credit to persons who apply or to discriminate against them in the fixing of the down payment, interest rate, duration, or other terms or conditions of a loan because of the race, color, religion, creed, marital status, familial status, sex, national origin; the physical or mental disability of such person or of any member, stockholder, director, officer, or employee of such person or of the prospective occupants, lessees, or tenants of the dwelling for which the loan application is made.

■ HUD FAIR HOUSING ADVERTISING GUIDELINES

Section 804(c) of the federal Fair Housing Act makes it unlawful to make, print, or publish or cause to be made, printed, or published any notice, statement, or advertisement with respect to the sale or rental of a dwelling that indicates any preference, limitation, or discrimination based on race, color, religion, sex, handicap, familial status, or national origin or an intention to make any such preference, limitation, or discrimination.

Table 15.2 summarizes current HUD guidelines as to certain phrases that will and will not create liability under this Section.

Ads should focus on the property advertised rather than on potential tenants or purchasers. It is better to say "swimming pool on-site" than "great place for swimmers." Care should be taken not to advertise in media that are directed solely toward a racially or religiously segmented geographic or economic market. If more than one local publication or electronic medium is used, the same phraseology should be used in all of them.

Advertisements may describe the behavior expected of prospective residents (for example, "nonsmoking" or "sober").

■ THE MARYLAND STATUTE

Maryland's fair housing law, Article 49B, Sections 19 to 39, has been found to be "substantially equivalent" to the federal Fair Housing Act of 1968 as amended. It is of central importance and is the source of much of the material in this chapter. The entire text may be found at *www.michie.com*. Choose "Michie's Code of Maryland," then scroll down to and choose "Article 49B," then "Discrimination in Housing." Look at §§19 to 39, which deal with housing discrimination.

T A B L E   15.2

Fair Housing Advertising Guidelines

Issue	Typical Phrases That Will Create Liability	Phrases That Will Not Create Liability
Race, Color, and National Origin	White family home No Irish Pakistanis welcome	Master bedroom Rare find Desirable neighborhood
Religion	No Jews Jews welcome Christian home Near Lutheran nursing home Any particular clearly religious graphic* No Muslims Muslims welcome	Merry Christmas Happy Easter Images of Santa Claus or Easter Bunny Valentine's Day graphic Kosher kitchen in building Chapel on site
Sex	Males only Females only	Mother-in-law suite Bachelor apartment
Handicap/Disability	No wheelchairs	Great view Walk-up apartment Walk-in closets Jogging trails Walking distance to bus stop Wheelchair ramps
Familial Status†	No children Adults only Couples only Singles welcome	Two-bedroom Cozy family room No bicycles allowed Quiet streets

* If a property refers to a religion in its name (Lutheran Home, Beth Torah Home) or a cross or the star of David appears, the ad should contain such words as, "This home does not discriminate on the basis of race, color, religion, national origin, sex, handicap, or familial status."

† Certain exceptions exist for age-qualified communities limited to 55- and 62-year-old+ adults.

■ EDUCATION REQUIREMENTS

Real Estate Commission General Regulations 11, 14, and 17 require that all license applicants, as a part of their educational requirements, be instructed in the human relations aspects of the practice of real estate, including study of fair housing laws and the effects of such undesirable practices as exploitation, steering, blockbusting, prejudicial solicitation, discriminatory practices, misleading advertising, and other related activities. All licensees (except those who exclusively perform commercial brokerage) are required to take 1.5 hours of continuing education in Fair Housing for each biennial license renewal.

QUESTIONS

1. James and Frances Wong, who are of Chinese descent, tell their real estate salesperson that they need a three-bedroom house in the $320,000 to $330,000 price range that is within walking distance of an elementary school. The salesperson, after identifying the Wongs as genuine prospects, finds a house on Judson Street that meets all the Wongs' requirements, but the salesperson knows that the residents of the neighborhood are unhappy about Asians moving into the area. The agent should
   1. refrain from bringing this particular house to the Wongs' attention.
   2. tell them about the house but suggest that they would be happier in another neighborhood.
   3. file a complaint with the Human Relations Commission.
   4. inform the Wongs about the availability of the house and arrange to show them the listing.

2. With respect to fair housing, all persons engaged in real estate transactions
   1. must be familiar with all applicable federal, State, and local antidiscrimination statutes and ordinances.
   2. carry errors and omissions (E&O) insurance to be protected.
   3. may refuse to be held liable.
   4. have the right to decide what is best for their customers and clients.

3. Two salespersons are trying to sell a residential property listed in a neighborhood that is predominantly Caucasian. They
   1. are acting properly by not showing this listing to white prospects.
   2. violate Maryland and federal laws when they decide whether to show a listing based on a prospect's race.
   3. need not introduce into the neighborhood anyone not of the predominant race of the neighborhood.
   4. should have a salesperson of the same race as the prospect show the property.

4. A broker approaches homeowners seeking to list their property for sale. They had not been thinking of selling, but the broker tells them, "The time to sell is now," because the neighborhood is experiencing a large minority group influx and that the value of their property "is sure to drop" if they wait any longer. This broker's behavior is
   1. blockbusting.
   2. steering.
   3. blind advertising.
   4. redlining.

5. A private club, by limiting the rental or occupancy of its lodgings to club members, as long as the club is not operated as a commercial hotel, is violating
   1. the federal Fair Housing Act of 1968.
   2. the Maryland Fair Housing Law.
   3. the Real Estate License Law.
   4. no State or federal laws.

CHAPTER 16

Closing the Real Estate Transaction

■ KEY TERMS

binder
homeowner
mortgagee

settlement officer
title insurance

title search
total payment

■ OVERVIEW

Whether it is called *settlement, closing, going to escrow,* or some other name, this event is the culmination of real estate brokerage activities. At this event, legal title to Maryland real property passes from sellers to purchasers and then to the lender. As a result of the closing, purchasers take on long-term debt, and sellers get funds from the sale of their property. From these funds, sellers typically pay commissions to their listing broker and satisfy outstanding mortgages and other liens against the property sold.

Listing brokers may divide their commissions with in-house affiliates who assisted purchasers, intra-company agents who represented buyers and sellers, or co-brokers who either assisted buyers as subagents or represented them as buyers' agents.

■ EVIDENCE OF TITLE

In Maryland, it is customary for buyers to order a **title search** and a **binder** (interim commitment) for mortgagee **title insurance** at the time of entering into a purchase contract. In most cases, the title (settlement) company orders the title search and

189

preparation of an abstract of title on behalf of the buyers. If the information in the abstract indicates marketable title, a settlement company that is authorized to do so by a title insurance company will issue a binder—a commitment from the title insurance company to issue a permanent policy at the time of settlement. Some attorneys issue their own certificates of title. Others simply indicate their opinion of title based on the abstract, without insuring the title. The issuance of title insurance is dependent upon a favorable interpretation of the abstract of title.

Lenders almost always require **mortgagee** (lender) title insurance for the protection of their position. In addition, State law requires that purchasers be offered **homeowner** (buyer) title insurance by the settlement officer at every residential closing. Buyers who decline homeowner title insurance are asked to confirm their refusal in writing. For the different characteristics and functions of each of their policies, the student should consult the principles text.

■ SETTLEMENTS

Most purchase contracts and sale agreements are closed in the office of a title company, the buyer's or seller's attorney, the mortgage lender, or the real estate broker. Closing in Maryland is usually performed at a meeting involving buyers, sellers, agents, and a settlement officer. "Closing in escrow," as described in the principal text, is generally not practiced in Maryland.

Real estate brokers or their salespersons normally are present at settlement, although the interaction is—and should be—principally among the officer conducting the settlement, the parties to the agreement, and any attorneys present. Licensees are present for whatever nonlegal services they may be asked to render; to provide personal support for their clients; and, of course, to receive the commission checks to take to their companies.

■ CLOSING AND TAX STATEMENTS

The buyers' or sellers' attorney or a settlement company officer will prepare the necessary *closing statement*. Licensees should know how these statements are calculated to estimate accurately sellers' expenses of sale and net proceeds from the transaction. They should also be able to estimate for purchasers the amount of additional cash needed at closing to complete the purchase. They should be able to understand and explain to customers and clients every entry on the settlement sheet almost always used: HUD Form #1.

Closing costs are apportioned according to statute, where applicable, and/or by contractual agreement. Typically, the seller is responsible for such property charges for the day of closing as ad valorem taxes, special assessments, and utilities. By federal law, all owner/sellers must provide the closing agent with their forwarding addresses and Social Security numbers. Corporate sellers must provide their corporate tax identification numbers.

If Maryland property is being sold by an out-of-state owner, Maryland statute requires that 6 percent of the total payment to the seller be withheld. **Total payment** is defined as the consideration for the property, reduced by mortgages paid and other costs of the sale; essentially, it means the seller's bottom line: "cash to seller." The amount withheld is prepaid Maryland income tax on any possible capital gain or other income tax liability the seller may owe to the State. If the seller is not a natural person but an "entity," such as a corporation, partnership, LLC, or trust located in another state, the percentage to be set aside is 7 percent. A seller claiming to be a resident of Maryland is required to sign an affidavit to that effect at closing. Since it is easier to collect taxes from an owner who lives within the State, sellers who have their permanent residence within the State at the time of closing will not have these amounts withheld.

Buyers and sellers must sign an affidavit as to the accuracy of information they have given that will be reported to the IRS. Typically, the person conducting settlement will request photo IDs of the principals. Copies of these IDs are maintained in the title company's records. Licensees should make sure that their sellers are prepared to provide all the required information at the time of settlement. The closing agent or title company can answer any questions that may arise.

■ EVIDENCE OF RELEASE

Within 30 days after closing, **settlement** (title) company **officers,** who are responsible for disbursement of funds, must mail or deliver to the sellers evidence of having recorded the *release of mortgage*. If the recording of release is delayed beyond the 30-day period for causes beyond their control, settlement officers must mail or deliver to the sellers a letter explaining the delay. They must send another letter for each additional delay of 30 days. Failure to follow these rules may subject them to audit of all their accounts by the court.

However, if persons conducting closing properly disburse all funds entrusted to them in the closing procedure within five days, no such evidence is required unless specifically requested by purchasers or vendors. Vendors and purchasers are to be informed in writing of these requirements before the deed is delivered at closing.

Settlements in Maryland must be performed by, or under the supervision of, an attorney. This does not mean that an attorney is present or has even seen the paperwork. It does mean that there must be an attorney responsible for the preparation and execution of closing and the proper disbursement of funds. To be recorded, deeds on Maryland realty, as mentioned in Chapter 10, must be prepared by an attorney or by either the deed's grantor or grantee. "Prepared by an attorney" may well mean "prepared by personnel trained and supervised" by the attorney who is responsible for their performance at closing. Supervision does not always have to be done in person. The student is reminded of the "evidences of reasonable and adequate supervision" required of real estate brokers mentioned in Chapter 3.

Representation

Whom do settlement officers represent? They usually owe certain fiduciary duties to several parties but exclusive loyalty to none. When they order and evaluate the abstract of title, they owe the purchaser due care. When they issue title insurance, they are acting as agents of the title insurance company. In collecting taxes for the state and federal tax information for the Internal Revenue Service, they have responsibility to gather and handle those funds and that information with due care. They owe the sellers the duty of paying off old liens and recording releases of liens on behalf of the old mortgagee and buyers the duty of recording their new deed. They must also record any mortgages that were given to lenders at settlement. In addition to their duties to all these parties, settlement officers represent themselves and their title company.

QUESTIONS

1. Residential closings in Maryland are
    1. usually performed by an escrowee.
    2. always performed by real estate brokers.
    3. always performed by title company clerks.
    4. always performed under an attorney's supervision.

2. Proof of release of debt on a property after a closing MUST be sent to
    1. the county courthouse within 30 days of closing.
    2. purchaser within 5 days of closing.
    3. seller within 30 days of closing.
    4. the former mortgagee within 5 days of closing.

3. An attorney who personally conducts settlement
    1. owes all parties due care in execution of closing duties.
    2. represents the seller.
    3. represents the buyer.
    4. may represent both the buyer and the seller.

4. In Maryland, title search is usually ordered
    1. at the direction and expense of the seller.
    2. at the direction and expense of the purchaser.
    3. by the salesperson who prepares the contract.
    4. by the broker of the listing client.

5. When the property being closed is sold by an out-of-state corporate owner,
    1. the buyer is no longer protected by the Maryland Guaranty Fund.
    2. the buyer must set aside 6 percent of the consideration.
    3. the closing officer must withhold 7 percent of the seller's proceeds of sale.
    4. the closing officer must withhold 6 percent of the consideration.

Maryland Real Estate License Examinations

■ OVERVIEW

Passing the state licensing examination is a major challenge for persons seeking a real estate license. Every applicant would like to pass the exam on the first try, not only to speed up the licensing process but also to reduce the cost of taking it over, minimize inconvenience, and avoid embarrassment.

The salesperson license examination can be taken only after 60 hours of prelicense instruction. A total of 135 hours is required before the broker examination. These requirements must be met *before* taking the examinations.

Table A.1 shows a summary of the key features of the exam.

■ THE REAL ESTATE LICENSE EXAMINATION

PSI Examination Services Inc. (PSI), Las Vegas, Nevada, an independent testing service under contract with the Commission, prepares and administers the licensing examinations. PSI's testing program is adapted to each state's real estate license laws and practices and to the priorities of its licensing agency.

TABLE A.1

Summary of Facts about Examinations

Exam	Portion	Number of Questions	Total Time Allowed	Minimum Number Correct Required to Pass	Fee Regular	Fee Express
Salesperson	National	80		56		
	State	30	120 minutes	21	$65	$75
	Both	110				
Broker	National	80		56		
	State	40	120 minutes	28	$65	$75
	Both	120				

Candidates receive two scores for their examination: the state score and the national score. The passing grade set by the Commission is currently 70 percent on each. This means the salesperson candidate must answer at least 56 out of 80 questions on the national portion correctly and 21 out of 30 on the state portion. Broker candidates must correctly answer 56 out of 80 on the national and 28 out of 40 questions on the state portion. Salesperson and broker candidates have 120 and 110 minutes respectively to complete the entire exam. (Statewide, between 60 and 65 percent of all candidates taking the salesperson exam for the first time pass both portions.)

The *national* section of the examinations for both broker and salesperson contains questions based on general real estate information. Subjects include Property Ownership, Land Use Control and Regulation, Valuation and Market Analysis, Financing, Laws of Agency, Mandated Disclosures, Contracts, Transfer of Property, Practice of Real Estate Brokerage, Mathematics, and Specialty Areas.

The *Maryland (State) section* contains questions based on Title 17 of the Maryland Annotated Code (the Brokers Act), as well as questions relating to the General Regulations and the Code of Ethics established by the Maryland Real Estate Commission. Test questions deal with duties and powers of the Commission, licensing requirements, and business conduct. Questions relating to Environmental Issues, Water Rights, Listing and Buyer Agreements, and Common Interest Ownership Properties are also found in the State portion.

Because tests are not preprinted, they can be generated daily from a computer database. Thus, they can be continually updated and the order of items rearranged.

■ APPLICATION PROCEDURES

Students obtain the "Candidate Information Bulletin and Application Forms" for the examinations, from the school where they take their class. They can also be downloaded, by a student who registers there, from the PSI Web site: *www.psiexams.com*.

The Bulletin also contains directions to the six testing centers in the State and a number of sample questions. Those who have passed the required prelicensing course and are ready to take the examination should mail the completed application form, together with evidence of passing the prelicense course, as well as the $65 testing fee and any other required documents, to

PSI Examination Services
ATTN: Examination Registration MD RE
3210 East Tropicana
Las Vegas, NV 89121

Failure to follow exactly the instructions on the registration form may result in students' not being scheduled promptly for the examinations they request.

The registration fee for taking a Maryland Real Estate Licensing Examination (either broker or salesperson) is $65. Payment can be made to PSI by personal check, money order, company check, or cashier's check.

Candidates who have previously provided complete certification of eligibility to PSI may register by mail or through Express Registration on the telephone, by fax, or on the Internet. These applicants may be persons who failed all or part of a previous exam or whose initial application form was incomplete but was accompanied by proper proof of their completion of the education requirement. A $10 fee is charged for Express Registration in addition to the basic $65 for the examination. A valid VISA or MasterCard is needed.

First-time applicants are to send their registration forms, other necessary documents, and the registration fee directly to PSI. In return, PSI will mail them (usually within two weeks) a Registration Confirmation Notice. This notice explains how to make an examination appointment. Once this appointment, including place, date, and time for examination, has been made, an applicant may still request changes. Do this by calling (800) 733-9267 two or more days before the scheduled testing date. All examinations—even if delayed—must still be completed within 90 days of original registration, or the candidates must reapply and pay another registration fee. The expiration date is shown on each student's Confirmation Notice.

The Registration Form asks for information that will be relayed to the Commission so it can process the license applications when candidates pass their tests. It also asks for certification that the candidate has successfully completed the mandatory educational hours. In addition, it contains a statement of *irrevocable consent*, which is required from applicants who live outside Maryland.

Applicants must answer the Registration Form questions to the best of their ability. The form is then signed as an affidavit, subject to the penalties of perjury.

■ TESTING PROCEDURES

Candidates may take an examination at any of the several testing centers located in Maryland. All candidates must bring positive identification to the testing site. This identification must include at least one government-issued picture ID with the candidate's signature on it—such as a driver's license, state ID, or passport. The second (additional) form of ID could be a credit card with the candidate's signature and preprinted legal name. *All* IDs must have exactly the same name as the document certifying completion of the required prelicense education and the Registration Form, including the same middle initial and same use of generation (Jr., Sr., II, III, etc.).

PSI uses a computerized testing system approved by the Commission. On conclusion of the testing session, the computer will show candidates whether they passed or failed; official notification of examination results, however, will be mailed to candidates. The computerized real estate examinations are administered every business day during the week at most locations. There is no "walk-in" testing.

Candidates take their examinations seated at specially designed, semiprivate computer work stations. On-screen instructions provide a 15-minute tutorial in the use of the keyboard. About as many keys are used as are found on a touch-tone telephone. Taking the test requires no computer skills. Instructions appear on the screen to guide the candidate through each step of the test. Both the salesperson and the broker test allow a total of 120 minutes—90 for the national, 30 for the state. Note that for brokers, there are 40 state-related questions, not 30, for the 30-minute period. There is an on-screen clock for the candidate to watch.

No notes, books, cell phones, pagers, or children are allowed in the examination center. Silent, nonprinting, nonprogrammable, battery-operated calculators are permitted, but they must not have alphabet keys. There is no smoking, eating, or drinking at the center. A candidate who tries to copy a question or an answer or to communicate examination content to another person may be disqualified and possibly subject to legal action for violation of copyright laws.

When candidates first take the real estate exam, they take the state section, then the national. Candidates who have already taken the exam but passed only one of its two sections are permitted to reregister and retake the group of questions—state or general—that they need to pass. Candidates must pass both sets of questions to be eligible for a Maryland real estate license.

■ TYPES OF QUESTIONS ON EXAM

The tests use multiple-choice answer format. An incomplete statement or a question is presented and is followed by four possible choices. Applicants are sometimes asked to find the *one correct answer*. At other times, they must find the *one wrong answer*. Here are examples of each:

■ EXAMPLE 1

Which one of the following cities is the capital of the state in which it is located?

1. New York City, NY
2. New Orleans, LA
3. Lincoln, NE
4. Scranton, PA

■ EXAMPLE 2

All the following are even numbers *EXCEPT*

1. 118.
2. 230.
3. 734.
4. 437.

The questions given here are not representative of those on the examination. Examples of more difficult questions and problems have been included in the chapters of this book so that you will become familiar with them and be better prepared for the examination.

The PSI testing approach is designed to assess reasoning processes as well as factual real estate knowledge. In answering examination-type questions, consider all answer choices carefully and eliminate the least likely ones instead of randomly selecting an answer. However, it is better to guess than to give no answer at all.

The purpose of the examination is to provide a measure of your knowledge of real estate and thereby allow you to demonstrate your qualification for licensure. You should try to answer all questions without spending too much time on any one question. The fourth answer choice for each math test item is often *None of the above*. Do not be surprised by it.

Here are the answers to the model questions:

		1	2	3	4
1.		[ ]	[ ]	[x]	[ ]

		1	2	3	4
2.		[ ]	[ ]	[ ]	[x]

■ MORE HELP IN PREPARING FOR THE LICENSE EXAMINATION

The author has tried to prepare you for the Maryland Real Estate License Examination by including in this book the kinds of items usually found on the test. Familiarity with the test items, however, will not in itself ensure a passing score. Your most important preparation for this examination involves thoughtfully studying real estate principles and practices and brokerage laws and regulations.

Concentrate on learning the material by studying the principles text and this book. When using the tests and exercises in these books, be sure that you find and *understand* the correct solutions for any questions you miss. Use the answer keys and explanations of answers in these books thoughtfully.

Dearborn™ Real Estate Education publishes other instructional materials in addition to *Modern Real Estate Practice* and *Maryland Real Estate Practice & Law* that are especially designed to aid you in passing the licensing exam: *Mastering Real Estate Math, Study Guide for Modern Real Estate Practice, Guide to Passing the PSI Real Estate Exam,* and *Maryland Real Estate Exam Prep.*

Practicing with the interactive software, *Real Estate Exam Prep: North Atlantic,* which includes Maryland, will give you the experience of answering on-screen questions similar to state exam questions while seated at a computer keyboard, the way you will take your test.

■ TYPICAL MARYLAND-SPECIFIC TEST ITEMS

The Maryland-related questions throughout this volume are in the format found on the real estate licensing exam. Use them to identify strengths and weaknesses in your knowledge.

List the items you miss and use that list as a guide for further intensive study of the text. Sometimes, you may want to test yourself on an entire list of questions. Other times, you may wish to attempt the items one by one, checking your answers as you go. Decide why every correct answer *IS* correct. In items that ask you to find the *WRONG* answer, do so, but then try to learn all you can from the three *CORRECT* answers to the same questions. Make intelligent use of all practice questions and the answer keys.

Practice Exam

APPENDIX

B

1. When a salesperson whose license has not been renewed negotiates a sale of real property, the commission is payable to
   1. the broker only.
   2. no one.
   3. the salesperson only.
   4. the broker and the salesperson according to prior agreement.

2. If a salesperson license is issued on September 20, 2008, it will expire on
   1. September 20, 2010.
   2. September 20, 2012.
   3. April 30, 2010.
   4. March 1, 2012.

3. When prospective purchasers first arrive at a brokerage office to inquire about real estate assistance, the Brokers Act requires that they be treated as
   1. customers.
   2. clients.
   3. agents.
   4. factors.

4. Salespersons' licenses must be
   1. kept in a safe place by the salespersons.
   2. carried by the salespersons.
   3. displayed in their brokers' offices.
   4. maintained in personnel files by their brokers.

5. The maximum amount that a claimant may collect per transaction from the Guaranty Fund on one transaction is
   1. unlimited.
   2. $250,000.
   3. $25,000.
   4. $10,000.

6. Under the Junk Fax Prevention Act, a person who sends a fax
   1. need not allow the recipient to "opt out" of getting more faxes.
   2. may have received the recipient's number from a fax-spamming company.
   3. may send the fax only between 9 AM and 5 PM.
   4. must have an established business relationship with the recipient.

7. Membership on the State Real Estate Commission includes
   1. only licensed salespersons.
   2. only licensed brokers.
   3. unlicensed persons and licensed brokers and salespersons.
   4. persons appointed by the Attorney General.

8. Maryland real estate salesperson and broker licenses are issued
   1. by the local Board of REALTORS®.
   2. to all applicants who have successfully completed required educational courses.
   3. by the Maryland Association of REALTORS®.
   4. by the Real Estate Commission.

9. Ethical standards that must be observed by all Maryland real estate licensees are set by the
   1. National Association of REALTORS®.
   2. State Real Estate Commission.
   3. Maryland Association of REALTORS®.
   4. local boards and associations.

10. When a partnership owns a real estate brokerage firm, which statement is *FALSE?*
    1. The broker is responsible for the real estate brokerage activities of the partnership.
    2. The broker must have a contractual or employment agreement with the partnership.
    3. The broker must be one of the partners.
    4. The broker must be designated by the partnership as its broker of record.

11. When builders sell houses they have built and own, which of the following is *TRUE?*
    1. They need not hold real estate licenses.
    2. They must be licensed if they sell more than six per calendar year.
    3. They must be licensed brokers.
    4. They may be licensed as salespersons but not affiliated with brokers.

12. A developer desiring to convert an apartment building that is more than five years old into a time-share project in Maryland *MUST*
    1. give each tenant 180 days' notice.
    2. give each tenant 120 days' notice.
    3. not give tenants any prior notice.
    4. notify each tenant within ten days after filing the Public Offering Statement.

13. The responsibilities of real estate licensees do *NOT* include
    1. fair treatment of third parties.
    2. competence in performance of duties.
    3. giving of legal guidance.
    4. loyalty to their principals.

14. In which states do lenders receive defeasible fee interests in mortgaged land?
    1. Title theory states
    2. Lien theory states
    3. Modified lien theory states
    4. Trust theory states

15. Under the Maryland Real Estate Brokers Act, the Commission may impose a specified maximum penalty per violation. The penalty can be as much as
    1. $25,000.
    2. $15,000.
    3. $5,000.
    4. $1,000 and/or one year's imprisonment.

16. The amount of commission set in a listing agreement is determined by
    1. Maryland statute.
    2. the local Board or Association of REALTORS®.
    3. mutual agreement between the parties to the agreement.
    4. the Real Estate Commission sitting in executive session.

17. Earnest money deposits received by salespersons of a firm must be
    1. deposited in their trust accounts.
    2. given to the sellers of the property.
    3. placed in their broker's safe.
    4. given to their broker for prompt deposit in the firm's trust account.

18. Which of the following statements about tenancy by the entirety in Maryland is *NOT* true?
    1. If husband and wife divorce, the tenancy is terminated.
    2. Both spouses' signatures are required to sell such property if both are living.
    3. Upon death of either spouse, the form of ownership converts to tenancy in common.
    4. Only a legally married husband and wife can own property as tenants by the entirety.

19. When a broker receives a full-price offer from a prospect and, at the same time, a less-than-full-price offer through a cooperating agent, the broker should present
    1. only the full-price offer.
    2. only the offer from the other broker's customer.
    3. both offers.
    4. the first offer received and then, if it is rejected, the other offer.

20. The law requiring certain contracts for the transfer of an interest in realty to be in writing to be enforceable is the Maryland is the
    1. Written Instrument Law.
    2. Parol Evidence Law.
    3. Statute of Limitations.
    4. Statute of Frauds.

21. In Maryland, a land installment contract need *NOT*

    1. be recorded by the vendor within 15 days after it has been signed.
    2. include all terms of the transaction.
    3. be signed by the vendor and vendee.
    4. be filed with the Real Estate Commission.

22. A licensee's presenting the Commission's form "Understanding Whom Agents Represent"

    1. informs prospective purchasers and lessees of the various ways they can be served by real estate brokerage firms.
    2. creates a representation agreement between the agent who presents the form and the prospect to whom it is presented.
    3. gives a licensee the prospect's permission to engage in a transaction involving dual agency.
    4. ends a licensee's presumed buyer representation of a prospect.

23. Material facts learned from a client remain confidential until

    1. the client dies and the estate is probated.
    2. the agency relationship (either presumed or contractual) is terminated.
    3. the Statute of Limitations has expired.
    4. the facts becomes common knowledge from other sources.

24. When does Title 17 require the Commission's form, "Understanding Whom Agents Represent," to be presented?

    1. At first contact with a prospective purchaser or lessee
    2. At the first face-to-face contact between the licensee and a prospect
    3. Not later than the moment a prospect expresses the desire to look at a property listed with the licensee's company
    4. Not later than the first scheduled face-to-face meeting between the licensee and the prospect

25. Agency relationships can be determined (legally inferred) from

    1. ministerial actions of a licensee.
    2. magisterial guidance from a licensee.
    3. payment or promise of payment to a licensee.
    4. a prospect's expectations of a licensee.

26. Which of the following statements about rental security deposits is *FALSE*?

    1. The landlord must pay the tenant 3 percent per annum simple interest on these funds at the end of the lease.
    2. Interest on security deposits is computed and compounded at six-month intervals.
    3. The portion of the deposit not withheld must be returned to the tenant within 45 days of end of occupancy together with an accounting of how any withheld portion was spent.
    4. Tenants may recover three times the amount of security deposit improperly withheld by the landlord, plus reasonable attorney fees.

27. Licensees may have their licenses suspended or revoked and/or be subject to fines by the Commission for all of the following *EXCEPT*

    1. drunken driving convictions.
    2. accepting net listings.
    3. performing acts of brokerage on an expired license.
    4. failure to be current in court-ordered child support payments.

28. A licensee representing a client buyer

    1. owes certain statutory duties to the seller.
    2. cannot be compensated by the seller.
    3. can be regarded as a cooperating agent and therefore the subagent of the seller.
    4. does not need a written representation agreement to qualify for compensation.

29. In purchasing a condominium, the most important document given to the buyer is the declaration. The declaration usually does all of the following *EXCEPT*

    1. authorizes a board of directors to administer the condominium affairs pursuant to the bylaws and to assess the owners so as to maintain the condominium adequately.
    2. describes the condominium units and the common areas and any restrictions on their use.
    3. establishes the undivided interest percentages.
    4. sets forth the rules for activities of unit occupants.

30. The condominium declaration
    1. must be recorded to place the property under a condominium regime.
    2. cannot be rescinded once it is recorded.
    3. can be changed only with the unanimous approval of the council of unit owners.
    4. must be printed in a daily newspaper before changes may be made.

31. In which of the following situations is deficiency judgment permitted when a property sells at foreclosure for less than the mortgage debt?
    1. Judicial foreclosure
    2. Nonjudicial foreclosure
    3. FHA loans
    4. All of the above

32. Brokers' choices of how to handle *contested* earnest money deposits do *NOT* include
    1. putting their client's interests ahead of the other party's because of their fiduciary duties.
    2. deciding to let the money remain in their trust accounts.
    3. notifying both buyers and sellers how they intend to distribute the contested funds.
    4. not distributing the money as they proposed if one of the parties gives proper notice of protest.

33. Rental security deposits may
    1. not be withheld by the landlord for unpaid rent.
    2. be kept during the lease in the landlord's personal savings account to earn interest.
    3. be withheld by the landlord to cover estimated damages at the end of the lease.
    4. be withheld by a landlord for the actual amount expended to repair damages caused by tenants.

34. According to Title 17, all the following could be considered "evidences" of reasonable and adequate supervision by a broker *EXCEPT*
    1. a proven pattern of the broker's physical presence in the broker's office, 9:00 AM to 5:00 PM, seven days per week.
    2. availability of company policy and procedure manual in each office containing, among other things, rules for handling funds of others and the requirements of fair housing laws.
    3. existing records of every-other-month training meetings provided for all the broker's affiliates together with a record of those attending and a list of topics presented.
    4. a paper trail showing that all contracts are approved by an experienced supervisor before being presented.

35. An agency agreement listing a Maryland property for sale
    1. may contain a provision for the broker to keep all the sale proceeds above a certain amount as the brokerage commission.
    2. is proper if it is signed by the owner of the largest share in a property that is owned by several owners.
    3. may indicate that the amount of brokerage commission to be paid will be negotiated between owner and broker after an offer is presented.
    4. may not require notice from either party to activate its termination date.

36. Which of the following statements about usury in Maryland mortgage loans is *TRUE*?
    1. There is no interest limit on first mortgages involving Maryland real estate.
    2. There is no interest limit on second mortgages involving Maryland real estate.
    3. There is no interest limit on land (installment) contracts involving Maryland real estate.
    4. Interest limits imposed on mortgages are not imposed on deeds of trust.

37. A pair of prospects who enter a Maryland brokerage office and ask help in finding a house to rent
    1. are considered by Maryland statute to be represented by that brokerage firm.
    2. are considered customers by Maryland statute.
    3. will owe a "reasonable and customary" brokerage fee if the firm finds them a property that they lease.
    4. must be given the Commission's form "Understanding Whom Agents Represent" immediately upon their arrival.

38. When Maryland real estate licensees renew their licenses, they must attest to having completed
    1. at least 3 hours of continuing education in fair housing.
    2. at least 1.5 hours of continuing education in ethics.
    3. a total of at least 15 hours of approved continuing education courses.
    4. at least 6 hours of continuing education on changes in federal, State, and local laws.

39. Maryland's requirements for a real estate broker licensee's office include all the following EXCEPT that
    1. it be a place where the firm regularly conducts insurance sales.
    2. it have a sign visible to the public that includes the words *Real Estate*, REALTOR®, or *Realtist*, whichever is applicable.
    3. records of all trust monies, kept in a secured area, available to the Commission's inspectors on demand.
    4. it have on display the license of the broker and every affiliate who works out of that office.

Associate Broker John Buonasera, known as "Mr. B," has published a flier to attract business. Below is the entire ad.

> Come to Mr. B for all your real estate needs: Buying, Selling, or Renting.
>
> Use my services and you will be pleased. Results guaranteed!
>
> I charge 2% less than most other REALTORS® for my excellent service.
>
> My personal assistants and I are available to you at all hours to answer your real estate questions and meet your brokerage needs.
>
> Call my cell phone, toll free: 1-888-555-5555.

40. Which of the following statements about his advertisement is *FALSE?*
    1. The ad makes it clear that Mr. B is not the broker of the firm.
    2. The ad is improper, because Mr. B doesn't mention the designated name of the broker whose firm he works for.
    3. The ad is improper, because Mr. B gives his own phone number and not that of the firm.
    4. The ad is improper because, although a nickname like Mr. B may be registered with the Real Estate Commission, his legal name, John Buonasera, must also be shown as it appears on his license.

Complaint Procedure

Possible Steps in Handling Complaints Against a Licensee

1.	Complaint is received by Real Estate Commission (REC).
2.	Complaint is reviewed by REC designee, usually the Executive Director.
2.1.a	OR: If complaint is deficient in form (i.e., unsigned or not made under oath), it is returned to complainant as rejected with explanation for the rejection.
2.1.b	OR: If complaint lacks facts alleging prima facie case, it is returned to Complainant as rejected with that reason given.
3.	Complaint is adjudged by REC designee to be in good form and to contain facts that suggest a violation of Brokers Act or REC Regulations has taken place.
4.	REC designee refers complaint to a hearing panel of the REC.
4.1	REC informs Complainant that the complaint is being processed.
5.	Hearing panel examines the complaint, and if the panel finds it is worthy of action, refers the matter to Investigative Services for investigation.
5.1	OR: Panel concludes that the facts do not warrant further pursuit of the complaint. Complainant is notified of this finding of insufficient grounds, and that the complaint is rejected. There is no right to appeal this finding.
6.	Licensee who is being complained about (the Respondent) and Respondent's broker are informed of the complaint and asked by the panel for written comment.
7.	Investigative Services investigates and reports its findings to the hearing panel.
8.	Hearing panel examines the report from Investigative Services and the responses from the Respondent and Respondent's broker. Panel concludes that Respondent has violated law or regulation and **sets the matter in for** (schedules) a hearing.
8.1	OR. Panel concludes that the facts do not warrant further pursuit of the complaint and that the complaint is rejected. Complainant is notified of this decision. There is no right to appeal this finding.
9.	Panel notifies Respondent and Respondent's broker of the scheduled hearing and informs them of their rights to be present, to respond, to be represented by counsel, and to have witnesses subpoenaed (at Respondent's expense). They are also informed what the charges are and the possible penalties that could be imposed. Respondent must have ten days' notice prior to the hearing. Complainant is also notified.
10.	In almost every case, the hearing is held before an Administrative Law Judge (ALJ). It is open to the public. Written and/or oral testimony is given. An Assistant Attorney General (AAG) presents the Commission's case. Respondent has opportunity to be heard in defense or mitigation. ALJs base their conclusion on **preponderance of evidence. Hearsay evidence** is admitted but weighed with discretion. The AAG and the respondent's attorney may both rebut testimony and give summations. No decision is announced at the hearing. Hearing is conducted according to the Rules of Procedure of the Maryland Office of Administrative Hearings. [COMAR 28, Subtitle 02.01—C, a 16-page document.] Some days after the conclusion of the hearing, the **proposed decision** of the ALJ is sent to the REC.

11.	A *new* hearing panel is given the proposed decision to review along with the case record. Panel adopts (or modifies) the proposed decision and sends it to the Respondent and the Complainant, giving each one notice of the right to file an exception within ten days.
12.	If either Complainant or Respondent takes exception within ten days, the panel sets a date for a hearing at which the parties can present arguments against the decision and rebut each other's argument. Parties must have 14 days advance notice of this hearing.
13.	The panel that sent out the proposed decision hears the arguments taking exception to the decision. The panel reaches a decision.
14.	Some days later, the panel notifies parties of its decision rejecting the exception and issues a **final written order.**
15.	Parties submit to the decision contained in the final written order.
15.1	OR: A party **appeals** to the **circuit court.** (The appeal alone does not create a **stay** of the decision for a licensee.)
15.1.a	AND: Appellant (one who is appealing), if a licensee, petitions the circuit court for a stay of the decision (perhaps delaying the suspension or revocation of appellant's license). Court usually grants this request and seeks a bond not exceeding $50,000.
15.1.b	AND: Circuit court denies the appeal and lets final order stand.
15.2	BUT: Appellant carries appeal to Court of Special Appeals.
15.2.a	AND: Court of Special Appeals affirms the final order.
15.3	BUT: Appellant carries appeal to Court of Appeals.
15.3.a	AND: Court of Appeals sustains the final order.
15.1.2 or 3	OR: Any of the three courts could have granted the appeal and set aside the final order.
16.	Appeals are exhausted; final order will be executed by the REC.
	End of Case

Note: These steps address a violation of the statute or the regulations in which no financial reimbursement was sought from the Guaranty Fund.

APPENDIX D

Maryland Real Estate– Related Web Sites

■ KEEPING UP-TO-DATE

Print materials like this volume are up-to-date when written and printed. However, changes in laws, regulations, and the business environment are constant. In various chapters of this book, Web sites (URLs) been given for specific topics. Here, in Appendix D, several "master" Web sites of great value are listed. They can aid students who become licensees in meeting their responsibility to remain current on all real estate matters. These sites are veritable springboards into a wealth of information for the student of Maryland real estate brokerage. Most are listed according to the entity that maintains them.

A discussion follows each Web link.

The Maryland General Assembly

www.mlis.state.md.us

This is the main source of information for everything that happens in the legislative branch of Maryland government. It gives the dates for the annual sessions and the number of senators, delegates, and districts. It enables its readers to identify their legislators by giving their own zip codes and to contact any State legislator by e-mail.

The site lists all bills that have been introduced in the State legislature from 1996 to present. It gives the status of current bills and the ultimate disposition of all bills from previous sessions. Bills are indexed by subject, statute affected, sponsor, and bill number. When asked to choose, select a topic such as "Agents and Brokers," "Real Estate Brokers," or "Real Property."

The site also sets forth the order of business for both the senate and house, their current agendas, and hearing schedules. It lists all the bills either signed or vetoed in the most recent session. In the case of a veto, a link is given to the letter in which the State governor explains the veto.

In every instance above, the actual texts of bills can be brought to the screen and then printed out or saved to disk.

State of Maryland Home Page

www.maryland.gov

At this site, choose "Online Services" near the top right corner; next, choose "Alphabetical Index." Here are over 100 live links to Maryland business, geographic, economic, and legal information. The home page also gives links that connect the student with the executive branch, the Maryland judiciary, the Maryland State Law Library, Maryland State departments, agencies, boards and commissions, and important agencies of the federal government. It also links to each Maryland county for local government information and business developments.

Office of the Secretary of State Division of State Documents

www.dsd.state.md.us

This Web site provides links to the Code of Maryland Regulations (COMAR), which offers the entire text of every State agency regulation together with suggestions on how to search; *The Maryland Register,* the official publication of the State government where changes to COMAR are published; and the *Annotated Code of Maryland,* where the Brokers Act can be found in the *Business Occupations and Professions Article,* at Title 17. Any of this information can easily be downloaded and saved.

The Maryland Real Estate Commission

www.dllr.state.md.us/license/occprof/recomm.html

Here, the student will find the names of Commission members, their terms, and the area of the state each licensee-member represents. At this site, the Commission makes available forms for complaints against licensees and forms for license renewal. It provides a means of inquiring about licensees by name. It contains information about licensing requirements, examinations required, license reciprocity, continuing education, and requirements for reinstatement of expired licenses. It also gives direct access to the current year's new laws and administrative changes that impact real estate licensees. It also links to COMAR and to the *Annotated Code.*

Maryland Statutes Text

www.michie.com

This site gives immediate access to the text of every Maryland statute and those of nine other jurisdictions, including Delaware and the District of Columbia. It does not, however, give the *catchlines*—the section and paragraph titles that appear in the bound volumes. Nor does it provide the commentary and explanations found in the *Maryland Annotated Code.* It is not indexed, but it has an internal searching device. Parts of any statute can be downloaded but only one segment at a time.

The State Department of Assessments and Taxation

www.dat.state.md.us

Billed as "Maryland's Largest Source of Real Estate Data," this site not only gives information about Homeowners' Tax Credit, Homestead Tax Credit, and Renters' Tax Credit but also the assessment of every parcel of real estate in Maryland. It also explains the semiannual payment schedule.

The site provides average sale prices of residential properties sold by county and by quarter for the last several years. Rates for the transfer tax, recordation tax, and tax stamps are also provided county by county.

The Maryland State Archives

www.mdsa.net

At this site, portions of nearly 700 volumes of the State archives can be viewed by the student by choosing "*Archives of Maryland Online.*" Or choose "*Maryland Manual On-Line*" for a complete guide to Maryland government. The "*Manual*" contains links to the three branches of Maryland State government as well as to county and federally related agencies. It is updated daily.

PSI Examination Services Information and Tutorial

www.psiexams.com

At this site, see "View the Examination Tutorial" (found at the bottom right corner of the screen) to see a tutorial about taking a licensing examination. It is a preview of the tutorial given to the applicant, on screen, at the time of taking the examination and pictures the keyboard used and the function of the most important command keys. The site also has a link to the locations of all the testing centers used for taking Maryland real estate licensing exams at "Locate Test Center." Students who register can download the "Candidate Information" booklet, which contains the application to take an exam.

APPENDIX E

Documentation Required in Maryland Residential Real Estate Sales Transactions

When prospects first seek assistance in locating property to purchase or lease	No document is in play at this point, but the law presumes that licensee represents prospects and owes them **fiduciary** duties, such as confidentiality and loyalty.
Before showing property	The Commission's agency relationship information form, **Understanding Whom Agents Represent,** must be presented at first scheduled face-to-face meeting with buyer (or lessee) and seller (or lessor). This is a disclosure form, not a contract to represent any party. Presenting and explaining it to a prospect is a logical moment to decline to provide presumed representation and to offer to represent prospects by written agreement. Merely presenting the form, no matter what boxes are checked, does not **end** presumed buyer representation or **create** any other agency relationship.
First written agreement	This is a written Agency Agreement to represent either buyer (or lessee) or seller (or lessor). This may require an amended (new) **Understanding Whom Agents Represent** form in situations where buyer representation and/or dual agency are undertaken and were not checked in an earlier form.
When brokerage firm represents opposing parties (i.e., is performing dual agency)	The Commission's **Consent for Dual Agency** form is signed by buyers (or lessees) and sellers (or lessors). An additional **Consent for Dual Agency** form is required for each property to be shown under dual agency, because the forms are both property-specific and owner-specific. This form is most often needed when the prospective buyer is a client. It is not used when the prospect is a customer and the licensee is acting as cooperating agent (the subagent of a seller).
Prior to submitting a written offer	Purchasers are to be given the following before an offer to purchase is signed: 1. The **Property Condition Disclosure/Disclaimer** form must be properly completed and signed by sellers. This is a duty of all sellers, but responsibility rests with licensee representing the seller, by a cooperating agent assisting the buyer, or by the licensee representing the buyer. A buyer not receiving this form prior to ratification of contract may rescind the contract at any time prior to applying for financing. *All* agents should ensure that the form is presented to the purchaser before the purchaser submits an offer. 2. The **Lead-Based Paint Disclosure Statement** and the booklet *Protecting Your Family From Lead-Based Paint Hazards* are to be given to purchasers of residential property built before 1978. This form is to *accompany* the contract of sale from this point forward. Licensees should get receipts from persons to whom they give this statement and booklet.
At time of contract	Copies of, or receipts for, disclosures given to all parties are to accompany the signed contract. These include **Understanding Whom Agents Represent,** and **Consent for Dual Agency, Property Condition Disclosure-Disclaimer** and, if applicable, the federally mandated **Lead-Based Paint Disclosure Statement** and a receipt for the information booklet *Protecting Your Family From Lead-Based Paint Hazards.*

Recent Changes to Title 17, Maryland Real Estate Brokers Act

Recent Changes to Title 17, Maryland Real Estate Brokers Act, and Other Laws Impacting Brokerage Services

Legislative Year and Act	Section Changed*	Content of Change
2008 SB 181	§17-322,328	**Summary Suspension of License–Grounds**
		Authorizes the State Real Estate Commission to suspend licenses summarily, if the licensees have been convicted of felonies or fail within ten days after conviction or within ten days following release from incarceration, whichever is later, to disclose such convictions.
2008 SB 132 HB 566	§17-303(d)	**Education Requirements for Licensure**
		Provides alternatives, in addition to classroom instruction, for prelicense education requirements: remote access satellite; closed-circuit video; computer, including World Wide Web; home study; etc., each when approved by the commission.
2008 SB 1008 HB 1557	§17-101(a) + many additions to §4.5 of the Business Regulation Article	Repeals requirement for all salespersons for homebuilders to hold a license from the Real Estate Commission
		Establishes Home Builder and Home Builder Sales Representative Registration Unit in the Consumer Protection Division of the Office of the Attorney General
2008 SB 762 HB 1316	§17-507	"Record Keeping by Licensees": Requires all real estate licensees to keep copies of listings and any other document obtained in connection with a transaction involving brokerage services for five years starting from date of closing or from date of listing, if closing does not take place.
2008 HB 1253 SB 844	Natural Resources 8-1801 Business Regulation 8-101	**Chesapeake Bay Critical Area Act**
		Gives the Critical Area Commission authority to update and enforce the law, allows the State to revoke the licenses of builders who knowingly violate the law, increases the no-build buffer zone for new subdivisions in rural areas from 100 feet to 200 feet, and tightens the rules about where new housing can be located.
2008 SB 216	Adds Real Property §3-104.1 and 7-105.1 Amends Real Property 7-105	[THIS LAW IS PROSPECTIVE AND DOES NOT APPLY TO MORTGAGES GIVEN BEFORE THE DATE OF THIS ACT (April 3, 2008).]
		Sets forth strict procedures for early, orderly, and complete notice to delinquent mortgage borrowers at each step of the way from default to foreclosure sale, with clear interpretation of the procedures and advice to borrower. Details costs to bring mortgage into reinstatement. Sets forth situations permitting summary foreclosure.

Legislative Year and Act	Section Changed*	Content of Change
2008 HB 626	§17-613	**Maryland Real Estate Brokers Act: Violations and Penalties** Adds §17-530 and §532 to the list of violations subject to criminal as well as to administrative penalties. Increases maximum administrative penalties from $5,000 for any offense to $5,000 for first offense, $15,000 for second offense, and $25,000 for the third. Also increases criminal penalty fines to the same extent and increases maximum imprisonment from one year for any offense to one year for first offense, two for the second, and three for the third.
2008 SB 217 HB 360 An Emergency Bill	*Real Property* *Added new Subtitle 4. Maryland Mortgage Fraud Protection Act* *Criminal Procedure moving Sections 13-401–13-408 under new* *Subtitle 4. Violations of the Maryland Mortgage Fraud Protection Act.*	**Maryland Mortgage Fraud Protection Act** Identifies behaviors constituting mortgage fraud, especially concerning false information entered into documents upon which loan approval is based. Victims include lenders misled by such information. Perpetrators include applicants and loan officers and lenders who proceed despite knowledge that the data is fraudulent. Penalties are $5,000 and up to 10 years in prison, 15,000 and up to 15 years (if involving a vulnerable adult) plus actions for treble damages and attorney fees. There is forfeiture and seizure of properties and all chattels and cash acquired by mortgage fraud of persons convicted.
2008 SB 218 HB 361 An Emergency Bill	*Commercial Law 13-301(14)(xxii), (xxiv)* *Real Property 7-301 amended most of newly renumbered Subtitle 3*	**Protection of Homeowners in Foreclosure; Prohibition on Foreclosure Rescue Transactions; Enforcement**
2007 HB 183	*Real Property 11B-115*	Provides that a violation of the Maryland Homeowners Association Act, to the extent that it affects a "consumer," is within the enforcement authority of the Consumer Protection Division of the Office of the Attorney General.
2007 SB 194	*Commercial Law 14-350-4-3508*	Imposes duties on a "business" to protect an individual's "personal information" and to provide notice of a security breach relating to an individual's personal information. "Business" does not include an entity that has an annual gross income of less than $1 million. The personal information may include records of tenants, including applications of prospective residential tenants for apartment complexes. Violation of this law, which takes effect January 1, 2008, is an unfair or deceptive trade practice under the Maryland Consumer Protection Act.
2007 SB 678/ HB 314	*Article 49B 11; 11A; 11B; 11C; 11D*	Creates a private cause of action in Maryland circuit courts for workplace discrimination that impacts all employers (regardless of size), including the real estate industry. A civil action may be filed by a claimant after filing an administrative charge or complaint or by Maryland Human Relations Commission on behalf of a claimant. Remedies available in a civil action under the bills include compensatory damages based on the size of the employer; punitive damages if the respondent is not a government entity and engaged in an unlawful practice with actual malice; and reasonable attorney's fees, expert witness fees, and costs. The bills also expand the remedies available through MHRC proceedings by authorizing compensatory damages based on the size of the employer (starting at 15 employees for 20 weeks/year).

Legislative Year and Act	Section Changed*	Content of Change
2007 HB 401	*Public Safety 12-1101-1106* and *Real Property 10-702(e)(2)*	Requires the seller of single-family residential real property to include in the statutory "Residential Property Condition Disclosure" form information on whether a carbon monoxide alarm is installed on the property. Specifically, the seller must disclose "if the property relies on the combustion of a fossil fuel for heat, ventilation, hot water, or clothes dryer operation, whether a carbon monoxide alarm is installed on the property." This measure also requires a carbon monoxide alarm to be installed in newly constructed dwellings for which a building permit is issued on or after January 1, 2008.
2007 HB 1288	*17-101; 17-207; 17-301;17-322*	Expands the definition of **real estate brokerage services** to include selling real estate as a sales agent for a homebuilder. Individuals who provide real estate brokerage services are required to be licensed by the Maryland Real Estate Commission. [Repealed in 2008.]
2007 HB 1326	*Title 16-101*	Requires supervising appraisers to be either certified residential or certified general real estate appraisers, meeting federal and State requirements that are more comprehensive than those for licensed real estate appraisers. *Licensed* real estate appraisers are no longer authorized to supervise trainees.
2007 SB 511/ HB 465	*Real Property 10-705*	Amends RP Section 10-705 to add conservation easements to the list of disclaimers in real estate sales contracts. The parties may rely on the recorded easement to stand as the disclosure or in lieu of providing a copy of the easement.
2007 HB 452	*adds to 8-110.1 in Real Property Article*	Terminates "Irredeemable" ground rents and makes previously nonredeemable ground rent property used for one to four residential units become redeemable on December 31, 2010, unless the holder files notice to preserve its irredeemability for ten years, etc. If and when redeemed the cost of redemption shall be the annual rent capitalized at 6 percent. "AN IRREDEEMABLE GROUND RENT SHALL BE CONVERTED TO, AND BECOME, A REDEEMABLE GROUND RENT, UNLESS WITHIN THE TIME SPECIFIED IN SUBSECTION (E) (F) OF THIS SECTION, A NOTICE OF INTENTION TO PRESERVE IRREDEEMABILITY IS RECORDED."
2007 SB 106	*Real Property 8-111.2*	Prohibits new ground rents (with certain exceptions) on one- to four-unit residential property.
2007 HB 489	*Real Property 8-110, 14–116.1, and 14–129*	Repeals certain waiting periods for redeemable ground involving property with four or fewer residential units. Creates requirement for a transferee who becomes holder of a ground lease to notify the leasehold tenant—within 30 days of becoming owner—of tenants' right to redeem the property and invite the tenant to contact the holder for details.
2006 SB 684 HB 1107	*added 17-3A (§1-§10)*	Allows a person holding a real estate license in another state and whose principal place of business for the provision of real estate brokerage services is outside of Maryland to apply for a "reciprocal license" to offer real estate brokerage services in Maryland.
2006 SB 384 HB 715	*17-518*	Provides that a licensed real estate salesperson with less than three years' licensure may serve as the manager of a real estate branch office under certain circumstances.
2006	*Real Property 9-102*	Expands existing laws and provides that a mechanic's lien may be established for the provision of building or landscape architectural services, engineering services, or land-surveying services. An improvement erected or repaired, rebuilt, or improved, to the extent of 15 percent of its value is subject to the establishment of a lien.
2006 SB 253/ HB 298	*Real Property 14-117(k)*	Requires a contract for the sale of residential real property to contain a disclosure advising the buyer that the property may be located near a military installation that conducts flight operations, munitions testing, or military operations that may result in high noise levels. Does not apply in Allegany, Carroll, Frederick, Garrett, Howard, Montgomery, and Washington Counties. The new mandatory text for contracts is "BUYER IS ADVISED THAT THE PROPERTY MAY BE LOCATED NEAR A MILITARY INSTALLATION THAT CONDUCTS FLIGHT OPERATIONS, MUNITIONS TESTING, OR MILITARY OPERATIONS THAT MAY RESULT IN HIGH NOISE LEVELS."

Legislative Year and Act	Section Changed*	Content of Change
2006 HB 1288	*Commercial Law 12-204; 12-410; 12-1007*	Specifies that a lender on a mortgage or deed of trust may not require a borrower, as a condition to receiving or maintaining a mortgage, to maintain homeowner's insurance coverage against risks to any improvements on any real property in an amount exceeding the "replacement cost" of the improvements.
2006 HB1620	*Real Property 8-203*	Authorizes a residential tenant to purchase a surety bond to protect the landlord against nonpayment of rent, damage due to breach of lease, or damage that exceeds ordinary wear instead of paying all or part of a "security deposit" to a landlord.
2005 HB 412 SB 192	*Real Property 10-702*	Newly defines **latent defects** to mean "material defects in real property or an improvement to real property that (1) A purchaser would not reasonably be expected to ascertain or observe by a careful visual inspection; AND (2) Would pose a direct threat to health and safety.... [This is a statutory requirement that sellers disclose latent defects about which they have actual knowledge. This is a statutory restatement of a common law principle.] Definition to appear in the residential property disclosure/disclaimer statement."
2005 HB 147	*Tax-General 10-912*	Changes the percentage of income tax to be withheld at settlement from the sale of real estate by a nonresident individual. Until this change, 4.75 percent of the total payment was required. The effect of the new formula created by this bill is to increase withholding to 6 percent as to nonresident individuals. (The 7 percent rate of withholding for "nonresident entities" was not changed.)
2005 HB 251	*Environment 6-801, 6-804, 6-817, 6-819, 6-819, 6-828, 6-830, 6-846, 6-850*	Reduces the elevated blood lead level that triggers notification by local health departments from 20 ug/dl to 15 ug/dl, strengthens enforcement authority, expands the current law to include exterior structures such as playground equipment and benches, etc.
2005 HB 374	*Environment 4-411.2*	Requires the Maryland Department of the Environment to provide a specified notice to the appropriate local health department upon a finding by the Department of specified oil contaminants, including MTBE, in groundwater samples.
2005 SB 630	*Transportation 21-1006*	Establishes that as of October 1, 2010, all signs designating a parking space or zone for individuals with disabilities must state the maximum fine for illegal parking and, as of October 1, 2010, each parking lot in the State must be compliant with the applicable codes.
2005 HB 464	*17-512*	Allows salespersons and associate brokers in the same brokerage firm to form limited liability companies (LLCs). Their broker is permitted, at their request, to pay commissions they have earned to the LLC. Previously, only professional service companies qualified for such payment.
2005 HB 865	*17-211, 306, 307, 311, 312, 313, 314, 316, 317, and 318* *Business Regulation Article 2-106*	Directs that, after July 1, 2006, fees paid to the Commission are to be forwarded to the Comptroller to accumulate in a State Real Estate Commission Fund from which the Commission's operating expenses will then be paid. (Since July 1, 2007, the Commission has been empowered to set almost every fee charged for license issuance, renewal, and so forth. Increases made by the Commission may not exceed 12.5 percent per year. Until the Commission changes the schedule, fees remain as previously established by the General Assembly.)

Answer Key

C H A P T E R 1
Maryland Real Estate License Law and Related Regulations

1. (3) Salespersons are not employed by owners but by brokers. They must work not only for brokers who are duly licensed but for brokers under whom *they themselves* are licensed.

2. (2) An affiliate's license certificate must be displayed in the office out of which the affiliate works. Affiliates' licenses are rarely if ever in their own hands. All licensees carry pocket cards, not licenses.

3. (4) Changes in office location, company names, or employment of an affiliate must be communicated to the Commission. Sharing of a commission, whether between brokers and their affiliates or between and among brokers, is not the domain of the Commission.

4. (1) Salespersons must not "split" or otherwise have commissions divided with anyone. Brokers pay commissions, but never—in whole or in part—to a nonlicensee.

5. (2) Freedom from broker control is not an IRS requirement for an IRS-recognized "qualified agent." On the contrary, broker control is vital for reasonable and adequate supervision required by license law. The other requirements are accurately stated.

6. (3) Only license renewal fees are paid every two years (biennially). Initial fees, as the name implies, are paid only at the beginning of licensure. This is also true of fees for the Guaranty Fund.

7. (3) It is a misdemeanor for which the penalty is not more than $25,000 and imprisonment for not more than three years. It *is* unethical, not a felony, and not a legitimate listing technique.

8. (2) The Commission has this authority over nonlicensees who perform acts of real estate brokerage. The same violation may *also* result in a fine and imprisonment if prosecuted by a *state's attorney* in a court of law.

9. (3) Unlicensed practice of real estate brokerage is a misdemeanor.

10. (3) "Puffing," intemperance, and slander of competitors are ill-advised, but Title 17 does not mention them. It does, however, forbid acts of bad faith.

11. (4) Title 17 regards a deliberately false statement to the Commission in a matter involving a Guaranty Fund claim a misdemeanor with a fine by the Commission of not more than $25,000 for a third offense; or a $25,000 fine and imprisonment for not more than three years for a third offense when prosecuted in court by a state's attorney. These stringent measures took effect October 1, 2008. Previous maxima were a $5,000 fine by the Commission and/or $5,000 fine and imprisonment for one year if prosecuted by a state's attorney.

12. (4) While out-of-state businesses such as corporations, LLCs, and partnerships may be licensed under special conditions to perform commercial brokerage, standard brokerage licenses are granted only to individuals.

13. (2) Neither the Executive Director nor the House of Delegates is involved. The State Senate provides "advice and consent" and the Secretary (of DLLR) provides advice to the Governor who actually appoints members to the Commission.

14. (2) All brokerage licenses expire two years from their date of issue. Previously salesperson licenses had expired on April 30 of the next even-numbered year. Broker licenses had expired on March 1 of the next even-numbered year.

15. (2) The Brokers Act is an exercise of the police power that protects the public interest. The "public" includes both consumers *and providers* of brokerage services.

16. (3) The Executive Director is chosen by the Secretary of Labor, Licensing, and Regulation from a list of three nominees submitted by the Commission. The Governor, the Senate, and the classified system are not involved.

17. (3) Ads placed by affiliates, or by their broker, for the sale of listed property must all clearly reveal the designated (official) name of the brokerage firm. Showing the affiliates' names, phone numbers, e-mail addresses, and/or Web site URLs is permitted only if the name and phone number of the brokerage are also meaningfully and conspicuously displayed.

18. (1) The Guaranty Fund must be maintained at not less than a $250,000. If it falls below that amount, an assessment for all new licenses and renewals is authorized.

19. (2) The three parts of the Code of Ethics refer to licensees' relations with the public, the client, and fellow licensees.

20. (2) The Commission has five licensee members and four consumer (nonlicensee) members.

21. (1) When the Commission is hesitant to issue a license to an applicant, they deny the request and offer the applicant a chance to be heard. Depending on the outcome of the hearing, the Commission either maintains its original position or grants the license.

22. (1) The Commission has statutory authority to set license and certain other fees associated with its operation. This authority, before being granted to the Commission, belonged to the General Assembly.

23. (2) In return for a fee, helping someone buy or sell Maryland real estate is an act of brokerage that requires licensure. The other three situations are specifically exempted from requiring a license.

24. (4) After being submitted to the Comptroller of the State, license fees are forwarded to the State Real Estate Commission Fund. This is an accumulating fund retained for the use of the Commission year after year.

25. (1) The law forbids individuals who hold real estate licenses from being employed by the Commission, and while employed by the Commission shall not perform acts of brokerage for which licenses are required. The Executive Director and field inspectors are examples of employees.

26. (1) It is the broker's responsibility to return such license certificates to the Commission whenever any salesperson or associate broker leaves the firm for any reason.

27. (2) Maximum recovery from the Guaranty Fund is $25,000 per transaction. Only actual losses are covered.

28. (4) The first three statements are true, but not *every* person needs a license to perform acts of brokerage. There are a number of categories exempt from the requirement.

29. (2) Sales associates may deliver brokerage services only through and under a *broker* under whom they are licensed—*not* an associate broker—and not *just any* broker. Salespersons may never operate brokerage businesses under their own names—unless they happen also to hold broker licenses.

30. (1) Attorneys who advertise publicly that they are in the business of providing brokerage services must hold broker licenses. A power of attorney given to an individual (by a buyer or by a seller) allows that individual to perform a single act of real estate brokerage. Salespersons for home builders need not be licensed; however, they must be registered with the Home Builder and Home Builder Sales Representative Registration Unit of the Consumer Protection Division of the Maryland Attorney General's Office (since October 1, 2008). Trustees conducting a trustee's sale of foreclosed properties are specifically exempt from the license requirement.

CHAPTER 2
Real Estate Agency

1. (2) Real estate brokers' *clients* are also called their *principals*. Brokers are their principals' agents.

2. (3) Such "dual agency" can be performed in Maryland real estate only when a broker appoints two such intra-company agents. Brokers may be agents of either buyers or sellers, but may not represent both *personally*. However the broker's firm may represent both buyer and seller if the broker designates two intra-company agents, one for the seller, and one for the buyer. The person who appoints the two ICAs cannot serve as one of them.

3. (4) The players are properly identified; Bettina is not a "single-agency" broker because she is performing "dual agency" here through her company.
4. (2) A broker who represents a client-buyer must disclose that fact to any seller or the agent of any seller he encounters.
5. (4) "Presumed buyer representation" (PBR) ends when a buyer asks to make a contract offer on a property. PBR begins when a prospect seeks assistance to rent or buy residential property. PBR does not end when prospect is shown the property of another firm. PBR also ends when a prospect is to be shown a property listed with the salesperson's broker's firm.
6. (4) The only way a broker may represent both buyer and seller in the same transaction is to appoint two intra-company agents—one to represent the buyer and the other the seller. Neither a salesperson nor a broker can personally represent both buyer and seller, even with their "permission." "No harm" is "no excuse" for a broker's improperly conducting dual agency.
7. (4) It is a violation of privacy under the Americans with Disabilities Act to state that a present or former occupant of a property under consideration by a purchaser had or is said to have had HIV, AIDS, or AIDS-Related Complex (ARC). No fiduciary duty is breached by withholding such information or opinion.
8. (3) Title 17, the Brokers Act, requires disclosure not later than the first scheduled face-to-face meeting with buyer or seller prospects. The rule for REALTORS®, by contrast, is disclosure of representation at the first contact. To wait until an offer is made—or until a party requests disclosure of representation—is to violate the law and also to risk possible collapse of a settlement, with consequent litigation, and costly disciplinary action by the Commission.
9. (3) Agents must obey their clients, not their customers. The other three duties are owed to customers.
10. (2) Only firms with a minimum of three licensees may engage in dual agency under Maryland law because there must be two intra-company agents appointed by a broker. The broker may not "self-appoint" to be an intra-company agent. Ministerial duties do not support a charge by either party of disloyalty or undisclosed dual agency.

CHAPTER 3
Real Estate Brokerage

1. (2) If price is shown, so must be the amount of the annual ground rent and the cost to redeem the lot.
2. (1) An ad *may* show the name of the listing salesperson but *must* show the broker's designated name. Showing the asking price is optional. One MLS member may not advertise properties listed by other members.
3. (4) The statute calls for brokers to have a definite place of business and to maintain there an office for regular conduct of business and maintenance of records. Commission regulations state that a mail drop, answering service, or mechanical answering device, together or separately, will not meet this requirement.
4. (4) Only a licensed real estate broker may operate a Maryland real estate brokerage firm.
5. (1) All ads must contain the *designated* name of the broker. It may or may not be the broker's legal individual name. But it must be the name shown on the broker's license as issued by the Commission.
6. (2) Licensed brokers of firms, the persons primarily responsible for actions of the firms and their affiliates, are not *required* to perform any of the other three functions. Neither are they *forbidden* to perform them.
7. (1) If a salesperson's name appears in an ad, the designated name of the broker must also be clearly and conspicuously displayed. If the salesperson's phone number is given, the clearly identified phone number of the firm must also be shown.
8. (2) Unless there are instructions to the contrary, earnest money deposits held by a broker must be placed—and kept until properly disbursed—in a non-interest-bearing account in an insured, approved Maryland depository institution. The other choices describe forbidden actions.

9. (4) The broker's signature is sufficient by itself, although other combinations of other licensees and non-licensees are permitted, providing that at least one is a licensee.

10. (3) Unlicensed persons such as personal assistants may *assist* in the holding of open houses by providing security for the licensee conducting them or handing out printed materials, but may not *conduct* open houses. They are permitted to do the other listed functions.

CHAPTER 4
Listing Agreements and Buyer Representation Agreements

1. (1) A net listing is forbidden in Maryland real estate brokerage. The other three are permitted.

2. (3) Chapter 5 of the Regulations of the Commission, entitled *Supervision,* requires that the Residential Property Condition Disclosure and Disclaimer Statement be completed at the time a licensee lists the property. It is to be completed by the client, not the licensee. Later completion is a violation.

3. (2) The buyer may rescind the contract before application for a loan is made. If no loan is needed, right of rescission could last until settlement. If buyer receives the statement after the contract is fully signed, the buyer has five days from receiving it to rescind. However, if the buyer proceeds to complete a mortgage loan application, that ends the right IF the lender informs the buyer that by applying he or she loses the right. If the lender fails to do so, the right goes on. If the lender "wakes up" and tells the buyer sometime AFTER loan application is made, buyer has another five days. Obviously, it is important to get the statement to the buyer before the buyer submits the offer.

4. (2) Before the firm may offer a property for sale, a completed copy of the listing must be given to the seller. Advertising the property is one way of "offering a property for sale."

5. (1) A Maryland affiliate must hold a Virginia license and be working for a Maryland broker who is also licensed as a broker in Virginia. The other choices do not qualify.

6. (3) Forms published by a multiple listing service are copyrighted and may be used only by its members who subscribe to that service. A person using such a listing agreement would, of course, *also* have to be a licensee.

7. (3) To be valid and to conform to the Brokers Act, listing agreements for Maryland real estate must be written (not parol), signed by all owners and by an authorized representative of the brokerage firm, and state the compensation to be earned either as a percentage of the selling price or as a dollar amount. Automatic renewal provisions are forbidden.

8. (4) Buyers who receive the form prior to submitting their offer may not rescind the contract based on that offer because of something revealed in that form. The three "rights" of rescission, shown in the other choices, do not exist.

9. (1) The rate or amount of commission, as established by negotiation between broker and client, must be clearly stated in the listing contract. There is no "established" rate imposed—or even suggested—by government or by the real estate industry.

10. (3) The General Regulations of the Commission, supported by the Brokers Act, require listings on Maryland residential property to be written. Listings create agency relationships, and must contain definite termination dates requiring no notice from either party.

CHAPTER 5
Interests in Real Estate

1. (3) These easements are for the purpose of keeping the land on which they are purchased in agricultural use. This, in turn, benefits the environment by slowing "suburban sprawl."

2. (4) A minimum of 20 years' *continuous* use is required by Maryland statute; 25 years' continuous use meets *and* exceeds that requirement, but 25 years' *intermittent* use does not.

3. (4) Prescriptive easement is recognized. The other three choices, examples of legal life estates, are not recognized in Maryland.

4. (1) An owner whose land is bordered by a navigable river owns to the average high-water mark but may construct a pier that reaches farther out. This *riparian* owner owns the pier but not the water or land

beneath it. Although he has the right to use water from the stream, he may not prevent the water from passing through by a dam or other means of diversion. No wharf is to be constructed without approval of the governmental agencies that have authority to grant or to withhold such permits.

5. (4)   State real estate transfer taxes help fund the purchase of agricultural easements.

CHAPTER 6
How Ownership Is Held

1. (2)   Maryland is not a community property state.
2. (3)   It will be construed to be and treated as tenancy by the entirety.
3. (2)   When one dies, the survivor becomes owner in severalty. Concurrent ownership of any kind requires more than one owner.
4. (1)   Chapter 4 of the Regulations of the Maryland Real Estate Commission requires time-share developers to register with that body.
5. (2)   Unless a higher proportion is specified by its controlling documents, condo bylaws require a two-thirds vote of the council of unit owners. Notice and quorum restrictions may apply.
6. (3)   Rental conversion to condominium requires registration with the Maryland Secretary of State.
7. (2)   Those who purchase a new condominium from its developer may void their contracts right up until settlement if they have not received the Public Offering Statement. If they proceed with settlement, they lose the right to void their agreements. Other statement choices are incorrect.
8. (2)   They have a ten-day right of cancellation for any (or no) reason.
9. (4)   All these documents must be delivered to the purchasers not later than 15 days before closing. When they have been delivered, purchasers then have seven days to cancel without any announced reason.
10. (3)   The Maryland Attorney General's office mediates most forms of condominium disputes among these parties.

CHAPTER 7
Legal Descriptions

1. (1)   References to the recorded plat of subdivision are sufficient to describe lots within that subdivision. They are used in listings and sales agreements.
2. (2)   A location drawing shows that the improvement is actually on the lot and other basic facts. Placing fences, however, requires a boundary survey, which is usually more expensive.
3. (3)   This description is dignified by reference to the recorded plat of subdivision for its details. The other choices lack such material details as adequate boundaries and other dimensions.
4. (4)   This description makes use of distances, compass directions, and monuments to describe a parcel in outline—all characteristic of metes-and-bounds surveys.
5. (3)   Most Maryland legal property descriptions use either the metes-and-bounds or the recorded plat of subdivision method. For convenience, street addresses and post office box numbers may appear, but they are not part of the actual legal description. Baltimore City, however, uses a system of parcels on numbered blocks.

CHAPTER 8
Real Estate Taxes and Other Liens

1. (4)   Some jurisdictions at each of those levels have been enabled to levy taxes on Maryland real estate. This authority comes from state enabling acts.
2. (2)   Each parcel of residential Maryland real estate is reassessed once every three years at full market value. An out-of-sequence reassessment may be performed when a property has undergone significant improvement.
3. (3)   Contractors have six months from the *completion* of their work to record a notice of lien. Six months after March 15 would be September 15.

4. (4) The other statements are accurate.

5. (1) For situations involving a first-time home buyer, the transfer tax is reduced from 0.5 percent to 0.25 percent and is charged to the seller. Therefore, the seller pays 0.25 percent. (0.0025 × $400,000 = $1,000.) This charge may not be shifted to the buyer.

CHAPTER 9
Real Estate Contracts

1. (1) The Maryland Statute of Frauds requires that all contracts for transfer of interests in property for more than one year be in writing and signed. The sales contract transfers equitable title to the buyer and thus falls under this law. There are widely used industry contracts, but there is no "standard" contract. All parties must sign.

2. (2) *Parol* means *oral*. A licensee who fails to reduce agreements between parties to writing violates the Brokers Act. An oral agreement to purchase might be valid (enforceable in court) under very specific, limited circumstances.

3. (1) Licensees dealing on their own behalf must disclose their licensee status (the fact that they are licensees) to the other party. Typically such disclosure is written into the contract being used.

4. (4) The others are all required.

5. (3) Inclusion of the notice is required in *all* counties, even those "excluded" by the notice.

CHAPTER 10
Transfer of Title

1. (3) Maryland requirements for adverse possession include open, hostile, continuous possession for 20 years under claim of right or color of title.

2. (4) All three are true. Even when a valid will is left, a widow or widower who receives less than her or his intestate share can contest the will under the Law of Descent and Distribution.

3. (4) Deeds are valid *between the parties*—the "party of the first part" and the "party of the second part"— even without recordation. That means they can be enforced by either one against the other. But *recorded* deeds protect grantees against *third* parties.

4. (3) To be recorded, a deed to Maryland real estate must have been prepared by the grantor, grantee, or an attorney. It must show (or be accompanied by an affidavit showing) the full consideration. Only a typewritten will may be recorded.

5. (4) Although often witnessed by three, a will with only two witnesses satisfies Maryland law. The other three statements are false.

CHAPTER 11
Title Records

1. (4) Instruments that affect land partially in each of two counties are recorded in both counties.

2. (2) Customarily, title search is ordered by the settlement company on behalf of the buyer and at the buyer's expense.

3. (1) Deeds and mortgages affecting Maryland land are recorded in the office of the county clerk of circuit court.

4. (3) These instruments are recorded in the grantee and the grantor index. They typically refer to previously recorded transactions. The selling (or the listing) broker's name is not a matter for recordation.

5. (2) Witnessing does not take the place of the required acknowledgment before a notary. A deed must be notarized to be recorded.

C H A P T E R 12
Real Estate Financing

1. (2) The Federal Equal Credit Opportunity Act forbids refusal of credit to an applicant based on the applicant's religion.
2. (4) Maryland law requires that his lender grant James a six-month extension if he requests it.
3. (2) Under Maryland law, courts may not foreclose on an unrecorded mortgage. It is the lenders' (mortgagees') obligation to record their mortgages.
4. (1) Mortgages and deeds of trust are the two ways that lenders secure almost all Maryland residential loans. A bank would not be involved in an installment contract unless it were selling property it owned. Real estate trusts and deeds of release have no relation to the situation described.
5. (3) Banks, savings banks, and savings associations are required by state law to credit the borrower's escrow account with passbook rate (or 3 percent—whichever is greater) interest annually for first mortgage loans for which they hold servicing duties.

C H A P T E R 13
Leases

1. (2) Absent a provision in the lease to the contrary, common law provides that a tenant's right of possession is uninterrupted by transfer of ownership of the leased fee.
2. (1) Maryland statutes require that landlords credit tenants' security deposit accounts with 3 percent per annum. Therefore, a deposit of $2,400 would earn $72.
3. (1) A lease for seven years or less need not be recorded, but a lease for more than seven years must be recorded.
4. (2) An annual ground rent of $720, capitalized at the rate of 6 percent, suggests that the value of the land alone is $12,000 (720 divided by 0.06). By not *selling* the land to the buyer, the builder can lower his price for the property by $12,000, to $228,000.
5. (2) Arthur will own a house situated on a rented lot. He will hold a leasehold estate in the land with ground rent as stated.
6. (2) One who pays rent for the land she possesses holds a leasehold estate.
7. (1) One purpose for which ground rents are created is to make the purchase of a developer-built house more affordable. The buyer *"buys"* the house but *rents* the lot, rather than buying the land outright.
8. (2) The annual ground rent divided by the capitalization rate gives the cost of redemption. Example 2 is the only one of the four that satisfies this formula. ($600 divided by 0.06 = $10,000.)
9. (4) Court seizure and sale of a residential tenant's personal property for unpaid rent is called *distraint*.
10. (1) Five percent of one month's rent is a penalty for late payment allowed by Maryland statute. The other provisions may appear in a lease, but they are unenforceable in court.

C H A P T E R 14
Environmental Issues and Real Estate Transactions

1. (2) Leakage from USTs (underground storage tanks) pollutes the ground and groundwater rather than the air.
2. (3) The two objectives are interrelated because preservation of open space is an important method of preserving ecological balance.
3. (3) Revitalization of older neighborhoods is intended to slow "sprawl" into the open countryside. The plan tends to increase housing density. It does not emphasize development of new areas.
4. (2) State law enables local jurisdictions to impose environmental regulations that are even more strict than those of the State. To take effect, however, the local regulations may *not* be *less* strict.
5. (4) Addressing environmental issues involves multiple levels of government as well as overlapping geographic jurisdictions.
6. (3) State agencies seldom allow local governments to approve any disturbance of the land in a "buffer zone." The buffer zone is 200 feet and the critical area, 1,000 feet.

7. (2) Where a critical area ends, a 200-foot buffer zone begins.
8. (2) There must be no other way to accomplish a worthy objective before filling of wetlands is permitted.
9. (1) Environmental regulatory actions tend to make *less* land available for real estate development.
10. (2) Even though the notice itself excludes *certain counties* in its warnings, the notice must appear in residential sales contracts in *every county*.

CHAPTER 15

Fair Housing

1. (4) Any warning about hostile attitudes in the residents of the neighborhood would tend to discourage the purchasers and therefore amount to *steering*.
2. (1) Persons involved in real estate transactions are bound by all antidiscrimination laws. They are held to have "constructive notice" because ignorance of a law does not excuse its violation.
3. (2) To show the property to prospects based—either positively or negatively—on their race is a violation of fair housing laws. It is *steering,* regardless of its motivation.
4. (1) *Blockbusting* is attempting to frighten present owners into selling (listing) their properties. Although it is typically done for financial gain, that is not a requirement for prosecution under the Brokers Act.
5. (4) The situation described is one of the "exceptions" built into the 1968 Fair Housing Act. Maryland has parallel exceptions in its fair housing laws.

CHAPTER 16

Closing the Real Estate Transaction

1. (4) Closings in Maryland are performed under the supervision of an attorney. This does not mean the attorney has to be physically present.
2. (3) The settlement officer is required to account to the seller for the payoff not more than 30 days after closing.
3. (1) No matter whom an attorneys performing settlement represent, they owe all parties due care in conducting the closing, disbursing funds, and so forth.
4. (2) Title evidence is usually ordered on behalf of and paid for by the purchaser.
5. (3) Seven percent of an out-of-state corporate seller's net proceeds must be withheld by the closing officer. If the seller were "an individual" rather than "an entity," it would be six percent.

Practice Exam

1. (2) No commission can be claimed by a firm based on the activity of a person who should have been properly licensed but was not.
2. (1) Licenses are issued for a period of two years from their date of issuance.
3. (2) Based on "presumed buyer/lessee representation," they are owed client-level duties.
4. (3) Salespersons' and associate brokers' licenses must be displayed in the brokers' branch office out of which each works.
5. (3) The maximum loss that is covered is $25,000 per transaction.
6. (4) Since 2005, the amended law has allowed unsolicited fax advertising if the sender has an established business relationship (EBR) with the recipient and the recipient has given the fax number to the sender with permission to use it.
7. (3) Membership of the Maryland Real Estate Commission is composed of five licensee members (either salespersons or brokers) and four consumer (nonlicensee) members.
8. (4) Although passing the courses is required, not all who pass apply for a license and not all who apply are granted one by the Real Estate Commission. The Brokers Act (Title 17) empowers the State Real Estate Commission to issue salesperson, associate broker, and broker licenses.
9. (2) The State Real Estate Commission has authority over *all* Maryland licensees, while the Association of REALTORS® has authority only over its members. Not all licensees are REALTORS®.

10. (3)   A partnership wishing to provide brokerage services must find a broker and designate that person as the broker of their firm. The broker could be one of the partners, but need not be. No unlicensed partner, however, may participate in any act of brokerage.

11. (1)   Although many builders use licensed brokers to sell their homes, the builders don't need to employ licensees or to be licensees. Changes in the law in 2008, however, require them and their salespeople to register with the Home Builder and Home Builder Sales Representative Registration Unit, an agency in the Attorney General's Office.

12. (2)   The Maryland Time-Share Act requires that a developer converting a residential rental building into a time-share holding give its residents 120 days' advance notice and provide them with other assistance in certain circumstances.

13. (3)   Unless they are also qualified to practice law in Maryland, real estate licensees are forbidden to give legal advice, although they often explain common contract provisions.

14. (1)   In a title-theory state the mortgagees (lenders) receive "bare legal title" to mortgaged property. However, they agree (in the mortgage defeasance clause) that their claims will be extinguished by borrowers' paying off the debts secured by their mortgages.

15. (1)   The *Commission* may impose a fine as much as $25,000 for a third offense and/or suspend or revoke the license of the offender. Violations prosecuted by the *Attorney General*, on the other hand, may result in fines as much as $25,000 in addition to possible imprisonment for periods from one to three years.

16. (3)   It is a cardinal principal of federal and state antitrust legislation, that competing providers of a service such as real estate brokerage are not to establish, try to establish, or even discuss with one another, the fees they charge the public.

17. (4)   Salespersons should never maintain trust accounts for customers' or clients' money. Neither should earnest monies be kept in the office safe. Such deposits must be *promptly* (and in no event, after longer than seven business days) deposited by the broker or the broker's designee in the firm's trust account.

18. (3)   Tenancy by the entirety involves only two persons: a married couple. When one of two dies, the one left is alone and has no one to hold "in common" with. The survivor's ownership thus is *in severalty*.

19. (3)   The fiduciary duty of brokers requires that they put the benefit of their clients (in this case, the sellers) ahead of their own. If the seller clients can see all available offers, they can choose the one that is best for them and not be maneuvered into accepting an offer that would most benefit the brokerage firm.

20. (4)   Maryland's Statute of Frauds requires that, to take effect, transfers of any interest in real property for more than one year must be in writing and signed.

21. (4)   No legal requirement about land (installment) contracts requires contact with the Commission. The other statements are true.

22. (1)   Representation agreements are not created by delivery of this form. Neither does presentation of the form end presumed buyer representation or give permission for dual agency. Each of these requires a separate written agreement. The form in question merely tells the one to whom it is delivered whom the licensee presenting it is already representing. It also explains the ways parties can be represented or served by licenses.

23. (4)   Neither death of a client nor expiration of an agency agreement ends the requirement for agents to maintain confidentiality. That requirement ends by permission of the client or by the information's becoming common knowledge from other sources. The Statute of Limitations does not address this matter.

24. (4)   The Brokers Act, Title 17, specifies that the form be presented "not later than the first scheduled face-to-face meeting with a prospect." In contrast, the REALTOR® Code of Ethics requires that agency representation be disclosed even sooner—"at first contact."

25. (2)   Neither payment or promise of payment of consideration, nor the delivery of ministerial (servant) acts, can be held to create an agency relationship. On the other hand, a customer who receives expert (magisterial) guidance from a licensee could infer that an agency relationship exists.

26. (2) The interest is computed in six-month intervals but is *not* compounded. The other statements are accurate.

27. (1) Although heinous, drunken driving is not one of the offenses listed in Title 17 as warranting penalties. The other three offenses *are* bases for such disciplinary action by the Commission.

28. (1) Licensee duties to nonclients include honesty, reasonable care, and disclosure of material facts. A seller's brokerage fee may properly be shared with the agent of the buyer, even though that agent is not a subagent of the seller. Compensation for representing a buyer also requires a written agreement with the buyer.

29. (4) The declaration is a document separate and distinct from both a condominium's bylaws and from its rules. It does not contain either the bylaws or the rules. The other three statements are accurate.

30. (1) A property is placed under a condominium regime (governance) by recording its declaration.

31. (1) Deficiency judgments for a lender are possible when foreclosure has been court-supervised (as it is in judicial foreclosure). Such judgments are not available to lenders in cases of nonjudicial foreclosure and of foreclosure of FHA-insured loans.

32. (1) The good-faith duty of fairness to both parties prevents brokers from putting the interests of their clients ahead of those of the adverse party in deciding to whom contested earnest money will be paid. Title 17 makes the other three alternatives available to the broker in such situations.

33. (4) Security deposits may be withheld for actual costs of repair for tenant damage to the rented property over and above normal wear and tear *and for unpaid rent*.

34. (1) The mere physical presence of a broker, no matter how many hours are invested, is not one of the evidences of reasonable and adequate supervision listed in Title 17. No credit for attendance! The other three choices are each found in that statute.

35. (4) Maryland law requires that "listing" agreements contain (among other things) a termination date that is effective without further action by either broker or client. "Automatic" extension provisions are forbidden.

36. (1) There is no limit on the interest rate for first mortgages. Second mortgages and land contracts are limited to 24 percent. Deeds of trust, used in place of the traditional mortgage, are subject to the same limits as mortgages.

37. (1) Renters receive "presumed representation" (just like buyers) for which no fee may be claimed. The law no longer regards "walk-ins" as customers. Although the statute says, ". . . not later than the first *scheduled* face-to-face meeting," it is prudent to give unscheduled walk-ins the agency disclosure form immediately.

38. (3) Biennial renewal for a licensee requires a total of 15 clock hours of approved courses. Among these must be at least three hours of ethics, three hours of legislative update, and—except for exclusively commercial licensees—one and one-half hours of fair housing. In place of fair housing, commercial licensees may take one and one-half hours of class presenting the Americans with Disabilities Act.

39. (1) It must be the place where the firm regularly conducts *real estate*, not *insurance*, transactions. The other three requirements are stated accurately.

40. (1) On the contrary, the ad gives the impression that associate broker Buonasera *is* the head of a firm, its broker. The other statements about improper advertising are accurate.

Index